AS WE COME MARCHING

• • • • • • • • • • • • • • • • •

People, Power

Progressive Politics

Edited by
Steven Langdon & Victoria Cross

Windsor Works Publications
Ottawa • Windsor

Windsor Works Publications

346 Randolph   147 Strathcona
Windsor, Ontario   Ottawa, Ontario
N9B 2T6   K1S 1X7

Canadian Cataloguing in Publication Data

Main entry under title:
As We Come Marching: people, power & progressive politics
Includes bibliographical references.
ISBN 0-9699026-0-3
1. Socialism — Canada.   2. New Democratic Party.
3. Canada - Politics and government —1993 -
I. Langdon, Steven.   II. Cross, Victoria, 1956 -

HX109.A7 1994   320.5'31'0971   C95-930029-5

Cover Photo: Murray Mosher/Photo Features, Ltd., Ottawa, Ont.

Design: Dinah Greenberg

Printer: Our Times Publishing, Ltd., a unionized, worker-owned and operated printshop co-operative, 390 Dufferin St., Toronto, Ontario

This book was printed on acid-free recycled paper, using vegetable-based ink.

Larry, this one's for you!

Larry Bauer grew up rough and ready in Essex County, Ontario. He emerged as a key leader in the Canadian Auto Workers (CAW), locally and nationally. His immense personality, dedication, and commitment to working people and their families were evident in his relentless battles for (and sometimes with) others. Daily, Larry grappled with the tough questions. He pushed hard, argued, challenged himself and others, and took risks. Larry never stopped trying to do the right thing for the working people he represented or the community in which he lived.

Larry Bauer died in May 1994, days after being re-elected President of CAW Local 444. Our last conversations with him were about this book, its content and direction.

We miss him.

Contents

The Political Economy of Change

Foreword

. . . .

Bread And Roses

As we come marching, marching, in the beauty of the day,
A million darkened kitchens, a thousand mill lofts gray,
Are touched with all the radiance that a sudden sun discloses,
For the people hear us singing: "Bread and roses! Bread and roses!"

As we come marching, marching, we battle too for men,
For they are women's children, and we mother them again.
Our lives shall not be sweated from birth until life closes;
Hearts starve as well as bodies; give us bread, but give us roses!

As we come marching, marching, unnumbered women dead,
Go crying through our singing their ancient cry for bread.
Small art and love and beauty their drudging spirits knew.
Yes, it is bread we fight for — but we fight for roses, too!

As we come marching, marching, we bring the greater days.
The rising of the women means the rising of the race.
No more the drudge and idler — ten that toil where one reposes,
But a sharing of life's glories: Bread and roses! Bread and roses!

Poet and novelist James Oppenheim wrote "Bread and Roses" after seeing young women mill workers carrying a banner reading "We Want Bread And Roses Too" during the Lawrence, Massachusetts textile strike of 1912. The Lawrence textile strike remains one of the key events in North American labour history. There, the Industrial Workers of the World successfully organized unskilled workers (mostly young women) across craft and ethnic lines, despite opposition from the powerful and wealthy, the bitter cold of

New England, and violent police attacks. At Lawrence, women demonstrated immense courage as they were jailed, beaten, and sent their starving children to far-away safety organized by a network of supporters. The workers won their strike with a range of tactics and deep solidarity that respected the cultural differences found in the variety of ethnic communities.

No matter what, the workers marched, sometimes by the tens of thousands. And when they marched, they sang — often singing the same song in several languages at once. Their non-violent "passive resistance" tactics became a hallmark of the labour, civil rights and anti-war movements. Oppenheim's poem has been set to music by a number of people. We know of four versions; there are likely more.

Over the years, "Bread and Roses" has become an anthem for both the labour movement and the women's movement. It expresses the courageous spirit of working people and their families as well as the deeply-felt egalitarian dreams that fuel that militancy.

That's why we chose "As We Come Marching . . ." for our book's title. It reflects the determination and ultimate optimism which this book expresses.

We have developed this book because neither of us is prepared to accept that "there is no alternative" to the neo-conservative — capitalist — agenda and ideology. For over a century, the major countervailing alternative to capitalism has been socialism. "Socialism" is an analytic assessment of economic, social and political relationships involving class, race and gender — even geography — represented in a range of perspectives and thought. We don't believe "socialism" is monolithic, nor do we deny the complexities or even some of the possibilities found in "capitalism". Thankfully, Canadian socialism is infused with the democratic spirit and energy of several generations of activists, and we can look to our own vital North American history for the guideposts to carry us into the future.

To us, our democratic-socialist vision is one of hope. That vision is the affirmation of the ability of ordinary people to make and shape our own history through communities, unions, farm organizations — and our political parties, and therefore, government at all levels — as a vehicle for expressing people's will.

We are also pragmatic. It's very important to meet the needs of the moment. Vision is an essential underpinning, yet alone, it is not enough. We know there is a broad-based democratic left in Canada that is not explicitly socialist. That's one reason, after all, the New Democratic Party was created. But right now, the Canadian left does have some serious thinking to do about the vision we express, the strategy we take, and the tactics we use. It's time for some healthy talking and listening. It's time to assess where we are, look at the work we do, and figure out what needs to happen next.

When we listen, we hear thousands of voices singing out for real change: economic change, political change, social change. Those voices believe there are alternatives to neo-conservatism. Despite the dire statements of some, we believe Canada's left remains a vital, powerful force.

This volume is the first effort for Windsor Works Publications. The following collection includes the ideas of others who have also been reflecting on the future. We chose to include the visions of people we both respect, not solely those with whom one or both of us agree. We want to explore the debate in the left, not to provide the final word in that debate. We're aiming in good faith towards a common ground, even though finding common ground on some issues means we might agree to disagree on others. As was true with the workers in Lawrence, we believe there is real power in finding unity in our diversity, and realizing that while we march forward in shared cause, we can sing in different languages.

We have special thanks for the various unions, labour federations and individuals right across this country who have helped finance this initiative. Thanks to the contributing authors who have also been immensely generous in their support when all we could offer was gratitude.

Thanks too, to the Our Times Publishing Co-operative. They helped us through this new experience with patience and fortitude. Thanks also to Suzie Sulaiman and Stephanie David, Jonathan Langdon, Lisa Schmidt, John Shields and Hawley Neuert. As always, our spouses with whom we share our lives, Shirley Seward and Len Wallace, have given us fundamental support and critical help.

Steven Langdon, Victoria Cross
Autumn 1994

Introduction:
Bread and Roses in 1995

by Steven Langdon and Victoria Cross

A t a trade union convention, or a gathering of the women's movement, you might hear people sing "Bread and Roses." Usually, not everyone knows all the words, but a few strong voices will rise above the crowd singing "Yes, it is bread we fight for — but we fight for roses, too!" in full voice.

These few words house a compelling image that speaks to both the pragmatic and the romantic in each of us; the stomach and the soul. It is a song that many socialists sing because the fight for social justice throughout the world has always been a twin quest. It is a fight for economic gain for the many, not the few. It is also the fight for a finer human community, for social gain for all.

As we enter 1995 in Canada, the democratic-socialist quest for these changes has reached a fundamental crisis point.

It is a crisis of ideology — what we believe. It is a crisis of strategy — how and with whom we work and plan together. It is a crisis of tactics — what we agree are the right methods to win our goals. How did we get in this mess?

There is an immediate answer, though it is not the only answer.

In the past decade, most Canadians have been governed for some years by New Democrat provincial and territorial leaders, from British Columbia and Yukon, through Saskatchewan and Manitoba, to Ontario. Federal New Democrats under Ed Broadbent achieved the highest social democratic support ever in Ottawa, and almost reached the status of official opposition.

Yet, in 1993, federal New Democrats were crushed, losing every seat they held in Ontario by large margins and suffered massive losses in the western provinces. The party remains below 5 per cent in national polls.

There is a widespread view, especially in Ontario, that this electoral disaster was above all a judgement on the performance of Ontario's provincial regime.

Queen's Park journalist Thomas Walkom wrote in his tough critique, *Rae Days*: "By its actions and words, the Ontario NDP government dashed the hopes of all those who fought for and believed in an alternative to the orthodoxy of the Liberals and Conservatives, the banks, the Business Council on National Issues, and the editorial board of the Globe and Mail. In effect, the Rae government said to the country: It's pointless to argue with the dominant ideology; acquiesce and get it over with; you have no choice."[1]

As New Democrats, as activists, we had always offered choice. We were the alternative to the prevailing ideology.

Walkom stresses the impact of this difficulty in the 1993 federal election, "Rae's government was a living rebuke to (Audrey) McLaughlin, a disavowal of this, the cardinal assumption behind the NDP. 'We had no choice,' Ontario NDP Ministers would say as the government backtracked on its promises."[2]

The result for many Canadians today is a perception that the New Democrats and their allies are deeply confused, and have lost political direction. Like a Stephen Leacock figure-of-fun, New Democrats have leapt on their horse, and rushed off in every direction.

That confusion — and what lies behind it — represents a stark challenge to the party's future, and to the future of those movements that have found a home in the New Democratic Party, or helped create it.

This book seeks to help in meeting that challenge, by contributing a range of views on how Canada's New Democrats can renew their vision in years ahead.

But that is only one aim of this book. The quest for social justice and economic change — for socialist alternatives — in Canada has never been the monopoly of a political party. Rather, it has been the implicit or explicit goal sought by many progressive Canadians in a broad movement for a better community, involving labour unions, environmental action groups, farm bodies, women's organizations and many other people. Along the way, these goals were sometimes expressed through political parties, but all these movements have a vital life with or without an electoral vehicle.

This book is about the power of people to reshape Canadian politics. Despite the massive 1993 federal defeat, and Ontario actions that stir deep controversy, this book says progressive Canadians must not lose hope. We can fight the prevailing ideology and win.

Time and again throughout our history, ordinary people have made tough decisions to fight back against the elite. There have been defeats, but there has always been the remarshalling of energies, the refocusing of priorities, the creative application of new approaches, structures, forums — or the remaking of old ones. Canada's left is not dead.

As this collection shows, there is energy and vision on the left, across Canada. Women and men are organizing to seek progressive goals and to resist unjust attacks. Visions of better public services, strong environmental priorities, different ways of governing our country, and the urgent need for new jobs are motivating people.

And change is coming — in ways that put less stress on sheer electoral politics — and greater priority on policies based on democratic citizenship and community-based economic development.

Around the world, other socialists face similar challenges.

But our challenge is to realize our ideals in Canada. How can we capture the imagination of most people, and move from defensive battles and hopeful visions, to shaping a caring, co-operative community in real-world Canada?

A Vision of Change: Toward a Green Community for People

The progressive movement in Canada has been at its most energetic and effective when there has been a broad, unifying vision that could pierce the particulars of day-to-day politics, and convey a dramatic concept or concern to all Canadians.

It's that kind of vision or broad theme that democratic-socialism must again articulate in Canada.

In recent years, progressive Canadians have pigeonholed themselves into mosaic movements — forming alliances — but not driven by a broad, common vision. There has been a women's movement, various wings of the labour movement, a Black movement, a gay-lesbian movement, a farm movement, and so on — all of them with energy and effectiveness, but forming a mosaic fighting for change, rather than a movement shaped by a collective ideal born of a sense of shared struggle. This lack of unified purpose has worked against us. These movements have won important gains. But as we remain in our separate spheres, we have become vulnerable to a devastating criticism from our enemies. It is when we act separately that we hang together — summarily convicted without trial of the false charge that we act only in "special" interest, not in the interest of the whole of society. We need a thematic approach that can unite all of us for a broad goal.

In contrast, Canadian nationalism in the 1960s, or the opposition to the U.S. Free Trade Agreement, or the NDP campaign for "ordinary

Canadians" were broad, unifying ideas for progressives that cut across lines of segmentation and somehow brought many Canadians together.

The first section of this book presents a variety of views or visions; the second section describes various types of organizing and fight back campaigns. The authors describe what worked — or didn't. In the third section, we start the discussion about what can be the basis for a renewed economic agenda for Canada. In all, we see great possibility and hope in what we read.

Daryl Bean shows how crucial fine public services are to the well being of Canadian communities. Mae Burrows stresses environmental priorities and how they can contribute to jobs. Buzz Hargrove and Leo Gerard present the views from the key industrial unions in Canada — the unions that have historically played a crucial role in the life of the New Democratic Party and beyond. Pierette Landry writes from Montréal, to comment on Québec's future, and the rest of Canada. Kathy Baylis shows how the push to preserve family farms clashes headlong against corporate interests. All of the writers touch upon, to a greater or lesser degree, how we relate to one another, in our nation, in our unions and organizations, and between generations and cultural or social groups.

Can we discern here the basis for an overall theme? A point-by-point agenda? Not clearly.

But there are three strands that intertwine in many articles: Environmental and economic security for the future; the community — however broadly (or narrowly) it is defined — as fundamental to analysis and action; and the importance of community or public services to making our society human, humane and creative.

Our present society is highly globalized, more insecure in environmental and jobs terms, and increasingly fragmented and individualistic. But to survive, the world surely needs societies where we sustain our environment, give our communities more say in shaping the future, and establish more secure futures for ordinary people.

Environmental emphasis, a vibrant public sector, a community-based jobs strategy, and respect and protection for our rural and farm families — this combination represents a broad direction around which to build a new-style democratic-socialism. We might sum it up as aiming to build a green community for people.

That emerging vision is a sharp break with elements of the past conventional wisdom of Canadian social democracy. This view is also sharply divergent from the Rae-style neo-liberalism that some see as the future for New Democrats.

The past conventional wisdom of the social democratic left stressed national planning (an all-inclusive national industrial strategy, for instance), Keynesian-style manipulation based on high rates of national economic growth (pushed by deficit financing to increase total consumer demand) as the key to achieving full employment, and a drive for general social security through universal social programes in health, education, housing and income support.

The "new competitiveness" mode of thinking has marked the so-called Rae or Ontario model of thinking, although in a confused way. Ontario's government has moved away from demand management aimed at higher consumer demand in favour of a technocratic centralization focused on the supply side of the economy. As have their counterparts in the U.S. and other nations, the Rae government has also chosen to manipulate labour-supply and attempts to limit labour's demands. There has been a marked push for deals with corporate giants (Walkom details the efforts in pharmaceuticals in particular) to try to attract the promise of new investment to Ontario. The stress has been on building a more competitive, modernized economy — and social services and the public sectors generally have been seen as burdens to cut back and to target more precisely to save money.

There have been positive dimensions to the Rae experience, which critics such as Walkom do not recognize enough. Some are: a very aggressive public sector housing effort; the push to include all segments of Ontario in appointments to boards, commissions and public service positions; the labour law revision; and ad hoc, but important moves to preserve jobs in threatened northern communities. But the top-down style of governance, and the breathtaking reversals of policy that have marked Rae's government make his brand of social democracy with a corporate agenda an unlikely vision for the Canadian future. It is not a vision for the democratic left.

A new-style democratic-socialism will see the world very differently than either the old NDP orthodoxy or the new NDP competitiveness agenda.

Environmental security must be the key focus. Nuclear accidents in Ukraine bring deadly fallout across Canada. The ozone layer in our atmosphere is under siege. Our precious oceans, inland lakes, and rivers exhibit signs of grave stress. Thousands of fishing families on our east and west coasts are devastated by environmental disaster; overfishing threatens to end a whole way of life forever. Our Great Lakes are turning into a chemical soup. Many argue our forestry and agricultural policies devour our future.

That's where consumer capitalism has taken us. Surely it is time to change direction, to stop seeing simple undifferentiated economic growth as the key to our communities and our jobs.

That's what environmental security is really all about — the notion of sustainable development, of a balanced, ongoing economy with a long term future. In 1987, the international Brundtland Commission said sustainable development is using your resources today so as to sustain those resources for ongoing use in the future.[3]

As Native Canadians have said, our responsibility for what we do today must continue to the seventh generation.

That doesn't mean a no-growth society or turning back the clock to some pre-industrial age. It does mean a society in which growth non-damaging to the environment — even geared toward improving the environment — is stressed. It means the use of renewable resources must be strictly tied to actually achieving their renewal and our technological choices are both environmentally friendly and as much outside narrow, bureaucratic control as possible.

It also seems to mean much more stress on service activities, "green" industries, and information and public sector roles in reaching full-employment goals (since these are generally non-threatening to the environment) — rather than the broad-scale acceleration of consumer demand that the old social democratic model stressed. It also rejects the individualistic, neo-liberal "competitiveness" model embraced by the Rae government, because vibrant and valued public sector activities are crucial in this new context.

As argued in "Debts, Deficits and Human Communities: *A New Approach*," the public sector can consider costs and benefits outside the marketplace in making decisions. Public goods, such as safe communities and clean rivers, can be stressed. Although they cannot be measured, catalogued, priced and sold on an individual basis, they result in widespread social benefit for most Canadians. Public sector intervention can assure resource depletion is considered in decision-making that cares about the seventh generation. Our society does a poor job of measuring the value of public sector activity, just as our system of National Accounts does not measure the contribution of household work to the quality of life in Canada, or the full impact of environmental benefits and costs of certain projects and activities.[4] That's one reason so many governments, even New Democrat governments, have found it easy to make public sector cuts — because the benefits of the activities are often long-term and hard to define precisely — especially in the short shelf-life of some governments. Yet these benefits are often ultimately so much greater than any measurable cost savings.

Take the decision to cut CBC news and local programming in Windsor. On the face of it, the government and a public institution saved money. But the Windsor area ceased to have any means to participate in the hard-core news of the nation, to "see itself" on the screen, and lost a tool to define itself within the community and outside it as an entity distinct from the massive nearby U.S. presence.

In "Essex Windsor Makes Its Own History," we see that the social costs were immeasurably higher than the savings involved in the cutbacks. Those social costs ultimately mobilized thousands of Windsor-area people to fight for a key public service that if lost, would risk deep damage to community cohesion. Windsor's unrelenting pressure won back this public service. (It was a last-gasp concession from the Mulroney Tories, but an essential victory nonetheless.)

The battle over the public sector goes on, worldwide. Murray Dobbin sketches the results of the neo-liberal/neo-conservative drive in New Zealand. He shows how the strategy of cutbacks there greatly increased poverty and unemployment, destroyed the sense of community throughout that nation — and resulted in substantially higher debt levels than when the Roger Douglas counter-revolution began.

Stressing the public sector doesn't mean mere defence of the status quo, as Canadian Union of Public Employees President Judy Darcy discusses in "The Labour Movement and Progressive Politics: *The Fight to Preserve Medicare*." That campaign articulated new roles for health care team members and saw community clinics taking increased responsibility for health care delivery.

The notion of community is fundamental to this new-style socialism.

We can see the power of community, and the enrichment the sense of community brings to the individual and to the larger world, in "A Griot's Tale: *Dedicated to Black Pioneers*," by Elise Harding-Davis.

So much of Canada's decision-making has been shaped by a small, dominant elite in Toronto, Montréal and Ottawa, that a fundamental thrust of the drive for a new society must be anti-elitist and bottom up. Sensibly, Canadians recognize that those at the top have run our economic, social and political decisions for a long time in Canada, without many recent remarkably positive results.

Now the people of Windsor, Brantford, Shefford, Rimouski, Moncton, Sydney, Corner Brook, Sudbury, Thunder Bay, Brandon, Saskatoon, Moose Jaw, Athabasca, Penticton and Yellowknife want their say.

It is at the community level that a new ethic can emerge — an ethic that understands that choices today shape the environment for years to come and can decide the quality and continuity of community life.

As Paul Hertel, Mike McLister and Maureen Curtis show, at the community level the threats by foreign corporate giants to community integrity can be fought, and somewhat mitigated. Through organizing local support, these activists have achieved progressive gains.

If Brian Mayes and Simon Blackstone are any indication, Canada's young people are prepared to make important sacrifices of time and energy to help a new vision of Canada come to life. While the writers don't pretend to speak for a generation, they demonstrate that we need recognize that to create "community" we may have to explore more fully the idea of active "citizenship" they begin to describe.

Coro Strandberg shows, basing her insights on her British Columbia experience, there are exciting examples emerging regarding community-based jobs development. Judy Wasylycia-Leis demonstrates community-based services are open to the democratic direction that must be a future priority.

Jobs can be built through small and medium businesses and co-operatives founded at the local level. The push for greater democratization of decision-making is answered, in part, through participation in community economic development and reshaping community services.

Neo-liberal and neo-conservative solutions will not meet this spirit, because, ultimately, they are top-down, technocratic solutions that administer cutbacks.

Yet, ironically, the right-wing forces in Canada's political culture have most successfully captured the deep-seated (and well-founded) skepticism most Canadians have for far away, behind-closed-doors decisions. It's time we reclaim our populist roots, and in so doing, show that the solutions offered by the Reform-based coalition are actually anti-community and anti-democratic in that they would weaken people's ability to shape what happens in their communities and thus strengthen large scale private interests.

Much community-based economic development can be grounded in green initiatives, such as alternate energy products, waste recycling technology, and services such as energy auditing. Sustainable development goals require a strong public sector to reflect and support the "public goods" character of much environmental development. As more fully described in "Debt, Deficit and Human Communities," important public sector financing initiatives are essential to both sustainable development efforts and a community-based jobs emphasis.

Organizing for Change: Toward Movement Politics

Politics in Canada is changing in important and irreversible ways, and the democratic left has to understand this if we are to begin to shape new social and economic realities.

Two broad trends appear at work. The first is an internationalization of the real political framework within which many decisions are being made. The second is more complex, and includes an explosion of traditional party bases of support that has made internal electoral politics in Canada much more fluid, and opened the door much wider to region-based protest parties. It also includes a related shift giving non-party groupings (like the women's movement) much more capacity for impact in the system.

The first trend, toward globalization, is evident in the powerful general economic directions set by the regular G-7 summit meetings, the International Monetary Fund (IMF) and the various international bank and lending consortia that deal with international debt questions for developing countries (such as the Paris Club). The slower-growth, anti-inflation strategy of the G-7 in response to the 1979-80 oil price crisis, for instance, was immensely powerful in setting the context for high unemployment and high interest rate policies in Canada and elsewhere during the 1980s. The relatively cautious IMF-centred strategies on Third World debt relief have also been crucial in slowing world economic activity and retarding export-led recovery.

Similarly, the international politics of the General Agreement on Tariffs and Trade (GATT) have reshaped Canadian farm policy (moving from supply management to high tariffs against imports in the short-run, and to more direct international competition for all producers in the long-run, as those tariffs decline). The continental politics of the North American Free Trade Agreement (NAFTA), too, take much decision-making capacity out of the hands of Canadian governments, such as the power to shape our own energy policy.

Simultaneously, a range of new environmental pressures can simply not be handled within one nation. Depletion of the ozone-layer, with its dangers for human health, could not be tackled by a single country. It required multilateral moves like the Montréal protocol by which phasing out of standard chlorofluorocarbons (CFCs) production was accelerated throughout the world. International action on the management of common-property renewable resources, like fish stocks, has clearly become essential — given the tragedy of the Newfoundland fisheries.

Meanwhile, political strategies have also had to become internationalized, in response to these new realities. Greenpeace takes its campaign against B.C. forestry practices to Europe, influencing the European Parliament and European purchasers; and Mike Harcourt and his British Columbia New Democrat government have to campaign in Europe, too, to present a different perspective. The James Bay Cree take their fight against Hydro-Québec to New England electricity markets; and again an international political response occurs, this time from Québec.

In "Small Town Ontario Environmental Activism," Paul Hertel illustrates the international context of the new politics. In his analysis of the fight to block the Fermi II U.S. nuclear power station, located in Monroe, Michigan, Hertel demonstrates that the close co-operation between Michigan and Ontario environmentalists helped the battles on both sides of the border.

Former Manitoba premier Howard Pawley stresses the critical implication of these changes in his article: this new cross-border reality of politics requires joint strategies and common goals among progressive groups in different parts of the world if the democratic left is to successfully challenge the dominant Canadian elite — because that elite is internationalizing its centres of power. Washington, New York, Paris, Bonn and Tokyo are coming to replace Toronto, Montréal and Ottawa.

For some, this change is difficult to understand, because the old benchmarks — the benchmarks of parties contesting on a national scale — are so weakened. So they say the "old" left/right distinctions are gone. But there are still poor people, still people without democratic rights, clean water, without a future that holds both food for the stomach and the "art, love, and beauty" mentioned in the lyrics of "Bread and Roses." There are still nations with relatively more of the good things in life, and people that have less, much less, of what the world can hold for all.

The left/right debate has not gone away. It has merely changed location, found a new address in the communities of the world, in the neighbourhoods, plants and offices of cities and small towns, in the rural life of every nation. Thanks to communication: television and computer screens; facsimile transmissions and phone lines; film and video, these issues are brought home to each of us, every day. Thanks again to such communication, the responses to social and economic challenges that people choose do not always occur in the old ways, in a top-down fashion that assumes someone or somebody else will speak for them. Just as nations, governments and economic decision-makers now engage in greater "lateral" communication, so do the rest of us.

In this reshaping world, given the extensive fluidity of party support, the easy response in domestic politics is twofold. There is either the easy politics of acquiescence — selling out past Canadian dreams, but with a "human face" and a self-deprecating style; or there is the easy politics of regional resentment — reacting against the powerlessness these international trends produce for people but without any alternate program of substance.

Today in Canada, the federal Liberal party follows the first easy course. Broadly, the Liberals provide the same philosophy of cutbacks, deficit reduction and harmonizing (and squeezing) social programs that international pressures pushed under the Mulroney government. They do it with different faces, and an "aw, shucks" style that contrasts with Mulroney's imperial self-pride. Only now, as the implications of large social policy cutbacks, tougher unemployment rules, and giving in on NAFTA begin to clash with Liberal promises in the 1993 election campaign, does this easy course become somewhat harder.

But not too much harder, because the official opposition parties in Parliament, the Bloc and Reform, have also taken the easy and natural course of being what they are — region-based protest parties. The Bloc questions social policy reform, not so much because it takes from the less-fortunate, but because it threatens Québec goals of full control over training policies. Reform questions the Axworthy proposals because they won't cut the deficit enough to guarantee keeping Alberta without a provincial sales tax.

But this is not 1955. Politics doesn't just happen in Parliament. The Canadian Labour Congress strongly condemns the social policy proposals. The Council of Canadians publishes huge newspaper ads featuring U.S. pictures of poor children left out of the neo-conservative social service system there. CBC Radio runs a long documentary by Murray Dobbin on what really happened in New Zealand as they took this direction, showing the growing unemployment, poverty and national debt that resulted. The Canadian Centre for Policy Alternatives, and Manitoba's Choices group, aim to develop a counter-budget to the Liberal cutback plan. In New Brunswick, students who will be hit hard by large tuition increases protest and picket the Prime Minister and the Canadian Federation of Students discusses a nation-wide student strike.

A political struggle is underway *outside* Parliament. No national political party takes the lead, but a "movement" of different groups takes shape.

As Buzz Hargrove and the Canadian Auto Workers (CAW) describe in "Labour and Politics: *Rethinking, Redefining, Rebuilding,*" social movements and radical-issue groups increasingly provide much of the energy and involvement of people on the left in Canada. This does not mean that political parties like the federal New Democrats are left out of consideration, but they become just one element in a much broader movement, in which there simply is no controlling centre.

Where does that leave democratic-socialists thinking about strategy?

Surely the focus has to shift more to such "movement politics", in terms of domestic organizing priorities, and (reflecting Howard Pawley's point) in terms of developing effective international links.

This is a difficult shift for some New Democrats to make. They argue that the NDP should stick to the old social democratic orthodoxy of building a mass party that, in effect, monopolizes the left social bases of support by leading the fight for change from Parliament. Such New Democrat traditionalists express real problems in working with the various social justice and issue groups — seeking instead an active party encompassing the important concerns of these groups, and mobilizing those interested in these issues to seek change through Parliament.

This view weakens the progressive left in the new context of a changed framework of politics. It was a view, for instance, that kept some key New Democrats from working closely with movement-style political groups in a fundamental battle like the fight against U.S. free trade — and thereby led to miscommunication and non-parallel strategy decisions that contributed greatly to losing that crucial, defining struggle.

Other New Democrats have argued you cannot ultimately trust the party loyalty of social justice or movement groups, so therefore the party should see the world in a less differentiated way and seek support indiscriminately, as does the Liberal party. At its extreme, this view even involves cutting all ties with the labour movement. You should not see your party as the advocate for any given groups, such New Democrats argue, in contrast to the old NDP orthodoxy.

But the reality *is* that there is a broad movement for social change, with more credibility than the New Democratic Party today, and in that movement, the Canadian trade union movement is seen as a close, key, and continuing ally. And most parts of the Canadian trade union movement continue to see the New Democratic Party as an ally, even a partner, in political action.

The real choice is thus between a party without a real, organized base (which Rae has constructed — or deconstructed — in Ontario) and a party that sees itself as part of a broader progressive movement, of which it is just one (mainly parliamentary) arm.

The old orthodoxy of the mass social democratic party (British or German style) seems no longer consistent with the new fluidity and the internationalism of modern Canadian politics. But democratic-socialists can still lead the New Democratic Party into full commitment to the new "movement politics" that is loosely structured around the labour movement in Canada.

Progressive Canadians need a broad new movement for change if we are truly to challenge for power — with some arms able to operate internationally, some arms able to focus on particular activist struggles here in Canada, and some arms to do the writing and circulating of ideas to keep our movement thinking, refining and reshaping our approaches. That broad progressive movement needs a strong voice in Parliament, too.

To bring together the elements of a coherent alternative to neo-liberal and neo-conservative capitalism we need that combination of vision and pragmatism stressed in our foreword — and we need the solid organized base of counter-institutions that the labour movement can provide.

The labour movement has itself changed. There are more women, more people of colour, more new Canadians and "white collar" workers in the labour movement. More than ever, the labour movement has become an arena in which other movements operate. The women's, gay/lesbian rights, and Black movements have worked within and changed labour's agenda. The Canadian Labour Congress' program has, on many issues, been ahead of the New Democrats'.

Time and again, the labour movement, which contains within it the elements of so many other movements, will take leadership, try new tactics, explore the new strategy of movement-based politics, and community-centred approaches. As did the Industrial Workers of the World, who organized the long-ago "Bread and Roses" 1912 Lawrence textile strike, today's Canadian labour movement has shown the flexibility and creativity that many New Democrats have not.

Michael Darnell outlines some of the aspects of the Great Lakes Fishermen and Allied Workers' Union (GLFAWU) struggle for recognition. It was a legal battle, a political battle and a battle between cultures that was successful, in part, because it involved the contributions of many unions, many individuals committed to justice, as well as the courage of the workers involved.

In the absence of real direction and shared analysis with a national political party, the labour movement has stepped into the breach and provided the direction for the broad, democratic left of Canada without, and sometimes in spite of, the New Democrats.

The labour movement has become even more central to the strategy that democratic-socialists choose, not less relevant. It is time for greater dialogue with the leading activists and thinkers in the labour movement, and a new, more closely shared agenda to develop.

For democratic-socialists in Canada to cut ourselves off from the labour movement would betray the history of our roots in

Saskatchewan (where M.J.Coldwell and Tommy Douglas came into politics through independent labour party involvement) as much as in Ontario (where the rise of CIO-style industrial unionism spurred the Cooperative Commonwealth Federation breakthroughs in the 1940s). It would also cut us off from the one powerful set of institutions in our society that inherently challenges the logic of capitalist profit-maximization day after day. For democratic-socialists to seek such a divorce would be bizarre and suicidal.

Even if we did not need such a strong and active base centred in the trade union movement to win Parliamentary power, we would need such an alternate framework of popular groups and union activists to carry through substantive changes once Parliamentary power is achieved. (The Rae retreats show how easily governments, once elected, can otherwise be forced to retreat from confrontation after confrontation.)

In our experience, it is at the community level that relations of trust, co-operation and partnership can best be built and developed into an ongoing movement for change. There, New Democrats can play a vital and equal role. Over nine years in the Windsor area, there was a close and co-operative partnership developed between federal New Democrats and the labour movement — focused around the Labour Council, but also involving close ties with the major CAW locals in the area (444, 200, 195, 1973, 89, 2027, etc.), with Canadian Union of Public Employees (CUPE) union locals, with Communications Workers, Postal Workers, and with many building trades' locals.

This partnership drew environmental groups that we helped develop (such as the Clean Water Alliance and Essex County Citizens Against Fermi II) into close ties with the labour movement that, in turn, spurred the labour movement to set up its own Environmental Action committees. The partnership also drew together labour-initiated job-oriented groups, like the Unemployed Help Centre, allowing New Democrat MPs to work hard in Parliament to obtain key training and job preparation support for Windsor-area workers. Small business also saw the leadership being provided through the labour-NDP partnership, and worked with us on many initiatives. The National Farmers Union (NFU) local in the area was drawn in, too, as were various anti-poverty groups.

It was on that basis that people in Windsor brought together a very large demonstration in early 1988 against the U.S. trade deal, and helped bring the whole community to mobilize against the closure of Windsor CBC.

So a new-style community based strategy is not just tied to local con-

cerns. It builds linkages, trust and co-operation around local movement politics; but may also lead to community based action on national and international political issues. The point is that this community
level of political action has a reality in concrete situations and real personalities that make progress in building an alternate vision for the
future possible — because we are not talking about something abstract
and unconnected to people's lives. We were instead working together
for a green community for people where they live and want to work.

The Political Economy of Change: Is There an Alternative?

Murray Dobbin describes the "TINA" phenomenon in analyzing the
tragedy of New Zealand. We hear of TINA often in Canada. "There is
no alternative!" is a refrain sung at all levels of government, right
across the country.

With the U.S. trade deal in place, with international capital so mobile
in response to perceived policy changes, and with the high federal
debt loads that Conservative and Liberal governments have accumulat-
ed (and consequent yearly interest payment burdens), can Canadian
governments do anything different?

Answering this broad economic and social policy question is another
fundamental challenge for new-style democratic-socialism. These days,
a widespread myth exists, even among many New Democrats, that the
progressive left can never have any credibility on economic issues to
win popular support. On the contrary, experience shows that when
New Democrats have won endorsement from people, it is because we
have built credibility on economic concerns. This has been possible
to do in the past, and must be done again if a broad progressive movement is to be successful.

When the Broadbent-led federal New Democrats captured the lead in
popular opinion polls in 1987, detailed question-by-question analysis
showed very high support for NDP positions on taxation (favouring a
new minimum corporate tax, and more redistribution built in the tax
system), on U.S. trade policies (stopping the trade deal talks and instead
working on sector-by-sector approaches like the AutoPact), and on
Canadian nationalism (more screening of foreign investment and
tougher efforts to ensure Canadian control in our cultural industries).
Overall, when respondents were asked which party they thought
would best "show leadership to tackle the big economic problems facing the country," 30 per cent chose the New Democrats, compared to
24 per cent for the Liberals and 21 per cent for the Conservatives.[5]

New Democrat provincial governments have also achieved excellent economic records — in Saskatchewan, where the Douglas-Lloyd government(s) of 1944-64 built a very efficient public service to manage the province's finances — and in Manitoba, where the Pawley government brought the province through the 1982-83 recession with the lowest rate of unemployment in Canada. Pawley has stressed that winning power in 1981 required that Manitoba voters came to regard the New Democrats as the best potential governing party on economic matters.

Our union brothers and sisters teach us that to effectively mobilize members to work for broader social change, leaders first must demonstrate real-world skill in grievance handling and bargaining. Ordinary people know that "Bread and Roses" go together. The labour movement has been very effective in winning gains for people, by presenting a vision that is firmly entrenched in the economic life of this nation — even the world. We should draw real strength from their lessons, and from lessons of the past, if we want our broad progressive movement to be successful.

But economic policy, as with new-style visions and organizing frameworks, must be community centred. That's what Coro Strandberg portrays in "Achieving Social and Economic Justice: *A Vision for Canada.*" Strandberg traces the wide network of community economic development efforts that are growing in Canada, and emphasizes this must be the focus for job expansion in the future. This is a strategy that places much initiative in local communities, rather than relying on broad expansion of consumer demand (through deficit financing, for instance) to achieve full employment.

The question of deficits must be confronted by the progressive left in building an alternative economic strategy. But our analysis must surely not follow the neo-conservative rhetoric and cutback priorities that Murray Dobbin shows bring so much human pain and injustice.

There isn't any doubt that huge new deficit increases to get Canadians back to work would not succeed. Such an approach would follow the old orthodoxy that Keynes showed could work in the stagnant 1930s. But now this would simply lead to high leakages from the Canadian economy — creating new jobs elsewhere. And the deficit increases would only be possible to finance with higher interest rates, which would tend to cut back productive investment (and new jobs that go with it) in Canada.

At the same time, significant cuts in the deficit, leading to reduced public services, are inevitably arbitrary and questionable. This is because as stressed in "Debt, Deficit and Human Communities" we do not presently measure the value of public sector benefits in appropriate and accurate ways. Judy Wasylycia-Leis, former minister of social development in Manitoba, in calling for a new democratic-socialist social and economic policy paradigm informed by socialist-feminist analysis, shows this point clearly in her article. Cutbacks force much care-giving out of the official statistics, because services are now provided by women in unpaid ways rather than through professional caregivers. The result is reduced incomes for women forced to give up paid jobs, less professionalized care, and more unemployed professional care givers — all representing social costs to the community. Yet the official statistics suggest the public has gained because it is now supporting less for this care. This official statistical picture is distorted and unreal.

The real economic issue, therefore, is not whether to increase the deficit. No one is arguing that this should be done. But the economic policy priorities should not be a blind stab in the dark to cut public services of all kinds.

There are, rather, at least two questions that must be faced. The first is how do we measure the real social benefits and costs of what the public sector does in Canada? Unbelievably, no one seems to have tried to answer that question for any of the public sector cuts made in this country. As Daryl Bean stresses in his article, there is a very strong case to be made for Canada's public sector.

And second, while that fundamental question is probed (likely with very different results than official statistics presently suggest), why help finance debts for the private sector in many ways through the tax system? Should we not redirect some of these tax incentives to help finance debts for the public sector, especially where public goods benefits are likely to be great?

"Debt, Deficit and Human Communities" traces the rapid increases in large corporate debt in Canada since 1980, and shows how the tax system encourages and helps this (by allowing companies to deduct their interest costs in calculating taxes, for instance by providing for super-fast write-offs of some of these debts against taxes owing — via accelerated depreciation, and by tax benefits for private investors in Canadian-owned corporations). The same article shows no such tax benefits help public sector investment in new environmental protection efforts, for example — although there are very high (but unmeasured) public goods benefits from these efforts.

There are ways to shift tax benefits from the heavy stress on the private sector to more balanced support for public sector investments as well. Establishing a national investment fund for public sector initiatives with high benefit-cost ratios, and permitting tax-free interest payments to be made on bonds floated by this fund, would encourage private investors to put some of their capital into such endeavours. These funds should aim particularly at sustaining our environment for the future and developing job alternatives to economic activities that are reduced or phased out because of environmental concerns.

The same capacity to attract private capital for community initiatives should be legislated for authorized community development councils that meet required participation and public purpose criteria. Again, the emphasis would be job-focused and shaped by goals of sustaining the environment.

At both levels, that of a national investment fund and that of community economic development, public enterprise and co-operatives should be seen as potentially important economic actors, as well as private businesses. Public enterprises have a mixed record, with some question marks (Ontario Hydro has become a power unto itself rather than a community development mechanism), and some positive examples (Air Canada in pre-privatization days). Co-operatives are a growing, important economic reality (including the printers of this book!). The point about both forms of enterprise, public and co-operative, is that they can consider social costs and benefits much more easily than most private businesses can — and that is potentially very valuable in a world of environmental priorities.

Economic mechanisms can be built, therefore, to help achieve green communities for people — without new tax levies or recurrent expenditure increases.

To do so, progressive Canadians must stress a new-style economic approach that is much more community based, puts less emphasis on Keynesian-style demand management, and sees the public sector as an important actor in a framework where social benefits and costs, and the provision of public goods (like environmental security) carry much more weight. Our job goals of full-employment can be realized in the context of this strategy, but not so much through accelerated economic growth, as through more meeting of community needs via community initiatives, and through the shift to a green economy emphasizing more services, more information management, more creative cultural work and more development of green technology.

A Time for Debate

This book is a song with many verses, and many singers. However, in the words of the old party managers, we are not "all singing from the same song sheet." Now is the time for honest debate, for differences, as we sort out how to go on. The reader will not find complete harmony here, but differing perspectives, approaches. That, too, may give the book its value.

Please don't stop by reading this book. Please tell us what you think. Better still, get together with other progressive people in your community and talk about what to do. Listen to other voices in your community, and act together to spur progressive change.

It is in that action, as we reflect upon it, that we can make progress as a movement.

Together, we can build green communities for people in Canada. It may seem a challenging task, given the reversals of recent years. It is also an exciting and audacious goal for the future for a progressive movement that can make a major difference in Canada. It is a way to begin a new century carrying forward the hope and vision of our predecessors, with action and plans that work in the here-and-now. We can have bread and roses, too.

ENDNOTES

1. Thomas Walkom, *Rae Days: The Rise and Follies of the NDP* (Toronto; Key Porter Books, 1994) p. 269.
2. Ibid., p. 5.
3. See excerpts in Michael Jacobs, *The Green Economy* (London; Pluto Press, 1991) p. 59.
4. See, for instance, one of the earliest critiques of what National Accounts measures — W.D. Nordhaus and James Tobin, "Measures of Economic Welfare," in Robert and Nancy Dorfman, eds. *Economics of Environment* (New York; W.W. Norton & Co., 1972) pp. 479-88.
5. This polling was done by the Angus Reid organization and was reported in Southam newspapers throughout Canada, in August 1987.

Visions of Change

. . . .

A new consensus must be forged which will not only rally progressive interests to a common cause but will provide a vision to inspire and motivate Canadian society towards a more socially and economically secure future.

Coro. T. Strandberg
Achieving Social and Economic Justice:
A Vision for Canada

The Labour Movement and Progressive Politics:
The Fight to Preserve Medicare

By Judy Darcy
National President
Canadian Union of Public Employees

A bowling alley seems an unlikely venue for social change. But on June 18, 1992, that's where a group of Prince Edward Island trade unionists, community activists and ordinary citizens gathered to watch a national TV action special about Canada's health care crisis, "Medicare Check-Up." The show was an exciting, high-profile event: a first for the labour movement.

But even more exciting for the program's main sponsors, the Canadian Union of Public Employees, were the on-the-ground community events to defend medicare that had preceded the show. Many of the people sitting in front of the wide screen in the bowling lane that night, along with their counterparts in other provinces, had spent much of the previous few weeks participating in community activities of all kinds in support of saving, and improving, Canada's most cherished social program.

There had been door-to-door canvasses to collect pledge cards in Prince Albert, Saskatchewan, and in Selkirk, Neepawa, Arborg and Rivers, Manitoba. There was a parade that wound its way through Pine Falls, Manitoba, shopping mall card collections in Kenora, and the performance of a play on health care issues in Peterborough, Ontario. There was a successful lobby to get the Nelson, B.C. school district to send a letter in support of medicare to the federal government and a kick-off campaign dinner in Hawksbury, Nova Scotia.

It was all part of an ambitious, multi-faceted campaign spearheaded by CUPE, and supported by the Canadian Labour Congress, the Action Canada Network, the Canadian Health Coalition, seniors', women's, and other social action groups, to protect and progressively reform Canada's universal health care system.

While the campaign had some notable flaws (in retrospect, more time, more resources and a greater effort to make it a broader labour movement and coalition effort in some provinces were needed), it remains a useful model for the type of long-term grassroots campaign that the labour movement and its allies must now wage to build support for an alternative to the lean and mean ideology of the corporate agenda. Given the serious political setbacks progressive organizations and the New Democratic Party have suffered at every level, we have to look at bold and innovative ways to go on the offensive against the right-wing tide that's sweeping across Canada. In a very real sense, we need to fight to reclaim the hearts and minds of Canadians, including those of many of our own members and traditional supporters.

These are precisely some of the things CUPE set out to do with the Keep Medicare Healthy campaign. In our initial brainstorming sessions we had to face some hard truths. First, we knew that while the vast majority of Canadians supported a universal health care system, most did not realize that then-Prime Minister Brian Mulroney and many provincial governments were stabbing medicare in the back through a series of budget cuts and policy betrayals. Medicare was not a hot public issue then. Yet CUPE's front line workers in hospitals, nursing homes and other health care institutions were telling us horror story after horror story about the effects of underfunding of health care on services and their jobs. Daily, they were watching Canada's health care system bleed to death. They told us about "budget" care replacing patient care, about impossible workloads and patients taking second place to the bottom line. They wanted Canadians to know that medicare was in critical condition.

One Manitoba nursing home worker told me that staff were given 6 1/2 minutes to get residents up, washed, dressed and ready to eat each morning. Residents had to be woken up as early as 5 a.m. in order to all be ready for breakfast. "The only way we can possibly do that is strap them in their chairs, hose them down and blow them dry," she said. "I am humiliated by the way I am expected to work. And I am paid to bring humiliation to the residents."

Needless to say, CUPE was also vitally concerned about what severe budget cuts, ad hoc restructuring, and the push for privatization and contracting out were doing to our members' job security. But we knew that defending the status quo just wasn't going to cut it. Rapid and radical change in the name of deficit reduction was the name of the game throughout Canada's health care system. To counteract the effects of these deep cuts, we needed to come up with some viable, progressive alternatives of our own, not a campaign that just said "No."

To make sure our message spread effectively, and was not seen as being merely self-serving, we had to reach out to like-minded groups and other unions. Going it alone was not an option.

So as a first step, we launched a major, coalition-based mobilizing and communications effort to raise public consciousness of the crisis and urge everyone to say "Yes" to saving medicare and improving health care.

While we advocated restoring previous federal funding levels to medicare, we also put forward a series of seven principles for health care reform, ranging from giving non-physician staff a larger role in patient care, democratizing health care institutions, putting an end to privatization of health care, and taking on the multinational drug companies, to getting doctors off piece-work, promoting alternative models of providing health care to the community that safeguard quality care and decently-paid unionized jobs, and encouraging a wellness care system that's serious about preventive care.

We wanted to re-direct the debate on health care reform away from strictly dollars and cents to a positive statement about the kind of health care system Canadians want to see. These principles were the heart of our vision of health care and we used them in all of our material, including the Keep Medicare Healthy kits and pledge cards that were distributed to CLC and CUPE regional campaign co-ordinators, CUPE locals and other unions and coalition groups. In the end, close to half a million cards were collected through community activities and by mail. They were later presented to the government in front of 100,000 people demonstrating on Parliament Hill May 15 against the corporate agenda just a few months before the 1993 federal election campaign.

The seven principles of reform were also the basis of our two-hour national TV action special, which garnered an audience of 431,000. (Not bad considering the opening of the 1992 Barcelona Summer Olympics attracted 1.3 million viewers.) The show received favourable media coverage (on the "entertainment pages" for a change!). It featured Canadian entertainers like co-hosts Eric Peterson and Shirley Douglas, Margot Kidder, Oscar Peterson and Bruce Cockburn, as well as prominent personalities, people from all regions and leaders of various groups affected by the health care debate: the women's movement, First Nations, progressive doctors and front-line health care providers. And 16,271 viewers actually picked up the phone — at 50 cents a call — to support the campaign to save medicare. Clearly, the campaign had struck a chord.

While all the community activities and communications efforts were going on, we also sponsored a research project to look at more detailed policy options for reforming the health care system. This was nitty gritty, "unglamourous" stuff. But it was indispensable. Our researcher worked with a planning group of CUPE staff and members and met with health care workers in every region to hear their stories and ideas. The results of the research were put into background documents and used for strategy discussions at our first national health care workers' conference, in February 1993.

Paying close attention to the ways in which the health care crisis was unfolding regionally was key to making people feel connected to the campaign. And, in fact, as the campaign evolved, it spawned several regional spin-offs spearheaded by CUPE health care workers — in Alberta, Saskatchewan, P.E.I., Ontario and New Brunswick — who found innovative ways to keep the issue alive in their regions and motivate Canadians to join the fight to keep medicare healthy.

On the national level, health care unions and coalition partners have also continued to build on the groundwork laid by the Keep Medicare Healthy campaign. While a House of Commons Committee debated the Tories' Bill C-91 which guaranteed further price-gouging by multinational brand name drug companies, busloads of seniors descended on Parliament Hill carrying huge card-board cut-outs of pills with their old and new prices clearly marked. During the last federal election campaign, health care unions and the Canadian Health Coalition organized a National Day of Action on Medicare. Across the country, thousands of health care workers wore two bandages on their uniforms (crossed in an X to encourage voting to save medicare) and challenged candidates and party leaders to sign campaign pledges to save medicare. (Only the NDP Leader, Audrey McLaughlin, signed.)

More recently, at CUPE's initiative, several health care workers' unions have been meeting to develop strategies to support the Canadian Health Coalition's efforts to save medicare, with an emphasis on training local activists to carry out a campaign that advances 10 Goals for Improving Health Care through activities from coast to coast. This campaign goes hand in glove with the CLC's action plan to educate and mobilize Canadians around an alternative program for job creation, health care and social policy reform.

Clearly, the labour movement and our allies are in it for the long haul. No one thinks that support for progressive reform of medicare, let alone for a comprehensive vision of a Canada that puts people ahead of the bottom line, can be won overnight or solely through catchy slogans, rhetorical flourishes and clever ad copy. Using these tactics alone will barely garner a ripple of interest from our own members, who are fighting just to hang onto their jobs and whose support for their union's and the labour movement's policies cannot be taken for granted.

We know we need to bring about a virtual sea change in public opinion. Without it, we can't hope to force governments to enact the social and economic reforms needed to make Canada a caring and compassionate country. That's a pretty tough challenge. But if we want to succeed, our efforts must go far beyond skimming the surface and focus on grassroots education and mobilization of our members and our diverse communities. The need to bring people together for common action has never been greater. We need campaigns that are flexible and creative, and break new ground. Our campaigns must take place not just on the national level, but on regional and community levels as well so that people can more readily see how broad social and economic issues touch them where they live.

But above all, if we want to build strong solidarity for meaningful change, our first task is to provide people with a strong, unifying core — a compelling and clear alternative vision, something they can fight for, over and above what they've been used to fighting against.

Assistance from Bozica Costigliola in preparing this article is gratefully acknowledged by the author.

Labour and Politics:
Rethinking, Redefining, Rebuilding —
The View from the Canadian Auto Workers

. . . .

Buzz Hargrove
President
National Automobile, Aerospace, Transportation and General Workers Union
of Canada (CAW Canada)

The Canadian Auto Workers (CAW) has always been an activist union with a key role in progressive politics, particularly in Ontario. The birth of the Canadian union 10 years ago heightened this role of the union, as the CAW became a centre of Canadian nationalist activism, and a source of renewed hope and spirit for the Canadian left.

There is a deep relationship with the New Democrats and its predecessor party, the Cooperative Commonwealth Federation. The CAW's role at the local, provincial and federal levels can't be underestimated, though electoral and party politics have always been only one element in the union's efforts to express the aspirations of working people. There were changes in the union's relationship with the New Democrats prior to the election of the Rae government or the 1993 federal election. Those events crystallized an already dynamic situation and sparked greater debate inside the union and among its democratic left coalition partners about how to bring forward an agenda for social, economic and political change.

The following paper was prepared by the president of the union, Buzz Hargrove, in discussion with others, and brought to the CAW's 1994 Constitutional Convention. There, delegates discussed it and ratified it. For CAW members, this paper represents the collective thought of the union. For those outside the union, this paper provides an essential picture of where Canada's largest private sector union stands.

Introduction: Acknowledging the Crisis

> *The Council endorsed the statement, but what was more signif-*
> *icant was the level of discussion and healthy debate that*
> *occurred. . . . people were critical, but they weren't looking for*
> *excuses to give up on the Party — they were looking for*
> *changes that would revive their enthusiasm . . . [they] under-*
> *stood that public debate — including public campaigns to*
> *push this government in certain directions — is both part of*
> *the democratic politics we believe in **and** the only way to actu-*
> *ally change things . . .*

Buzz Hargrove, covering letter to NDP Provincial Premiers and
Members of Provincial Parliament regarding his December,
1992 Council Report

There is a crisis in the Labour-New Democratic Party partnership.
That crisis was brought to a head in 1993 when the Ontario New
Democratic Party introduced its cynically misnamed "social contract."
But the crisis extends beyond that event and it extends beyond Ontario.

This crisis in social democracy is international. It's something confronting the labour movement throughout Europe as well as in
Australia and New Zealand. That's why even the International
Confederation of Free Trade Unions, officially representing over 110
million organized workers in 108 countries made it the central theme
of a conference last year.

The crisis is reflected in loyal activists who ask "what's the alternative?" but then can't themselves muster the excitement and energy to
win others over. It shouts out at us with the reality that, in the last federal election, the Reform Party — so fundamentally opposed to the values and needs of organized working people — won more votes from
unionized workers than did the NDP. During that federal election, the
NDP's share of the vote was under 8 per cent, less than in any election
since the formation of the New Democratic Party in 1961; less even
than the Cooperative Commonwealth Federation's poor showing in
1958 which led to its rebirth as the NDP; less, in fact, than any vote
the CCF itself received including its first electoral campaign in 1935.

The labour movement can't allow party loyalty to hide the truth that
the party — and therefore the politics of labour — are in deep trouble.
The real danger is not that by openly debating this fact the NDP might
be further damaged; the danger is that if we're silent, the party will
surely sink into irrelevance, seriously damaging the labour movement
itself along the way. We must ask ourselves what has happened and
why, so we can move on to address where we go from here:

- Why, after the miserable failure of the right to address economic and social needs, and the election of NDP governments in Ontario, British Columbia and Saskatchewan are we (the left) rather than they (the right) on the defensive?

- Why, after the breakthrough in Ontario and in spite of some very positive legislative steps, is the Ontario NDP government reviled by so many workers rather than seen as a party/government fighting — in difficult times and against powerful enemies — on their behalf?

- Why hasn't labour been able to deliver the vote? Are we just another interest group, concerned with elections to consolidate our own gains?

- Had we decided, in 1961, to work towards the long-term building of a socialist constituency — rather than winning the next election — would we be better off politically than we are today?

Why, in short, have we — the NDP and the unions — been so unable to capture, articulate, build on, and lead the anger and frustration that is so clearly out there?

The Ontario NDP Government: Who's to Blame?

> *What has become particularly clear is that the NDP does not just fall short in terms of the degree of reform expected and needed by the unions, but that it can actively undermine union power and solidarity. One cannot underestimate . . . the political significance, of an NDP government in particular, joining in the general attack on public sector workers and their rights.*

> *The Assault on Trade Union Rights, Freedoms*, Panitch and Swartz, 1993 (p. 178)

> *How many times has a labour movement supported a liberation movement, only to find itself betrayed on the day of liberation? There are many examples of this in Africa. If the African National Congress does not deliver the goods you must do to it what you did to the apartheid regime . . .*

> Nelson Mandela, "Address to Special Coalition of South African Trade Unions Conference," October, 1993

The crisis in the Labour-NDP relationship has been clearest in Ontario, though events in Ontario certainly have some parallels in British Columbia and Saskatchewan. A discussion of labour's relationship with the Ontario New Democratic Party (ONDP) government takes on an additional importance because Ontario's economy is so significant — it's the size of many countries (like Sweden's) — and because Ontario lies at the heart of economic power in Canada, affecting us all.

In spite of progressive moves on labour reform and other issues dealing with equity and justice, the government soon began sounding like other governments, making judgements based on expediency, and putting the main focus on the deficit.

If it weren't for the "social contract", the CAW might still be officially supporting the party. But it would have been a support sapped of the kind of enthusiasm crucial to any success. Nevertheless, the "social contract" happened and the significance went far beyond a simple disagreement on a particular policy.

The social contract was neither social nor a contract. It was a unilateral roll-back of existing collective agreements. As such, it not only took away the fundamental right to bargain from some 900,000 workers, but also set the stage for more of the same from other governments. If future governments do the same, will the NDP stand up in the house and shout "Shame!"? And by focusing public attention on public sector workers, the NDP essentially sent the message that it was this group of workers that was to blame for the deficit, undermining the already fragile public support for the work they do and the services they provide.

Above all, when this NDP government defended itself by arguing they had no alternative, they were, to all intents and purposes, working to demobilize anyone fighting to keep some hope for alternatives alive. The NDP was essentially "teaching" the most dangerous lesson of all: There is nothing we can really do; the right *is* right.

So who do we blame? We can be angry at the architects of this direction, but if we stop there we'll miss the point and find that the same things will happen again but with different players. Some frustrated activists view the problem as Bob Rae, or a caucus with not enough "real" workers, or bad advice from advisors. But the truth is that the Premier had the support of the overwhelming majority of his caucus; that the caucus had a uniquely large degree of working class representation; and — above all — that what was going on in Ontario had its parallel with what had happened and was happening with other social democratic governments around the world.

The basic problem is not so much "who to blame" as it is the *role and direction* of social democratic parties in opposition and in office. In opposition, they moved to the centre to get elected; in office they tried to become credible managers of capitalism, managers with a human face. But "managing" the system when corporate power had expanded globally, when you have a hostile bureaucracy, and especially when the system itself is in crisis, only leads to "managing the discontent" of workers and the population. The so-called new managers end up to be the sellers of the bad news, the distributors of the bad medicine.

Taking over the reins of government is an important *step* in affecting change, but in itself, it's a far cry from taking power. The corporations still decide where to invest and when to take away productive capacity; the media still decides what is relevant information; antagonistic bureaucrats retain a multitude of ways to sabotage policies they disagree with; a majority of the population may have cast protest votes, but remain wary of radical policies. In this context, if you have not been preparing to challenge the status quo, you end up serving it.

The Politics of Hard Times

> *A dramatic change has occurred in the world economy over the last two decades. What we are living through is not just another downturn or another temporary setback. We are witnessing a new direction for capitalism, one that has been redefining what progress means.*
>
> **Hard Times, New Times:** *Report to the 1993 National Collective Bargaining and Political Action Convention*

The assumption that dominated the post-war period was that capitalism would continue, in a relatively stable way, to provide a rising standard of living for ourselves and our children. As long as this assumption prevailed, the primary issue wasn't fundamental change in our society or a dramatic challenge to the establishment; it was ongoing reform, improving the level of equality, speeding up progress.

Not surprisingly, this shifted the focus of politics from being a movement to being an electoral machine. For unions, it meant accepting a particular division of activity within the party: the "party" made the fundamental decisions on electoral strategy and direction, and we provided the footsoldiers — the money and the bodies — to go door-to-door. Education of the membership was not about developing workers who understood capitalism and thought about organizing for change; that is, it wasn't about creating a mass base of dedicated socialists and dedicated supporters. Rather, it had the much more limited goal of officially endorsing the NDP and getting our members to vote "correctly" in the next election.

This strategy of downplaying longer term goals and vision backfired in two particular ways. First, during good times, workers could achieve improvements outside party politics: collective bargaining, lobbying and specific campaigns proved to be quite successful in making concrete gains (which is not to say that the NDP was irrelevant, only that its necessity was less pressing). Second, having based all its strategy on capitalist stability, the NDP was not ready strategically for dealing with capitalism in crisis times. In bad times, a party whose vision had wilted, that had built no movement behind it, and had no real strategy for progressive change, was extremely vulnerable to corporate pressure from the right.

At this time of crisis in the NDP, with the labour movement itself under attack, parallels to the thirties when both the CCF-NDP and industrial unionism were born are too obvious to ignore. Does that birth of our movement hold lessons for its revival?

Stepping Back: Our Roots as a Movement

> *There is a need for the party to become more involved in daily struggles which would attract many eager men and women who are really ready for a Social Democratic Party but have so far failed to be inspired by the CCF — and I don't blame them.*

David Lewis, letter of July 26, 1937

> *We must get away from the old idea of winning at any cost and by any method and steadily build up a convinced and educated constituency.*

J.S. Woodsworth, first CCF leader, letter of March 14, 1935

During the Great Depression, two points seemed clear to many of those frustrated and angry with the direction of our society.

1. The establishment was bankrupt in terms of solutions and vision. Business and governments had nothing to offer except more of the same, arguing for more cutbacks and "sound finance" (concentrating on the budgetary deficit, not the deficit in jobs, equality, or justice).

2. Finding and carrying out progressive solutions necessitated a break with the two old-line parties. These parties were dominated by the business class and if we really wanted change we need-

ed to build a party independent of business, one linked to farmers, the working class, and sympathetic intellectuals.

In 1933, the Cooperative Commonwealth Federation (CCF) came into being. It emerged at a time when various groups across the country were organizing to defend themselves and fight for change. Some of these groups stayed outside the coalition that became the CCF. Within the CCF coalition there was a very wide range of perspectives, yet one characteristic stood out. In those early years, a great many CCFers viewed themselves as part of a "movement" and structured their activities as part of a movement.

Only a movement, with its commitment to a new world, could generate the excitement and energy to build a new party. Only a movement, with a long-term vision and active in every facet of people's lives, could keep people going through the inevitable disappointments and ups and downs. And only a movement could eventually take on the issues of a fundamental change in the distribution of power and direction of society.

As a movement, the focus was on educating, organizing, mobilizing. Newspapers were established to disseminate information and analysis: during the thirties, the CCF had six newspapers in six different provinces supported by a central news co-op. Educational activity was paramount as reading lists were distributed, study groups formed, and leaders travelled the country not to get a sound-bite on the news but to teach and debate the issues. New people were constantly brought into "politics" by creating new institutions for fighting back — like councils of the unemployed. And over the next decade, one of the most significant new movements, the industrial labour movement, emerged to challenge corporations in the workplace and to unite with others fighting for change.

What is so striking about the present is the virtual absence of such activities in the culture or life of the NDP. When our union talks about political education, we generally mean what happens in Paid Education Leave (PEL), not in or through the NDP. When there is talk of organizing the unemployed it comes from unemployed groups themselves or from unions, not from riding associations. Who initiates and leads major national campaigns — like the fight against free trade and the 1993 demonstration for jobs? Is the NDP leading in the fight for reduced work time? How often or seriously does the NDP ever talk about having a left newspaper or even a left magazine to debate the difficult issues of our times? Is there any serious discussion within the NDP about how to mobilize young people?

The CAW and the NDP: Support and Tensions

> *Although the UAW (Canada) continued to pump money into the NDP in the aftermath of the 1980 federal election . . . the party moved away from social democratic principles towards a more conservative political image at the same time that the UAW was becoming more politically militant in its own actions and demands. As had happened so many times in the past, the UAW and the NDP were marching to the beat of two different drummers.*
>
> ***Plant to Politics: The Autoworkers' Union in Postwar Canada***,
> Charlotte A.B. Yates, (p.217)

The current tensions between the CAW and the NDP are not new. They have historical roots and parallels. Although the CCF had already fought its first election in 1935, the UAW Canada did not officially endorse the CCF until 1948.[1] One concern expressed by a significant section of the CAW was that the CCF viewed the labour movement as a "special interest group" rather than as a leading force for fundamental change.

From the 1950s to the present, the UAW-CAW's financial and organizational support for the NDP was consistent and impressive, yet certain tensions consistently recurred. In fact, during the term of each of the union's presidents, there arose a particular "crisis" in the relationship to the party. And each of these crises had a similar root: the contrasting responses of the union and the party to a particularly deep downturn or new phase of capitalist restructuring. If, during these periods, the party was also in office provincially, the tensions were all the greater.

The first major downturn after World War II happened in the late 1950s. While the party was looking to become more respectable, then Canadian Director George Burt, in his report to the (union's) Council, wondered whether "it is going to be more and more necessary for our government to consider taking over the resources of Canada and plan production for full employment" and went on to suggest that "we have gone past the stage where we can depend on the hit and miss methods employed by private enterprise."

It was in the mid-1970s that the post-war boom truly ended. The downturn signalled by "the energy crisis" represented a permanent change: shared material progress could no longer be assumed. A central part of the then-Liberal (federal) government's response was to directly limit workers' ability to make progress by imposing general wage controls. To the labour movement, this unilateral cancelling of the right to bargain over the price and conditions of our labour was an attack on one of our most basic democratic rights. The two NDP provincial Premiers (Allan Blakeney in Saskatchewan, Ed Schreyer in Manitoba), however, supported the imposition of wage controls. A furious Dennis McDermott attacked their position at the then-UAW Canadian Council and, frustrated with their assumption that we had nowhere else to go (with political support), mused in private about withdrawing support for the NDP at the next election.

In the 1980s, the major corporate project for restructuring centred around the Free Trade Agreement (FTA) with the United States. The CAW joined with others in labour and coalition groups to place this issue at the top of the national agenda. The NDP of course opposed the agreement, but gave it only secondary prominence in the 1988 election.

When both the United Steelworkers of America (USWA) and the CAW released strong criticisms of the party's spiritless response, something more than just another election post-mortem was at stake. The labour movement was suggesting that it, rather than the party, had been right about electoral tactics. More significant, it was the labour movement rather than the party that was bringing more people and more passion to politics, while raising the level and clarity of debate about what was happening to our country.[2] There was, in other words, the beginnings of a challenge to "subcontracting politics" out to the NDP; the labour movement's own leadership potential was stirring.

And then, during the deepest recession in Canada since the 1930s, with business aggressively attacking the labour movement and past social gains, the NDP won the provincial election in Ontario (and then British Columbia and Saskatchewan). It looked like the 1990s would — finally — mean the end of an era dominated by the corporate agenda, and a period in which both policies and political discussion would not be limited by competitiveness and deficits.

It was in the context of subsequent disappointments over how the Ontario NDP acted and talked that I reluctantly stated to our Council: "Our response must include withdrawing our support from the NDP *Government* of Ontario and to limit support for the New Democratic *Party* of Ontario to the very minimum levels that allow us . . . to maintain our affiliation."

For the first time in some 45 years, during which cracks in the relationship were papered over, the CAW took the decision to withdraw support from a section of the NDP. And more significantly, we opened the doors for a wide-ranging debate about politics and the NDP.

Redefining Politics

In addressing the issue of reviving progressive politics in Canada, three points seem especially important. First, that a strong and independent union movement remains the crucial base for any politics of the left. Second, that unions must extend their activity so that they truly become the center of working class life in their communities. Third, that the issue is not so much whether to participate in the NDP, as the purpose and role of a party of social change today: what kind of party do we need at this particular stage of capitalism?

Unions as Movement

> *Unions were born out of struggles to change the status quo. Our successes extended progress beyond unions themselves, and our struggles became part of a **social movement** for a more humane society here and for peace and justice internationally. These struggles were first steps towards developing the confidence that change is possible and that our vision of society is not just a dream.*
>
> **CAW Statement of Principles**

What places unions at the centre of any politics of the left are our financial resources; our organizational strength including people with the skills and experience to educate, reach out, mobilize and get things done; and our strategic role in the economy — the economy needs our members' labour.

Yet, unless we also have a progressive and independent view of the world, none of the above potential will bear any political fruit. A mobilized and independent union movement can affect politics directly — a potential we often underestimate. In the past, strikes and sitdowns have changed labour legislation (Rand formula, advance notice, severance pay) and union bargaining positions have affected national policy discussions (from Unemployment Insurance in the 1930s, to medicare in the 1960s, to fighting the "competitive agenda" in the 1980s and addressing reduced work time today).

More generally, without the counterweight of unions it would be so much easier for corporations to steamroller their agenda without debate or resistance. During the FTA debate, for example, it was unions — alongside coalition groups — that ensured that a national debate actually occurred around this historic issue and its impact on the future of our country. The point is that when we act as a countervailing force to the enormous power wielded by the economic elite in our society, we play a vital democratic — and therefore political — role.

Above all, we should recognize the impact of union activity on how our members perceive politics. Unless individual members learn on the basis of their daily lives that collective action can really matter, they will surely be cynical about any other kind of collective activity — including electoral politics. It's when we stake out positions that challenge the establishment, when we engage our members in resisting the corporate agenda, when we collectively fight to defend ourselves in the workplace and win new rights and better conditions through bargaining, that we develop the foundation of any meaningful politics: namely, the confidence that things can be changed, and the understanding that change requires solidarity.

That solidarity starts in the workplace and in the union, but given what we're up against, we must also firmly root it in the community. It's not just that we need broader support to avoid being isolated. It's also that our members have lives and community-based needs outside the union: the cost of housing, the degradation of the environment, the livability of our cities, what's happening to our kids in the school system.

There are two (overlapping) aspects of extending the union's role into the community. One, "social unionism," focuses on the union as an institution that *contributes directly* to the community beyond serving our own members: e.g., expanding the role of non-profit housing, supporting shelters for battered women, contributing to food banks and the United Way, organizing sports leagues and music camps for young people, financing a student centre at the local university campus.

The other "movement politics," emphasizes the need to join others — usually other working people in the community — to mobilize and fight around both specific issues (e.g., fighting alongside the unemployed and defending those forced onto welfare, coalitions to resist health care cuts or demand affordable and higher quality childcare) and a broader vision of social change.

Amongst other things, these activities create new vehicles for participation by those members not particularly interested in traditional union activities. This strengthens the union and expands participation in collective action or "politics."

The Party and the Movement

> *What kind of party does this require? It requires a party ready to defend its natural constituencies because that is the only way to build a social movement: . . . a party that recognizes*

that the fundamental importance of unions and the social movement is that they bring new people into politics; . . . a party that encourages participation and sees its primary function as fighting immediate battles, educating for change, developing the co-ordination and organizations for the larger battles. There are, I believe, a great many Canadians who would want to participate in the building of this kind of party.

Bob White, "Brief to NDP Task Force," 1989
(reviewing the 1988 Free Trade Agreement election campaign)

Where does electoral politics fit into all of this? Clearly the issue isn't to deny the critical importance of electoral politics; this is an area of struggle we absolutely can't leave to the corporate sector. Rather, the point is to emphasize that: a) there are forms of effective politics beyond the ballot box which should not be ignored or underestimated; and b) building movements also sets the stage for a *more successful* party politics.

An electoral strategy without a politics of building movements alongside it will, as we have learned, inevitably frustrate activists and alienate potential supporters. While social democratic parties might in certain circumstances get into office without a movement, the movement is the only guarantee that its mandate will be fulfilled. Only active movements can counter the predictable pressures a committed government will face and reinforce its determination to carry on. Where a friendly government is hesitant, only a movement can ensure that it feels the heat if it starts to retreat.

The NDP has often paid lip service to such a movement, remaining suspicious about its independence. There was no way to escape that tension. Movements (including the labour movement) can't be reduced to being a tool of a political party or they will wither and die. The NDP can only earn the support of these movements by having its own activists participate directly in the movements, and by demonstrating its ability in further building those movements.

This suggests dramatic changes in the party. It challenges the NDP to move beyond being just an electoral machine and to become an integral part of a movement-building agenda which extends into every workplace and every community. It demands that we transform structures, like riding associations, from being primarily fundraising bodies to forums that develop ideas and work to build the movements and solidarity groups engaged in those daily struggles — big and small — that introduce people to politics and nurture the confidence that change is possible. It means a party that takes on the competitive agenda, and that agenda's narrow focus on what society is about. It means working towards developing — at conferences, in riding associations, in public forums — the ideological perspective and alternative vision that can move people and unite them against the corporate agenda. It means a party open to the most wide-ranging internal debate on direction. And it means that, after a successful election, a party that remains ready to challenge even a "friendly" government when it threatens to leave us weaker, rather than stronger, as a result of its term in office.

It is these kinds of issues and challenges that lie at the heart of what to do about the NDP.

Summary and Conclusion

> *Corporations have raised the stakes and moved the issues to a whole new level. If we don't also move to a new level, then even just hanging on to what we have — never mind achieving real change — will get harder and harder . . . The only way we can move unionism to a higher level — one that can play a role in introducing those alternatives that really matter — is by building a labour movement and a social movement that can eventually challenge and transform power in our society.*

> **Hard Times, New Times:** *Report to the 1993 National Collective Bargaining and Political Action Convention*

The media — and not only the media — have raised the question of whether a politics of the left is still relevant. The question, given everything that is happening around us, is absurd. The right has controlled the economic and social agenda for the last 15 years. It has had its chance to try out its solutions, and it has failed — *miserably*. Its solutions are bankrupt, its vision shamefully small. The economy may or may not recover in the short run, but the crisis — a crisis in capitalism's ability to provide a better life for all — will continue. And that means that a politics of the left is not just "relevant," but *more* important than it has been for some time.

Yet we haven't been able to take advantage of this waiting opportunity. The irony is that the crisis in capitalism has also led to a crisis in social democracy. We have not come to grips with a capitalism that is too weak to provide for our needs, yet strong enough to undermine what we currently have. Having prepared ourselves only for a capitalism that will continue — however unequally — to prosper, we haven't developed the twin needs of a) developing an economic agenda that can effectively deal with bad times, and b) developing the necessary mass political base to carry it out.

How then can our union be most effective in redefining "poli. and reviving the party? It may very well be that we can be most constructive by example. This would be committing ourselves to the following three "projects," each of which challenges the NDP to change the range and direction of its politics:

1. Strengthening and building the union (especially given the dramatic changes in membership we're experiencing), by expanding our educational programs, increasing local input, and building the confidence to continue resisting the corporate agenda and confronting its perverse logic.

2. Basing the union, particularly at the local level, in the community and community struggles. This is crucial to prevent the union from being isolated, to bring new people (CAW and others) into struggles and therefore politics, and to build a foundation for national politics.

3. Playing a national leadership role in taking on the economic and political establishments, defining an agenda for fundamental democratization of our political and economic system, and contributing to mobilizing the mass social movement without which no real change will occur.

The issue isn't about being "pure" — as trade union activists we certainly know that the road to progress is paved with a good number of compromises. It's because we understand how difficult the problems really are that we view the central problem as one of building: building our union, building a movement, building the party — so the limits to what we can do today can, over time, be overcome.

ENDNOTES

1. The Canadian Brotherhood of Railway and Transport workers (CBRT), now part of the CAW, was the only union officially present at the founding CCF convention in 1933.
2. It should be pointed out that the economic nationalism and movement politics advocated in these labour critiques echoed arguments made in the early 70s by a group within the NDP, the Waffle. The Waffle was ultimately thrown out of the party for these views. Ironically both the USWA and the CAW, concerned with the Waffle's criticism of international (American-based) unions were very instrumental in that decision.

Achieving Social and Economic Justice:
A Vision for Canada

By Coro T. Strandberg

The consensus among progressive movements in Canada has broken down. The increasing impotence of the nation state in the face of globalization of capital plus the growing awareness within certain socio-economic sectors that their interests are not served by Canada's welfare state have both contributed to this breakdown. The progressive consensus has weakened. Social democracy is on the defensive. Public support and awareness of progressive alternatives are also mired in a confusion of rhetoric and alienation to the point that few can distinguish credible proposals from their alarming impostors.

A new consensus must be forged which will not only rally progressive interests to a common cause but will provide a vision to inspire and motivate Canadian society towards a more socially and economically secure future. But first, the components of this vision must be assembled into a comprehensive framework which is practical, achievable and which can provide the leadership critical for the next century.

This chapter proposes two key strategies and discusses their potential for creating a compassionate and healthy society: Economic Democracy through Community Economic Development and Accountable Capital through Social Investment Strategies.

First, it will provide a brief overview of some of the structural conditions and socio-economic trends which are shaping Canadian society, in order to provide the context for — and reinforce the urgency of — these proposals.

The Context

Poverty and Welfare

Over four million Canadians live in poverty. In 1992, 1.2 million children were poor. And poverty rates for single mothers with children under 18 years of age increased from 56 per cent in the late 1980s to 65 per cent by 1991.[1] The "Poverty Gap" — the amount of additional income needed to bring all Canadians out of poverty — was estimated at $13.6 billion in 1992.[2]

And with national unemployment at over 10 per cent (July 1994), no wonder we are seeing high welfare rates. In British Columbia, for example, about one in 10 people rely on income assistance, while in 1993 there were over three million people receiving welfare, one million of them children.[3]

This is up from the 691,500 in 1987. And those with the highest usage rates are typically those most disenfranchised in the labour market: youth, single parents, Aboriginal people and people with disabilities.

While the federal government has embarked upon a review of the social safety net, the public is skeptical about government's ability to have any real impact on these social problems.

Public Alienation

We are all aware of the polls which show that politicians command little respect in Canadian society. However, polls now show that anger towards the *system* is even more serious than that directed toward politicians.

The public believes that not only have governments failed to find workable solutions to economic and social dilemmas, but that they are not truly responsive.

Confronted with economic uncertainty, declining real incomes, rising poverty and growing welfare rates, Canadians are increasingly of the view that governments alone do not have the answers to their problems. Old institutional approaches do not work. To fill the void, new, accountable and enduring methods and structures must be found to reverse the alarming social and economic trends in Canadian society. To begin, national goals must be developed which will foster the fundamental conditions essential to social well-being.

Social Well-being

Any vision of social and economic justice must start with a definition of social well-being which is contemporary and builds upon current knowledge and experience. The Roeher Institute recently completed a synthesis and analysis of the goals and principles which underpin social well-being in modern Canadian society. They identified three key elements of the post-war framework: security ("people are secure when their basic needs for income, safety and support are met"), citizenship (conferring civil and political rights on individuals) and democracy (securing political stability and economic strength through the institution of parliamentary democracy and the legitimation of trade unions).[4]

The Institute then identified three new elements which provide the basis for a contemporary concept of well-being: self-determination, equality and democratization. Self-determination is the articulation of aspirations, the choices made in pursuing them and the development of people, communities and society for the capacities needed to achieve their aspirations; democratization is the process of enabling people to participate in decisions which affect their lives; equality is the absence of barriers to mutual respect and recognition between people "who are equally free from political control, social pressure and economic deprivation and insecurity to engage in valued pursuits and who have equal access to the means of self-development."[5,6]

To sum up the Institute's analysis, we can conclude that quality of life and social well-being depend upon: security, citizenship, democracy, equality, self-determination and democratization.

A new national vision therefore, must address the public's increasing alienation from traditional institutions/systems and build upon these six conditions of social well-being to create an environment for healthy and compassionate communities and families to thrive. Two key strategies which embody these principles while addressing the public distrust of government initiative are Economic Democracy through Community Economic Development and Accountable Capital through Social Investment Strategies. They will be discussed in turn.

Economic Democracy Through Community Economic Development

Individuals and communities are increasingly demanding greater control over their economic and social futures. The essential goal of economic democracy is to increase people's control, as individuals or as groups, over their economic welfare. Security, democratization, equality and self-determination — and therefore social well-being — can only be achieved through strategies which support economic democracy.

So while fine in theory, what does economic democracy look like in practice?

Community Economic Development (CED) is an essential, though not the only, component of a national strategy for economic democracy focused on improving the quality of life for Canadians, especially those marginalized from the economic mainstream. (Other key components include worker buy-outs, worker-controlled pension funds and state enterprise.) Often derided as being small-scale and insignificant in comparison to private sector enterprise and other macro-economic policy levers of government, when measured against the objective of economic democracy, CED is a key building block.

There are many definitions of CED, which suggest it is still a largely misunderstood approach. A definition which places it squarely in the economic democracy agenda is found in *Making Waves,* which notes that principles of social solidarity, individual and collective empowerment and control over local resources are prerequisites for a progressive definition of CED:

> *CED is a comprehensive, multi-faceted strategy for the revitalization of community economies, with a special relevance to communities under economic stress. Through the creation of organizations and institutions, alliances are created and resources are put in place that are democratically controlled by the community. They mobilize and direct local resources (people, finances, technical expertise and real property) in partnership with resources from outside the community for the purpose of empowering community members to create and manage new and expanded businesses, specialized institutions and organizations.*[7]

Aboriginal people are the Canadian leaders in Community Economic Development, which should come as no surprise given the focus on self-government, capacity development and empowerment. Freeing themselves from the chains of economic dominance which have bound them to conditions of abject poverty, Aboriginal people recognize the importance of gaining control of their economic destiny. To understand the potential and impact of CED strategies, their successes and failures should be studied.

Recent studies organize CED into six major models, all of which need to be present in order to create an environment which supports economic empowerment. These models include equity investment, debt financing, development finance and technical assistance intermediaries, human resource development, and planning, research, advisory and advocacy services.[8] Because the first four demonstrate the power of democratically controlled capital organized for social purposes they will be elaborated more fully below. This presentation does not review the considerable experience of community businesses, worker co-ops and other job-creating enterprises, not because their impact is not significant, but because the focus in this section is on the infrastructure and development vehicles essential to economic democracy and community well-being.

There are about 180 development corporations in Aboriginal communities and Tribal Regions establishing new community-controlled ventures through equity investments, the first major CED model. They have goals which emphasize profit generation for reinvestment purposes, job creation and the development of management capacity. Kitsaki Development corporation, owned by the LaRonge Indian Band, shows just how successful this approach can be. Since 1985 they have used joint ventures to secure ownership in key economic sectors in northern Saskatchewan and today control 13 ventures ranging from manufacturing and trucking to catering and insurance. By 1992, these ventures had yielded $17 million in gross revenues and created 500 jobs.[9]

Kitsaki and the other 180 Aboriginal development corporations have benefitted significantly, however, from federal government programs over the last few years and would likely not have survived without this support.

While there are fewer non-native examples, two well-known models are also located within struggling economies: Cape Breton and Halifax. New Dawn Enterprises, located in Sydney, Cape Breton began in 1975 for the purpose of assisting community revitalization. Its first project was the renovation of a deteriorated building into a mixed-use residential and commercial building. Since then, New Dawn has built a significant asset base in affordable housing, managing about $12 million in real estate, while creating and managing eight ventures, primarily in the seniors' market.[10]

The Halifax-based Human Resource Development Association (HRDA) is noteworthy for its unique use of welfare funds. Founded in 1978 by the Director of Social Planning who successfully proposed the diversion of social assistance payments to create businesses to hire welfare recipients, it has hired over 1,000 welfare recipients in its businesses through its holding company, HRDA Enterprises, Ltd. Since 1978, sales have totaled over $22 million, and today it has over 164 employees. A recent cost-benefit analysis concluded that for every welfare dollar received HRDA returned two to the sponsoring governments.[11]

There are some interesting provincial inroads in mobilizing community-controlled capital for equity purposes. Saskatchewan, for example, introduced its Saskatchewan Community Bond Program in 1991 which provides a provincial guarantee for investments (the principal is guaranteed, not the return) in a local Community Bond Corporation established for the purposes of creating or expanding a local business. The capitalized business must be Saskatchewan owned, the bonds are sold in $100 denominations and investments are capped at $50,000 or 10 per cent of any single issuance. A June 1993 report of the Community Bond Program indicated that $12.5 million had been guaranteed for 5,500 investors in 24 local corporations and 350 jobs had been created.[12]

The debt financing CED model provides loans or loan guarantees to entrepreneurs, worker co-ops and community owned businesses. Unlike conventional industrial incentives, CED lending institutions target their loans to those who are economically disenfranchised. Community self-reliance and empowerment are the twin goals of CED debt financing institutions; they are concerned about both the availability of services and goods and the availability of long-term jobs. Technical assistance provision is a key service offered by CED lending institutions, not only because business start-ups are notoriously difficult, but because the local entrepreneur usually lacks the skills for successful business development, and because, inherently, such businesses are established in high-risk communities.[13]

As with equity investment models, Aboriginal communities have a strong network of CED lending organizations, with 33 native "Aboriginal Capital Corporation" (ACC) lending groups. About $100 million is currently on loan or guaranteed, with another $70 million in additional capital recently available. Overall, there is more than $200 million available for Aboriginal business lending in Canada (1992 estimates).[14]

One innovative lending program which is generating considerable press is the Calmeadow Peer Lending Circle. Based on the successful Grameen Bank in Bangladesh which has assisted innumerable families and villages through peer-based, micro-enterprise lending, Calmeadow has piloted the peer lending model in urban and rural Canada. Borrowers form groups of four to six people who assess each other's ideas and decide how much and when each person is entitled to borrow (from $500 — $1000 at 2 per cent over prime) using each other's character as collateral. Future loans to the group depend on repayment of each loan, so the peer concept is critical. Today Calmeadow Foundation, established in 1983 by Toronto industrialist Martin Connell, provides financial backing and support for funds in rural Nova Scotia, Vancouver, Toronto and a First Nations Fund. So far, fewer than half-a-dozen borrowers have defaulted on the peer loans amounting to an overall payback rate of 98 per cent; over 500 new businesses have been started this way across Canada.[15]

The Nanaimo Community Employment Advisory Society started out as an employability training program in 1975 which created Colville Investment Corporation in 1980 to provide business development support, including lending and technical assistance. An Economic Council of Canada 1990 cost-benefit analysis concluded that the net benefits of public investment in Colville were demonstrable, having created 1000 jobs on an initial capital infusion of $1.5 million. However, Colville remains dependent on external government capital and is not yet self-sustaining.

The Province of Ontario has also launched an initiative in this field, recently establishing a Community Loan Fund program. Loan guarantees are provided through locally-controlled organizations to assist those not well served by conventional financial markets to establish businesses and create jobs.

Next to financial assistance, technical assistance (TA) is the most important ingredient for successful CED. TA includes staff and board training, organizational development, specialized business development services, inter-organizational networking and advocacy and brokerage services for CED organizations.[17] CED activity can only grow and strengthen if there are people skilled in the CED process and there is a dearth of training opportunities in Canada. Practitioners in the field look enviously at the American network of training, advocacy and support for CED activity; the Canadian capacity pales in comparison.

Nonetheless, there are a few noteworthy examples, one of which is the Vancouver-based Westcoast Development Group (WDG), the technical assistance subsidiary of the newly-founded non-profit Centre for Community Enterprise (itself privately endowed to act as a financial intermediary and sponsor of CED activities). WDG provides training and materials for building the capacity of local CED practitioners. Over 2000 people have taken its CED training programs and its materials are in wide circulation across Canada and the U.S.. They are presently endeavouring to link their training to an accredited educational institution and to develop training for experienced CED managers. They provide networking and database services and produce a quarterly newsletter, *Making Waves,* a Canadian authority in the field.[18]

Finally, development finance intermediaries round out the range of critical support services for CED. Well established in the U.S., having received government and foundation support for years, development finance intermediaries are few and far between in Canada. They may have regional, provincial or nationwide orientation, and have a mandate to underwrite the capital costs of community-based development projects. They do not typically design projects, but help package them to offer other investors or to finance themselves. Their balanced concern for social goals (e.g. local empowerment and capacity-building) and financial goals (financial stability) sets them apart from conventional capital sources.

One well-known example is the Québec Workers' Solidarity Fund (FSTQ) with over $550 million in assets and 141,000 shareholders, which since its founding in 1984 has invested $250 million in about 100 Québec firms, creating or maintaining 23,000 jobs, and boasting an annual average return of 7.13 per cent.[19] It is socially mandated in that it will invest in Québec businesses, preferably unionized, and is predominantly owned by Québec unionist shareholders. FSTQ has also established a foundation to train workers to enhance their workplace influence, and has invested in a small business development fund sponsored by local Montréal CED groups. While the success of FSTQ is based on Québec nationalist aspirations and not necessarily on community interests, nonetheless, it is a powerful example of workers' potential in mobilizing capital for social purposes.

No discussion of community-controlled capital would be complete without a discussion of the credit union system, and no discussion of credit unions would be complete without a lament for the considerable untapped potential of this sleeping giant. There are over 2,500 credit unions and caisses populaires operating out of 3,900 branches nationwide. Their aggregate assets total over $90.3 billion with a membership of over 9.7 million people.[20] Most credit unions, however, provide only personal financial services and have not extended their mandate to include the general economic health and well-being of their communities. There are a few notable examples, however, one of which is reviewed here.

VanCity Savings Credit Union is known and envied nationally for its considerable financial strength. Based in and serving the

Greater Vancouver area, VanCity boasted $3.8 billion in assets, $30.2 million in net earnings after tax and over 200,000 members by year end 1993.[21] While VanCity is clearly a prosperous locally-controlled financial institution, offering a competitive array of financial products and services, VanCity is perhaps better known for its "activist" board of directors who are committed to progressive social change for the Lower Mainland community. Under this leadership VanCity founded the successful socially-screened Ethical Growth Mutual Fund (now owned by the national credit union system and expanded to include four other screened mutual funds which together total $234 million in assets), established a socially responsible real estate development company, (which has won numerous awards for its innovations in affordable housing, including incorporating social housing for single parents in the redevelopment of one of its branches), created a Community Foundation (now nearly $3.5 million in assets, which supports job creation, non-profit enterprise and affordable housing through grants, loans and technical assistance), and is now looking for creative ways and means through which its branches can support community and co-operative enterprise development.

This is an example of community-controlled capital at work, but while VanCity's social and business achievements are considerable, it is dwarfed by the Mouvement des caisses Desjardins based in Québec, a vast integrated financial network with nearly $60 billion in assets, owned and administered by its members. Offering insurance, industrial and commercial investment, trust, securities brokerage, securities transportation, credit card processing and foreign exchange services, this network of more than 1,500 caisse populaires located throughout Québec and francophone communities in other provinces, boasts a membership of five million and is governed by 18,800 volunteer directors. The largest private sector employer in Québec, with 38,000 employees, the Desjardins Movement is a leading economic and social force in Québec, proving the strength of co-operation, solidarity and vision.[22]

The size and strength of the Desjardins system, founded on a commitment to enhance the economic and social well-being and empowerment of Québec communities and individuals, shows the real potential of a focused, unwavering strategy for economic self-determination, equity and democratization — contemporary prerequisites for social well-being.

Economic democracy through community economic development, thus, is a key ingredient for an economically and socially secure future for Canada's children, families and communities. As a strategy, it is still in its infancy and a full network of technical and financial intermediaries, equity and debt institutions and human resource development and planning, advocacy and advisory services does not yet exist. Indeed, the public is by and large not aware of any alternatives to the conventional private sector models and the untapped capacity which exists in community-controlled capital. Of the nearly 10 million credit union/caisses populaires members nation-wide, how many, for example, remember to vote at credit union elections? How many progressives, for that matter, run for their board of directors?

A community economic development strategy requires vision, community commitment and the support — but not dominance — of government agencies. Federal and provincial governments should find ways and means to support community enterprise. Ways to assist include: amending charities and cooperatives laws to provide a legislative framework to encourage CED, providing financial assistance (seed capital, loan guarantees, tax incentives, etc.) in support of CED intermediaries and development corporations, education and promotion of CED as an economic alternative, and financial management training in CED practice.

This discussion, so far, has ignored the critique of CED that says it only serves to promote small-scale capitalism, that it creates low-wage, low-skilled jobs and maintains the prevalent economic power relations. These are valid concerns and reinforce the need to ensure CED institutions remain committed to the social goals on which they were founded. Indeed, nothing else could make so strong an argument for economic democracy: the only means for ensuring the integration of social goals is by active community/member/consumer or stakeholder participation.

Admittedly CED on its own is not enough. CED is a long term strategy, which calls for patient capital and a long term view. Years of neglect, generations of poverty and centuries of conservative economic thought must be overcome before substantial results are achieved and success can be declared.

However, there are other strategies, which, when integrated with a CED approach, can substantially improve the social and economic returns to communities and significantly enhance social well-being. One approach will be explored briefly below and proposed as a powerful tool to increase the social returns of capital.

Accountable Capital Through Social Investment Strategies

When the bad real estate investments of a single corporate family can tumble nations' economies and devastate the lives of countless families and small businesses, it is long past time to start asking questions about the public accountability of capital. The repercussions of the Reichmanns' troubled investments in England's Canary Wharf are still being felt two years later, as affected families and businesses work their way out of the financial difficulties which came in the wake of the empire's losses. When Olympia and York — Canada's largest private property developer — finally filed for bankruptcy protection in the spring of 1992, its debts were estimated at more than $20 billion.[23] The full extent of the losses will probably never be known.

While there was a hue and cry at the time about the secrecy and lack of accountability of investment decisions, there were few, if any, questions about the inherent right of capital to pursue self-interested profit maximization objectives exclusively. As argued by Milton Friedman, and largely unchallenged today, as long as corporations act legally, their sole over-riding purpose is to seek the highest financial returns for their shareholders. If this argument is left unchecked, given the globalization of capital and the inability (reluctance?) of national governments to regulate and monitor corporate activity, the public interest will soon become irrelevant, if it isn't already.

While this is a desolate picture, there are some hopeful signs that this future is not inevitable. Successes of the environmental movement are a case in point, where through grassroots organizing, corporate behaviour is held to account for its environmental impacts. A striking recent example is that of the European Greenpeace movement which exposed on the international stage, the clear-cutting practices of forest companies in British Columbia. That these high profile protests have had a significant impact on corporate behaviour is evident in the acceptance of B.C. forest companies to an increase in stumpage fees on trees harvested in public forests (an anticipated $2 billion over five years) in order to fund enhanced forest management practices, environmental restoration, increased value-added for forest products, retraining for forest workers and community adjustment measures.

However, in spite of the impact of such noteworthy examples, opportunities to increase the accountability of capital and corporate decision-making exist more in the future than are evident in practice. Any vision which aspires to sustain the environment and improve the quality of life of families and communities, especially those which are economically marginalized, must have a strategy for increasing the accountability for capital and corporate decision-making. To fail to do so is to bury our collective heads in the sand. Again, the principle of self-determination is key: to support social well-being, people need more control over decisions which affect their lives.

A few strategies which hold some promise for increasing accountability and responsibility of the corporate sector are touched on below.

Social Cost Accounting

It has long been understood that many corporate decisions ignore social and environmental costs. What is not understood is that this is not inevitable. Missing, however, is the methodology by which we can reliably and verifiably measure the social and environmental impacts of various business scenarios. That, and the political will to require social cost accounting to be factored into corporate decision-making.

One means to advance this approach would be to require companies to include social audits in their annual financial reports. The Society for Certified Management Accountants (CMA), based in Montréal, is working towards this end. Every year they evaluate hundreds of corporate annual reports in an effort to assess companies for socially-responsible performance. They look for investment in human resources (training), employment equity results, environmental practices, equitable wage ratios, community contributions and other social outcomes.

Social auditing is not an easy undertaking. There are few models and little expertise available to provide assistance in establishing social auditing frameworks. Measuring social outcomes is a complex and elusive science, a field left empty by corporate financial auditors. The CMA model is the only Canadian standard for social auditing available, and it is little known. Of course, if a demand were created for social auditing and social cost accounting formulae, no doubt auditing firms would find a way to deliver!

One of the long-term benefits of increased social reporting is that public pressure can be brought to bear on under-performing companies. With increased scrutiny often comes improved performance; peer group competition alone can have considerable influence.

A Canadian Community Reinvestment Act

American banks may not be happy with the Community Reinvestment Act (CRA), but it has led to some impressive results. When it was officially documented that American banks were engaged in "red-lining" — the practice of making credit available on less favourable terms on the basis of where people lived — Congress passed a law requiring banks to demonstrate increased local investment before authorization to expand was granted, deposit insurance applications were approved or mergers and acquisitions sanctioned. Third parties may also file challenges to applications based on poor CRA performance. Since the CRA was passed in 1978, more than $18 billion has been invested in communities in more than 70 U.S. cities.[24] Today, partly as a result of the CRA, there is an extensive network of community loan funds, community development corporations, community land trusts, micro-enterprise programs and other financial vehicles channeling resources to improve the socio-economic conditions of disadvantaged communities.

While admittedly, Canada's neighbourhoods do not have the same degree of socio-economic inequity, we can nonetheless point to similar red-lining conditions in our inner cities, in struggling resource-dependent and single industry towns, in aboriginal communities, in depleted regions and with certain population groups, such as women and others who lack assets or a credit history. We could similarly require our financial institutions to demonstrate their investments in community enterprises, small and micro-businesses, and in equity group businesses as a condition of business expansion or other license.

Some have suggested the federal government could encourage community investment by requiring banks to lend a percentage of the deposits covered by Canada Deposit Insurance Corporation in local communities for mortgages and local development, and to provide low-interest loans for affordable housing. The Financial Democracy Campaign in the United States has proposed that banks operate with licences, the renewal of which would be based on service records to the local community, in addition to financial and managerial soundness.[25]

Investment Power

Billions of dollars are held in pension and mutual funds across the country and the total is increasing exponentially. Channeled in socially-responsible and socially-useful directions, this financial clout can significantly improve social and environmental conditions. Again the U.S. experience is more developed. There are a multiplicity of socially-screened funds in existence. There is also an established U.S. social investment benchmark — the Domini Social Index —which is starting to demonstrate that socially screened investing need not result in reduced financial returns. The DSI has out-performed the Standard and Poor 500 and other corporate indicators over the last five years. Toronto-based Michael Jantzi Research Associates (MJRA) is developing a similar index to begin measuring socially-screened Canadian corporate performance.

Investments can be negatively screened — away from companies with poor labour or environmental records, from military, tobacco, and nuclear investments — or they can be positively screened — where investments are made in companies with exceptional employment equity records or which are developing alternative environmental technologies, for example. Clearly, as the force of these investments gains strength, corporate behaviour will need to pay attention to these concerns.

A limiting factor in social investment is the lack of information available on a national basis. Government record-keeping is scarce or difficult to access. A framework is needed to assist social researchers in compiling reliable, verifiable and current data on labour relations, environmental performance and employment equity. MJRA's Canadian social investment database is the first attempt in Canada at an analytical framework to track social and environmental issues on a standardized basis. Governments will need to increase the reporting requirements of companies to facilitate a strong social investment movement.

Lastly, there is a growing interest in shareholder activism, a corporate governance approach in which large institutional investors (churches, state and union sponsored pension funds, governments and others) use their financial clout to compel publicly held corporations to adhere to socially and environmentally responsible practices. Through resolutions, voting and letter-writing, these investors are increasingly starting to flex their financial muscles. However, Canadian securities law limits the nature of resolutions which can make it to the floor of corporate annual meetings to business-related resolutions only. A national framework which supports and encourages social investment in all its forms is essential to enhance the viability of this approach to increasing the accountability of capital. This national framework would need to include guidelines which encourage governments at all levels to similarly consider the social and environmental impacts of their investments.

Consumer Awareness

Eco-labeling is evidence of consumer demand for products which are consistent with their personal values. Consumers are looking for products which are environmentally friendly but lack the information to assist in their purchasing decisions. This consumer power can have a significant market-place effect, albeit with longer-term environmental results. However, it demonstrates the impact increased product information and awareness can have on buying behaviour.

The Council on Economic Priorities in the U.S. realized this demand and as social activists, they produced a consumer guidebook. *Shopping for a Better World: The Quick and Easy Guide to All Your Socially Responsible Shopping* provides the details on the social and environmental performance of over 2,000 products, 191 companies and 17 industries. Since 1988, over one million copies have been ordered.

While conscious consumerism is not an overnight strategy for social and economic well-being, with increased relevant and timely information, people are able to make consumer choices consistent with their personal values. Over the long term, this, too, is likely to have an influence on corporate behaviour. Federal packaging and labeling regulations can help spring-board this accountability approach to broader public awareness.

No doubt these strategies towards increased accountability of corporate decisions seem light weight in contrast to the faceless web of global capital. But then who would have predicted the end of South African apartheid? Was it not the critical mass of public opinion, the weight of capital disinvestment, the recognition of fundamental social and economic injustice which culminated in the historic election of Nelson Mandela as South Africa's President?

International Alliances

To be truly effective, however, a democratic vision for social and economic well-being requires an international strategy to regulate global financial markets and to counter-balance the flow of amoral capital. John Dillon, a researcher with the Ecumenical Coalition for Economic Justice in Toronto, calls for a new United Nations Conference on Money and Finance to recreate a stable monetary system and to introduce public accountability in the global marketplace. He believes governments need to re-regulate global markets in order to avert a repeat of the 1929 crash of the international monetary system, reverse the drain of wealth from less developed countries and to increase the share of global capital used to meet human needs and generate jobs.[26]

Alternative Trade

The baby-boomer generation, growing up in a more culturally diverse and well-travelled society than their parents, created a demand for cross-cultural products — world beat music, clothing, food and tourism. With this increased interest in ethnic and indigenous products, came the realization that they could also support their social values by buying through trading organizations which paid fair prices for products, pre-paid orders to assist credit access for poor people, offered "development dividends" (profit-sharing with producer-partners) and incorporated social and environmental interests in purchasing decisions. Globally, alternative trading represents over $545 million in sales, doubling its achievements in three years. Bridgehead, an alternative trading organization (ATO) owned by Oxfam Canada, saw its sales increase by 25 per cent in 1992-93 from $2.7 to $3.5 million, confirming the Canadian boom in "ethical consuming."[27]

A national strategy in support of alternative trade is a critical building block for a socially responsible economy. Key federal support would include favourable tariff treatment for ATO products, educational exchange programs to provide business training for people active in alternative trade and other means which assist ATO producers to become economically viable. And of course a strategy to encourage Canadians to celebrate multicultural diversity is essential.

Lastly, the Canadian social investment movement needs to forge links with socially responsible capital networks in Europe, America and elsewhere in order to not only provide a counter-balance to global capitalism, but to provide the financial strength to support community and co-operative enterprise in poor nations and poor communities around the world.

The creation of a climate which supports the accountability of capital and financial decisions and promotes socially responsible consumerism is a federal responsibility and key to the creation of a socially and economically just society. Our federal government and international institutions have fallen hopelessly behind transnational capital and its supporting technology in creating and controlling financial assets. Leadership and vision are required to address this alarming trend and to integrate social and environmental goals into our capital and economic systems.

Hope and Vision for the Future

Canadians need a vision for the future which can inspire and moti-vate them. They need a vision in which they have a strong role to play. They need to be assured that the country is proceeding down a path towards increased accountability of governments and of the corporate sector. They see and experience economic and social injustices in their communities and want to play a part in determining their own future.

Economic Democracy through Community Based Economic Development and Accountable Capital through Social Investment Strategies are not a panacea. They are not a complete program for economic and social well-being. They are not even mature strategies. They are, however, a key to a democratic and compassionate future, one which fully embraces the participation of disadvantaged and mar-ginalized communities. One which creates opportunities for local con-trol, self-reliance and mutual support. One which fosters social soli-darity. As a counter-balance to the international flow of amoral capital they have considerable — though untested — potential. As the basis for a popular social movement they have considerable promise.

They are vital to achieving social and economic justice.

Coro T. Strandberg is a director of VanCity Credit Union and active in promoting social investment strategies, economic democra-cy and corporate social responsibility.

ENDNOTES

1. National Council of Welfare, "Poverty Profile 1992" (Ottawa, Ontario: Government of Canada, Spring 1994), pp. 7-8.
2. Ibid., p. 47.
3. National Council of Welfare, "Social Security Backgrounder #2: Who are the People on Welfare?" (Ottawa, Ontario: Government of Canada, 1994), p. 2.
4. Roeher Institute, "Social Well-being" (North York, Ontario, 1993) pp. 3-8.
5. Ibid., pp. 28-39.
6. S. Lukes, (1980) "Socialism and Equality." In Sterba, J. *Justice: Alternative Political Perspectives*, as quoted in Roeher Institute, p. 37.
7. *Making Waves*, Vol. 5 No.1 Feb. 1994, p. 4.
8. Stewart E. Perry, Mike Lewis and Jean-Marc Fontan, "Revitalizing Canada's Neighbourhoods" (Vancouver, B.C.: 1993), p. 17.
9. Ibid., p. 21.
10. Ibid., p. 23.
11. Ibid., p. 24.
12. Ibid., p. 71.
13. Ibid., p. 31.
14. Ibid., p. 32.

15. Paul Waldie, "Peer Loans Find Ready Niche," *The Financial Post*, May 14, 1994, p. S32.

16. Stewart Perry, p. 37.

17. Ibid., p. 14.

18. Ibid., p. 62.

19. Ibid., p. 69.

20. B.C. Central Credit Union Statistics.

21. VanCity Annual Report.

22. Desjardins 1993 Annual Report.

23. Details in the paragraph are taken from: Walter Stewart, *Too Big to Fail* (Toronto, Ontario: McClelland and Stewart Inc. 1993) p. 71.

24. John Dillon, "Monopolizing Money: How Corporate Dictators of the World's Money Supply are Undermining National Economies," *The Canadian Forum*, June 1994, p. 10.

25. Ibid., p. 12.

26. Ibid., p. 11-12.

27. Bridgehead 1992-93 Annual Report.

Redistributing Power in a Changing Economy:
Defining a More Modern Militancy

by Leo W. Gerard
International Secretary-Treasurer
United Steelworkers of America

These are challenging times for social democrats. Around the world, basic social democratic policy objectives appear to be increasingly out of reach. Social programs are under attack. The rate of unionization, particularly in the private sector, is declining. Income inequality is increasing. And Keynesian-style economic stimulus has become increasingly ineffective. All governments, including those predisposed to reverse these trends, are faced with reduced revenues and are therefore constrained in their ability to respond. In this environment, high unemployment and low wage competition have become the dominant features of the economy.

At the end of the 1980s, most Canadian social democrats were content to blame the economic and social crisis on a succession of right wing governments. However, now that we have seen provincial New Democratic governments struggle with severe revenue crisis and an extremely hostile business community that is more able than ever before to act on threats of relocating facilities, it is time to take a more sophisticated look at our problems.

In the past 25 years, the framework within which the Canadian economy operates has been transformed. The mobility of goods, services, capital and technology has increased dramatically, leaving nations, regions and workplaces much more vulnerable to competition with each other for capital investment. In addition, dramatic productivity improvements in many sectors of the economy that have not been met by corresponding increases in wages and aggregate demand have left many workers unemployed or underemployed.

In this changed economy, our traditional methods of regulating economic activity are less effective. Unless social democrats identify new, more effective ways of regulating economic activity, our problems will get worse. We need new policies and institutions that will constrain low wage competition on an international basis. We need new approaches to stimulate economic growth so that full employment, a strong public sector and an equitable society are easier to achieve. We need to identify new ways to democratize the modern economy. In short, we need to develop and implement a more modern militancy.

Economic Change and Canadian Politics

Globalization, new technologies and the gap between productivity growth and wages has had an extensive impact on our economy. We have lost much of our branch plant manufacturing base. Our export-oriented resource industries, such as mining, fishing and forestry, generate far fewer jobs than they have in the past. The net inflows of foreign investment that Canada has historically enjoyed are being reversed as investors seek higher rates of return in other, lower cost countries.

The crisis in the goods-producing sector has had a particularly troublesome impact on public services. Our traditionally strong public sector has been squeezed by an increase in demand for services and transfer payments arising from job loss, and a severe revenue crisis arising primarily from stagnant wages, increased unemployment and prolonged recessions.

These problems affect all governments, regardless of their political stripe or ideological disposition. However, for right wing governments, the current economic environment is ideal for pursuing agendas that could not have been pursued in more prosperous times. For example, right wing rhetoric about deficits has effectively delegitimized the budgetary problems of governments that are starved for funds. The right correctly recognizes that these pressures are making it possible, in the guise of reacting to irresistible international pressures, to do things that would never have popular support on their own merits.

On the other hand, globalization, technological change and the growing ineffectiveness of traditional expansionary policies (particularly when practiced by provincial governments) have made life extremely difficult for social democrats. The crisis has forced three social democratic provincial governments, made up of dedicated unionists and social activists, to make budget related decisions they would have criticized Tories and Liberals for making.

Unfortunately, the response of many on the left to this crisis has been small in scale and partial in understanding. Consider, for example, the left's policy on trade. To the extent that the NDP and the rest of the Canadian left have dealt with globalization at all, attention has been focused on building opposition to the Canada/U.S. Free Trade Agreement (FTA) and to the North American Free Trade Agreement (NAFTA). At the same time, the party and many on the left have claimed a commitment to both the GATT and an undefined version of managed trade.

This is a curious trade policy to advance. Both NAFTA and the GATT are founded on the principle of seeking national treatment for foreign goods and services. While the investment-related provisions of NAFTA are more extensive than those of the GATT, both agreements will facilitate capital mobility and make it more difficult for social democrats to regulate economic activity. Since the GATT prohibits tariffs, quotas and many subsidies and performance requirements, one wonders what managed trade means.

Although the obvious contradictions in this position must be addressed, the more serious problem with this trade policy is that it fails to address the fundamental problem of increased capital mobility. Globalization was marching forward long before the FTA was even contemplated. In fact, since having access to another country's markets is an important means of attracting capital in an increasingly global economy, one might argue that the FTA and NAFTA are as much symptoms of globalization as they are causes.

Another flaw in much of the left's response to this crisis is a reliance on an over-simplified, ideologically-based analysis of our problems. While many on the left are quick to identify these economic trends as the goals of a "corporate agenda," too few acknowledge that the world has changed dramatically since most of our cherished policy goals were developed. We must realize that reversing these trends will require new policies and the creation of new institutions.

Beyond "stop free trade," "reject the corporate agenda," "deficits don't matter," "save the public sector" and "save medicare," what has the left been saying about economic policy? Surely there are more effective ways of responding to this crisis than with empty rhetoric and withdrawal of support for provincial NDP governments. Being ideologically pure and profoundly ineffective is not a viable option for social democracy.

Social democracy is about sharing power and creating a just society. It is not simply about preserving existing programs and challenging anyone who wants to change them. Social democrats must realize that if we can't find new and more effective ways to harness the forces of globalization and technological change, we won't be able to redistribute power. If we can't redistribute power, all the rhetoric and ideology imaginable won't prevent a continuing loss of faith in social democracy.

Coming to terms with Globalization

Technology has been one of most significant contributors to globalization. Desktop computers, hooked up over phone lines, have revolutionized both capital markets and the production of goods and services. Some $900 billion a day changes hands in international currency markets. Currency trading of such volume, 50 times greater than the volume of trade transactions, would not be possible without modern technology. Similarly, new technology now allows design specialists in Europe to spend lunch time shaping the design of machine parts engineered in Chicago that morning and then send them to tool makers in Taiwan in the afternoon.

Several years of debt crisis and IMF-sponsored structural adjustment programs have greatly enhanced the opportunity for capital to move to the South. Much time has passed since Salvador Allende's government nationalized Anaconda Copper in Chile. Investors are feeling more comfortable in parts of the world that once identified public ownership of key industries as central to economic policy.

The emergence of very large, truly international corporations has been another important factor. Most globally-traded manufacturing is done by firms with capitalization in the $8 billion to $80 billion range. The largest 350 multinationals account for some 40 per cent of the world's merchandise trade.

These trends have lead to significant international economic integration. The view of globalization held by most policy-makers and the business community is that it will increase productivity through greater economies of scale and a more effective use of world resources. This view holds that while there may be some countries that suffer more than others during the period of structural adjustment, the world as a whole will be better off.

However, as all social democrats know, this rosy prediction is not being realized and will not be realized until we find ways to regain control over economic activity. While there may be greater economies of scale for some industries, there is also tremendous downward pressure on wages, labour standards, levels of government regulation and sources of public revenue.

Mining is a good example. South American nations regularly use subsidies, low taxes and the promise of lower labour and environmental standards to lure Canadian mining companies to explore and develop operations in that part of the world. In 1987 members of the Mining Association of Canada spent over 80 per cent of their exploration budgets in Canada. By 1992 that number had dropped to 62 per cent and many MAC members believe it will be as low as 55 per cent by 1997. Since mining provides so many high paying and high skill jobs and accounts for over 16 per cent of our exports, this is indeed an unfortunate trend.

Trends leading to globalization started long before the FTA or NAFTA were contemplated and will not be reversed if the agreements are discarded. The real challenge to the left with respect to globalization is not to simply criticize NAFTA but to identify the institutions, alliances, trade agreements and international regulations that will harness these forces, and constrain destructive competition for capital based on tax concessions, subsidies, low wages, low environmental standards and union busting.

Some on the left are resisting this, clinging to old ideas of economic isolation and import substitution. Advocates of this approach ignore the fact that in an economy where 40 per cent of the economy involves trade, a self reliance strategy would require a restructuring of the economy far more radical than we are currently witnessing. It would also drive from Canada much of whatever capital is available to facilitate such a restructuring.

Finding ways to set and enforce international environmental standards, minimum levels of taxation and labour rights and standards will not be an easy task. Appropriate standards, methods of complaint, investigation and adjudication, and penalties will need to be developed on an international scale. However, we as social democrats and unionists must rise to the challenge. No one else is going to do it for us.

Social Democrats for Economic Growth

Sharing power and pursuing a just society is always easier in times of economic prosperity. In the prosperous 50s, 60s and 70s, social democrats could focus on fairness and let the economy take care of itself. That is no longer the case. In order to more effectively advance the equity agenda and offer hope to the unemployed and underemployed, social democrats must start talking about economic growth and wealth creation.

Much has been made of rank and file support for the Reform Party in the last federal election. Many social democrats believe this shift happened to some extent because of the NDP equity agenda. This problem must be addressed. I am optimistic enough about rank and file union members and party members to believe that the shift in support was more a symptom of fear than an outright rejection of equity principles. It is much easier to talk about giving more to women, ethnic minorities and the disabled when the economy is growing and wages are increasing than when they are not. When there is no growth, correcting for these inequities is seen as a zero sum game. Workers who are scared about their own futures won't find it easy to embrace these programs.

One way for social democrats to respond to this problem is to start focusing on economic growth again so that, among other things, equity goals can be achieved.

The left must also identify the role of private sector wealth creation in maintaining and enhancing society's ability to provide a decent standard of living. We have allowed the debate within the left on public vs. private ownership to eclipse this critical issue. Economist Lester Thurow is correct when he says "we can't sustain an economy by giving each other heart transplants, selling each other insurance, and taking care of each others children." While those sectors of the economy play a critical role in ensuring the economy functions effectively and have a very obvious impact on the quality of life in this country, we cannot sustain them unless the private sector produces and exports goods and services.

The relationship between technology and productivity on one hand, and employment levels on the other must also be examined. The number of person-hours required to make a ton of steel has been the most critical productivity measurement in the steel industry for a long time. Similar measures are used in other industries as well. By focusing, as corporations and governments do so often, on how to lower unit production costs by producing goods with fewer workers, we ignore the impact on aggregate employment.

The traditional view holds that increased productivity will generate wealth and a demand for new products which will generate new jobs in new sectors. However, increases in productivity have outstripped increases in demand for most manufactured goods in the past twenty years and the number of new goods and services have simply not taken up the employment slack.

Tackling the difficult issues of working time may be one of the more important ways to respond to the impact productivity improvements are having on employment. Controlling overtime, shortening the work week, and regulating part-time work and home work must be an integral part of the left's response to the current economic crisis.

Another is stimulating consumption and aggregate demand. Much has been made of the decline in the rate of productivity growth in Canada, but very little has been said about the fact that since the late seventies, wages have remained stagnant or declined in real terms as productivity has increased by over 1 per cent per year. We often hear individual employers complain that their employees are paid too much for the firm to be competitive, but perhaps one of our fundamental macro-economic problems is that workers collectively are not paid enough.

Domestic attempts to stimulate growth in recent years have usually failed to produce the desired results and have only added to budgetary problems. Social democrats will need to look at international approaches to stimulating the economy and determining what international institutions are necessary to implement these strategies.

The international monetary economy is awash with capital invested on a short term basis and whose movements influence interest rates and exchange rates more than the activities of individual governments. A new, stronger international financial system is needed to exercise controls over the speculative flows of capital, and to bring an end to the auction mentality that prevents real interest rates from coming down, even in the midst of a world wide recession.

Economic Democracy in the Modern Economy

Redistributing power at the Domestic level also requires new and innovative approaches. Social democrats should be trying to reharness domestic forces, with a view to creating good jobs and a just distribution of income and opportunity. To do this, systems must be put in place to redistribute power. Better labour laws, new sources of influence at the sectoral level and worker-controlled pools of capital are just a few ways to do this at the domestic level.

I do not believe that we can fully, or even largely, correct labour market inequities with tax policy and social programs. Giving working people a collective voice in the workplace and on public policy matters is an essential element of any social democratic agenda.

This task is made more difficult by the fact that the overall rate of unionization, particularly in the private sector, is declining. Private sector unionization declined from approximately 26 per cent to just under 21 per cent between 1975 and 1985. It has probably deteriorated further since then. Organizing efforts simply cannot keep pace with plant closures and downsizing. In other words, we expect that

80 per cent to 85 per cent of the private sector workforce will be unorganized by the end of this decade unless there are dramatic changes in the way we regulate collective bargaining.

The problem is our current system of collective bargaining. The Wagner Act model of collective bargaining, which focuses on site-by-site agreements, made sense when the objective was regulating collective bargaining in steel mills, automotive assembly plants and paper mills, but does not work very well for security guards, contract cleaners, bank workers and fast food employees.

The object of collective bargaining is to give workers a voice and to take wages and working conditions out of competition. In the small workplace segment of the economy and in much of the service sector, that can only happen with broader-based bargaining, perhaps on a sectoral or regional basis.

Social democrats also have to ask themselves what new vehicles should be developed to expand the role of working people in decision making. One way is through the development of sectoral initiatives like the Canadian Steel Trade and Employment Congress (CSTEC) and the Sectoral Skills Council. The potential for power sharing through these sorts of initiatives has only begun to be tapped.

In the case of CSTEC, workers, through their union, participate in the development of their own training programs, both while employed and if they are laid off. The result is worker-oriented assessment of training needs, the development of portable skills, the development of union-oriented courses and a high success rate in job placement for laid off workers.

Developing pools of loyal capital is another important manner to redistribute power. The largest source of capital in Canada is found in pension plans. Unfortunately, only a small portion of these funds are jointly or union trusteed. Thus, workers have no means of influencing the investment decisions these funds make.

Creative use of regulations on the investment of pension funds and changes to plan governance rules are important potential sources of power sharing that the left has not yet embraced. There is no reason why pension funds could not be managed to ensure they play an active role in Canadian economic development.

Labour Sponsored Investment Funds are another important source of loyal capital. While the Québec Solidarity Fund now has assets in excess of $1 billion and plays a key role in the Québec economy, the labour movement and social democrats outside of Québec have been slow to grasp the potential of such funds.

I believe that such loyal pools of capital, which could be focused on financing manufacturing entities, worker-owned companies and co-operatives in Canada, could screen investments based on social objectives and help address the problem of increased capital mobility.

Industrial Democracy — 90s Style

Redistributing power at the workplace is another issue that needs to be further developed and advanced. Social democrats and unionists in Canada have not done enough to take more control over decision making and workplace design. The result is that investment decisions are made without regard for the interests of workers, and job designs are based almost exclusively on cost and productivity considerations. Sharing power at the workplace must mean more than that.

Employee ownership can play an important role in the redistribution of power both by saving jobs in crisis situations and by giving workers the opportunity to gain some measure of control over the enterprise that employs them. At Algoma Steel, workers have increased control at three levels: at the shareholder level; at the management level; and at the shop floor level. As shareholders, workers have a right to veto certain fundamental business decisions, such as investing outside of the communities of Sault Ste. Marie and Wawa and the issuing of new shares that dilute workers' equity interest. At the management level, workers have a veto over the use of outside contractors, the content of training programs and the manner in which new technology is introduced. At the shop floor level, workplaces are being redesigned so that workers have greater discretionary authority to organize their work the way they want.

What I find most exciting about Algoma Steel is not just that it is worker owned, but that workers have significant control over several aspects of the operation. There is no reason why co-determination of this sort can not be practiced elsewhere.

Co-determination should not mean committees focused exclusively on identifying ways to improve productivity, it must mean accepting that workers have a different agenda. Creating a safe, healthful, equitable workplace, and building a strong union must be central to any co-determination model.

We need to do more work in developing worker-centred technologies that make the work experience more physically comfortable and increase the skill content of jobs. We need to design workplaces that accommodate and provide equal opportunity to women, aboriginals, ethnic minorities, the disabled and injured workers. We need to design workplaces that give workers more control over the content and pace of work and the opportunity to work with others.

We won't be able to achieve any of these objectives without increased influence in the workplace.

Developing and Implementing the Modern Militancy

The task we are faced with, reviving social democratic economic policy, is a daunting one. We live in a rapidly changing world in which traditional approaches to economic policy no longer work. We are required to take up a challenge, articulating a new economic order, that we have not taken up in the past.

We face a right wing that clearly has the upper hand. It has succeeded in giving its prescriptions the cloak of inevitability. It has a message that is seductively simple, and has a populist appeal.

If we are to respond effectively, we must not only move beyond empty rhetoric, we must maintain our commitment to the NDP and develop further our electoral strategies. It might be tempting to rely on outdated ideology and slogans like "the corporate agenda" as the basis for political action instead of a viable economic alternative simply because developing such an alternative seems difficult. It might be tempting to abandon provincial NDP governments struggling with real economic problems because it is easier than working with them to develop viable policies. However, a shallow ideological purity, when it comes at the expense of both a viable social democratic agenda and an electoral basis from which to pursue it, is not an objective worth pursuing.

If instead we can move forward, if we can develop and implement some of the strategies I have identified here and identify other ways to redistribute power in the new economy, then we will be rewarded. After all, we know that neo-conservatism and neo-liberalism serve such a narrow range of interests that, sooner or later, they will fail the basic test of democracy.

No Turning Back:
The Need for Change in Canada and Québec

By Pierrette Landry

The Canadian state began to intervene nationally on a grand scale during the Second World War. In the post-war period, it remained as intent as ever to continue planning Canada's future. Ottawa's intervention lead to many successes, including the transformation of Canada's economy into one of the world's most prosperous, allowing a majority of people to improve their quality of life considerably.

Unfortunately, by the end of the 1970s national intervention became increasingly unable to deal with much higher unemployment, deindustrialization and the erosion of Canada's living standards. At the same time, societal conflicts became more prevalent. One example was the battle over the Free Trade Agreement. Another is the malaise over Québec's future within Canada. While Canada has always had constitutional friction, it now has a crisis. The situation puts in question the ability of the Canadian experience to evolve.

The Canadian state in the 1990s is unwilling to acknowledge the negative realities that confront it. It refuses to admit that the 1982 Constitution is an obstacle to the accommodation of separate identities within the same territory. This essay will describe recent political trends in Québec and Canada, such as the Quiet Revolution, Bill 101, official bilingualism and the Charter of Rights and Freedoms. It will discuss the events following the 1980 Québec referendum, and examine the 1993 federal election. It will conclude with a discussion about the future of Québec-Canada relations.

Recent trends in Québec

The 1960s were the era of world decolonization. While many countries were becoming sovereign, Québec went through its own independence movement, the Quiet Revolution, a period of social and economic upheaval. The Québec state reinforced and modernized itself, enabling it to contribute to the development of various economic sectors, while increasing the number of francophone business leaders. The first reforms focused mainly on recovering control of Québec's natural resources. The creation and strengthening of Hydro-Québec became the first symbol of the state's efforts to diversify Québec's economy. In time, many new sectors were also developed, producing a phenomenon that has come to be known as Québec Inc. However, the 1990s' recession and the state's deficit problem have diminished this impulse.

The Québec government, determined to create a French-language "space," adopted the Charter of the French Language — Bill 101 — in 1977. René Lévesque considered it humiliating to have to adopt a law to protect the collective rights of Quebeckers. The social and economic reforms brought about by the state allowed Québec to be perceived as the home of French-speaking North Americans. The adjective Quebecker gradually replaced Canadian because French-speaking Canadians began to see themselves as a majority in Québec, rather than a minority in Canada.

Ottawa's vision: A Bilingual Québec in an English Country

As Québec transformed itself, relations with Ottawa became more tense. The situation remained manageable with compromises such as the creation, under Lester B. Pearson, of a separate Québec pension fund administered by the Caisse de dépôt et de placement. Its supporting role for the government and the private sector remains an important factor in Québec's development.

The election of Pierre Trudeau on April 6, 1968 marks a turning point in relations between Québec and Canada. One typical reform made under his mandate was the Official Languages Act, adopted in 1969. Its objectives were as follows: (1) to make francophones participate more equally in the federal public service; and (2) to spread the use of French among public servants, while permitting Canadians to be served in the language of their choice.

Unfortunately, an ambiguous legal text and political quarreling caused the first few years to be used mainly to clarify the law's interpretation. The hesitations ended with the adoption of a parliamentary resolution in June 1973. The right to work in one's own official language was limited to certain regions: the National Capital, designated areas including Montréal, and parts of the Eastern Townships, Gaspé,

Western Québec, Ontario and New Brunswick. The existence of these bilingual zones rests upon complicated calculations of the percentage of population speaking French. This is how English-speaking Canadians were supposed to be convinced of the need for bilingualism! The result of Trudeau's bilingualism is that French-speaking Canadians who live in or visit a region not designated bilingual cannot be served in their own language. Bilingualism is also perceived by many Quebeckers as a policy intended to avoid the promotion of French in most parts of Canada.

There are language requirements for all Public Service positions: bilingual, English essential, French essential, and French or English. The majority of public servants who work in Québec have bilingual positions or are bilingual. In 1993, bilingual positions numbered 54 per cent in Quebec, 8 per cent in Ontario and only 3 per cent in Western Canada. In some provinces, the percentage of bilingual jobs is as low as 1.4 per cent. In 1982, a Report by the Commissioner of Official Languages said that English remained the main working language of the federal Public Service, despite the increased proportion of French-speaking federal employees. As a result, Quebeckers usually say that federal bilingualism is a policy that applies mostly to them.

The Widening Gap

Québec's experience in self-affirmation reached a turning point with the 1980 referendum on Québec's association with the rest of Canada. The failure of the Yes side permitted then-Prime Minister Trudeau to unveil immediately his program to centralize Canada further. The British North America Act of 1867 would be patriated unilaterally.

The pillar of the 1982 Constitution was the Charter of Rights and Freedoms. There are four reasons why the Québec government opposed the adoption of the federal Charter. First, the amending formula depriving Québec of its traditional veto. Second, Section 23 provided a new way to enter provincial jurisdiction by affirming the right to receive education in the minority official language. Canadians educated in English in Canada could now have their children educated in English anywhere else in Canada, including Québec. This contradicted Chapter VII of the Charter of the French Language, which limits this right to parents who went to English schools in Québec. Third, the mobility rights contained in section 6 of the Charter might threaten Quebec's economic development policies. Fourth, the Charter did not recognize the uniqueness of Québec society in Canada and the equality of two founding peoples.

The Charter set into motion an irresistible momentum towards uniformity in the Canadian state. The provinces may override some of the Charter's dispositions only by paying the steep political price of using the famous notwithstanding clause (section 33). There was no referendum in 1982 to verify whether Canadians and Quebeckers approved the new Constitution, probably because the government was afraid to follow such a courageous path.

The Charter changed the role of the Supreme Court of Canada, giving it the power to decide the rights and freedoms of Canadians. The nine judges of the Court are chosen by the prime minister, making it a partisan organization. This can be interpreted as a major transfer of Parliament's decision-making powers to a judicial institution. The role of Parliament was completely transformed without Canadians even knowing what went on. It is frustrating to see that it is now up to a few unelected lawyers to decide how society works.

Individual rights now have priority over collective rights. Anyone may claim that his personal choice is a privilege, whether he be a worker disagreeing about the way his union fees are spent or an immigrant wishing to send his children to an English school in Québec. This fits well with the new perception that society is a mix of individuals either acting on their own or within a group: women, disabled, gays, environmentalists, etc. Individuals, in the name of the community at large, can claim that their rights are threatened by state homogeneity. They are encouraged to seek redress from judges, whose solutions for some become guidelines for all. We have created an automatic uniformity machine which makes it very difficult for a different vision to survive within Canada. Economic liberalism — through the North American Free Trade Agreement or GATT (now World Trade Organization) agreements — is the only *projet de société* governments are now supposed to get involved in.

The 1993 Federal Election

The Meech Lake and Charlottetown accords were two failed attempts to transform the new Constitution into a common project for English and French-speaking people of Canada. The symbol of Québec's distinct society did not pass the majority's test of what the Constitution should be. It is clear we live in a country very fond of constitutional and Charter ideals that make an abstraction of the other's reality. The election of 1993 may be interpreted as an endorsement of the Trudeau vision as embodied in Jean Chrétien. But the situation is not as rosy as partisans of a unitary vision would like us to believe.

Rather, the election confirmed an important metamorphosis of the traditional political cleavages that have existed since the war. Until recently, there were three elected political parties, two of which — the Liberals and Conservatives — alternated power. There are now five parties with members sitting in the House of Commons. Only one party has the support to govern Canada, so distant a consensus has become. And it can do so only with a well-distributed simple majority.

Faithful to those who voted for it, the Liberal party reminds Canadians as often as it can that the 1982 Constitution will remain as it is. We know that any reform would be very limited, and would only happen under the pretext that circumstances required it. Canada has a tradition of selecting ministers from all regions. It hopes this way to create a coalition of representatives from all parts of the country. Is this still possible? We have witnessed the rise of parties that not only disagree with the government's social and economic policies like the NDP did, but also express frustrations specific to some parts of Canada. In addition, regional representation is blocked by the ferocious party discipline that keeps debate within the executive branch of government and away from the public. The reality of representative government suggests that Canada's democracy has serious obstacles to overcome. Furthermore, the enormous pressure to make us "equal", applied through the 1982 Constitution, has only increased friction. Let's not soon forget the lesson of the Mulroney government: people are tired of being dictated to by a an unrepresentative elite.

Quebeckers' election of the Bloc Québécois (BQ) was motivated by a desire to make known to the rest of Canada the reasons why a growing number of Quebeckers are dissatisfied with the federal system. The BQ is also there to prepare the ground for change. Their vision rests upon a critique of the events surrounding the adoption of the 1982 Constitution; the contents of the Charter; and the inability of Canada to reform itself as demonstrated by Meech and Charlottetown. This is why all Quebeckers, regardless of ethnic origin or language spoken, are invited to plan together the building of a different society. According to the Bloc, many Canadian institutions, including the dollar, should be kept, thus implying a very advanced form of economic integration. Their interpretation of Quebeckers' frustration is that concessions such as the Official Languages Act are no longer sufficient.

Reform, the other new party, also wants change. One demand is that language and culture be under provincial jurisdiction. It perceives Canada as a mosaic of regions that would be best represented by a reformed Senate. In the name of efficiency, it also wishes the return of a centralized unilingual state like in the 1950s. Despite appearances, the federalism they propose is not very different from the present one. What they want is even more individualism and government *laissez-faire*. Their support remains concentrated in the West, but their effort to break through in other parts of Canada reveals a firm intention to replace the Conservative party. If the Liberals are forced to appear to reform the Constitution, there is no doubt that Reform's suggestions will be taken very seriously, just as they are in many other policy areas. Canada would be pushed even farther on the path to an American-style democracy.

Conclusion

Quebeckers are split. The separatists want a country. Others want real reform and believe it is still possible. Still others believe in the myth of a bilingual Canada and the promise of equality linked to the Charter. There are even a few ethnic nationalists, although they are a disappearing species, whether Mordecai Richler believes it or not. To that division must be added the political cleavages typical of today's society. The frustration of many Quebeckers has coalesced around the Parti Québécois (PQ). But not all PQ supporters agree with its message or its leader. Changes to that party are required to make it the vehicle of a real reform coalition. This makes the present situation hard to predict. Quebec is divided, as shown by the presence of both Jean Chrétien and Lucien Bouchard in Ottawa. Everything is possible, including a referendum on sovereignty or association with Canada.

The future does not look good. The Charter of the French Language is seriously threatened in the areas of education, immigration and commercial signs. The economic performance of Québec is the worst it has been in a long time. One third of Canada's poor live in Québec. The right for Québec to decide its own future is not recognized, as proven by arguments about the frontiers of an independent Québec. The debate is distorted by the media, an example being the endless enumeration of social and economic disaster that would fall upon Quebeckers in the event of separation. It is impossible for English-speaking Canada to understand that being bilingual does not and must not erase differences. The aspirations and personality of Québec remain invisible to the rest of Canada.

The country is under a lot of pressure. It is difficult to have real improvement, given the determination of the federal government to uphold the myth of the post-war economic and social miracle. The battle of economic diversification is lost. The fight against unemployment is not very successful. Social programs are threatened. The constitutional obsession with uniformity is a danger to anyone willing to be different. Nothing will change without a complete overhaul of the Canadian democratic system. Canada's historical realities, rather than doubtful idealism, need to be reflected in its Constitution. Québec's separation, or a major decentralization of Canada, will thus be talked about as long as the status quo remains.

Pierrette Landry is a Ph.D. Candidate at the Université du Québec à Montréal. She has worked as a researcher for two members of Parliament.

BIBLIOGRAPHY

Cohen-Tanugi, Laurent, La métamorphose de la démocratie, Editions Odile Jacob, Paris, 1989, 197 pages.

Commissaire aux langues officielles, Rapport — La langue de travail dans la fonction publique fédérale, Ottawa, décembre 1982, 43 pages.

Commissariat aux langues officielles, Les langues officielles — Les faits, Ministre des Approvisionnements et Services, septembre 1993, 28 pages.

Fitzmaurice, John, Québec and Canada — Past, Present and Future, St. Martin's Press, New York, 1985, 343 pages.

House of Commons Debates, Monday, April 18, 1994, volume 133, Number 051, 1st Session, 35th Parliament.

L'association du barreau canadien, L'adhésion du Québec à l'Accord du Lac Meech, Les Editions Thémis, 1988, 261 pages.

Leclerc, Yves, La démocratie cul-de-sac, L'Étincelle Editeur, Montréal-Paris, 1993, 191 pages.

Parini, Philippe, Régimes politiques contemporains, Masson, Paris, 1991, 294 pages.

Pelletier, Mario, La machine à milliards — L'histoire de la Caisse de dépôt et placement du Québec, Editions Québec/Amérique, Montréal, 1989, 330 pages.

Rémillard, Gil, Le fédéralisme canadien — Tome II — Le rapatriement de la constitution, Québec/Amérique, Montréal, 1985, 721 pages.

Sénécal, Gilles, Territoires et minorités, Association Canadienne française pour l'avancement des sciences, Montréal, 1989, 123 pages.

Zylberberg, Jacques, and Emeri, Claude, eds., La démocratie dans tous ses états — Argentine, Canada, France, Les Presses de l'université Laval, Sainte-Foy, 1993, 654 pages.

Breaking the Barriers:
Reshaping Environmental Activism —
Mae Burrows in Conversation

. . . .

by Mae Burrows
with Victoria Cross

Mae Burrows is the Environmental Director of the United Fishermen and Allied Workers' Union (UFAWU), a 6,000 member union representing fishers and shore workers in British Columbia. Burrows also serves as the director of the T. Buck Suzuki Environmental Foundation. The foundation undertakes environmental research and community outreach as the union participates in environmental organizations, campaigns and public education efforts. In addition, Burrows teaches, is working on her Masters' degree, and with her partner, raises their son.

In July 1994, Mae Burrows shared some thoughts about her work with Victoria Cross. In preparing for this discussion, carried on over several days, phone conversations and cross-time-zone, back-and-forth facsimile transmissions, Burrows joked about the number of hats she wears. "Sometimes I feel like a hatrack," she said, displaying her good-humoured and down-to-earth approach to the task of changing the world.

Cross: What's the key element of your work?

Burrows: The work I do is interesting because we don't buy the corporate line that has set the agenda for the public debate of "jobs vs. the environment." It isn't like that, at least for our members. A healthy environment will sustain jobs in the fishing industry generation after generation — this is true sustainability. Good environmental practices go hand-in-hand with commercial enterprise, the foundation of the fishing industry.

Cross: Am I hearing a new approach, an approach that seeks to create a different dialogue about the environment? Out east, mainstream press and television seems to be reporting only the strife, the anger between British Columbia's working people and those in the environmental movement. The B.C. government is portrayed as besieged from all sides, working for fair compromise with no help from anyone. Yet, with your work, you seem to be interested in bringing working people and environmental activists together. What's going on, as far as you can see?

Burrows: Unfortunately, most governments have been loathe to take a leadership role in this area. Usually, it is the citizen groups that must lead the way, and force governments to follow. This is often very difficult because governments at all levels seem to go out of their way to limit the vision and choices that citizens have. Obviously, citizen groups don't have equality with corporations, and even within the context of "consultation," equality is implied but rarely delivered since governments tend to react to the players with the most power — the corporate sector.

Governments pay too much heed to the corporate paradigm — it has to be jobs or the environment — and a sustainable economy cannot start from this perspective. When politicians present only two options, we know we are being manipulated. They have bought into the jobs vs. environment argument, which is the ultimate manipulation of capital to perpetuate its control.

This may be only natural in the sense that the government is reacting to those with the most power, as they are doing in the case of Alcan's Kemano II project, which I will discuss shortly. Left-leaning governments assume we will continue to support them because we have no other choice. That's a very disempowering assumption to work with.

Cross: You use the word "disempowering." The UFAWU has a reputation for having a high level of involvement on the part of the membership. How does that work, what's your approach?

Burrows: I see the UFAWU as being a leading force in attempting to redress those issues and change the paradigm to jobs and the environment. I hope this is evident in the work I do with fish habitat and water quality. The campaigns we undertake are always directed at a community and grassroots level. They deal with issues very close to people's homes and surroundings. They are issues about reforming logging practices which harm salmon streams, water quality issues, stopping industrial pollutants from flowing into water bodies. We also do hands-on marsh cleanup projects, to try to restore healthy wetlands and marshes for fish and other wildlife in the Fraser River estuary.

Cross: How long has the union been at this? When did this all start?

Burrows: The Foundation was established by the union in 1981. It was named after Tatsuro "Buck" Suzuki, a person of great stature in both his environmental and union work. He was a Fraser River fisherman who did river cleanup work in the 1950s, long before ecology and environmentalism were the popular activities they are today. He was prominent in UFAWU, serving 11 terms as vice-president, one as president and was often a full-time organizer. He was also active in the Japanese-Canadian Citizens Association. He was a wonderful person to name the foundation after and he is always a source of great inspiration to me in my work.

Because of the commitment of Suzuki and others, the union has a long history of leading coalitions to redress issues of inequality for working people, especially on the environmental front. The Kitimat Oil Ports Inquiry, the Moran Dam, pulp mill pollution: these are some of the major issues the union has been involved with over the years. They were all important, but they pale in importance beside an issue with which we have a long history — Alcan Aluminium's Kemano dam and diversion.

Cross: Please set the stage on this one, give us some background so we understand where we are today a bit better.

Burrows: The Nechako River, located in west-central B.C., is a major tributary to the Fraser River, one of the most important salmon rivers in the world. In 1950, the provincial government of the day gave Alcan rights to all the water in the Nechako and other, adjacent rivers, in exchange for establishing an aluminium smelter in Kitimat, 50 miles away.

Alcan dammed the Nechako, reversed its flow westward through a 10-mile long tunnel through the costal mountains, built a hydropower station and the aluminium smelter, and started producing aluminium, diverting about 30 per cent of the Nechako's flow. In the process, Alcan flooded out the Cheslatta Indian band and decimated some stocks of Fraser River salmon.

As part of the deal, Alcan will receive a perpetual license for all of the water it will be using to operate the facilities constructed by the end of 1999. Alcan will then have the right to use this amount of water forever.

Cross: What is Alcan doing now?

Burrows: With its corporate eye on the looming 1999 deadline, Alcan moved to increase the amount of water it sucked from the Nechako from 30 per cent to 87 per cent. It couldn't use this water to produce power for aluminium, since aluminium markets were declining, but it hit on another use for the water — producing electricity for sale to BC Hydro. During the late 1970s, Alcan drastically reduced the river flow to generate more electricity which it sold to Hydro. The reduced flow was disastrous for fish, and the federal Department of Fisheries and Oceans (DFO) obtained a court injunction requiring Alcan to allow enough water to flow to protect fish. Alcan complied with the injunction until 1985. DFO was preparing for a major court battle when suddenly, in 1987, a secret meeting held in Vancouver between DFO, Alcan and the provincial Social Credit government — which had actually encouraged Alcan to stop obeying the injunction — resulted in an agreement that allowed Alcan to drain up to 87 per cent of the Nechako, the amount of water it had originally wanted. The agreement flew in the face of dozens of studies done by DFO scientists which concluded that such low flows would be an unmitigated disaster for the fish.

Cross: But the government is different now . . .

Burrows: In 1991, the government of British Columbia changed hands. The Socreds were out and the New Democrats were in. What would be the NDP approach to Kemano II? During the election campaign, NDP leader Mike Harcourt had promised to hold a full environmental assessment of the controversial project.

That didn't happen. Instead, Harcourt commissioned NDP lawyer Murray Rankin to assess the political and financial consequences of not proceeding with Kemano II. Rankin took a very conservative approach and recommended that the project had to proceed, otherwise the government would be liable for Alcan's costs and claims. Figures like $500 million were bandied about. Credible legal opinions were available which suggest that Alcan's claims could be successfully challenged in court. There were also economic arguments which could be mounted to counter Alcan's costly compensation threats. The government could have taken a pro-active leadership role in protecting a sustainable fishery and agricultural industry, as well as the unquantifiable value of preserving the biological diversity of our precious salmon resource. Instead, the government took the low road and started by capitulating to Alcan's threats.

Cross: I'm sure UFAWU is not alone, probably Alcan isn't either. How has this battle shaped up? Who are the players?

Burrows: The project was significant for its supporters: Alcan, obviously, the unionized construction workers who would get the short-term jobs to build the project, the Kitimat Chamber of Commerce and other local businesses.

Opposing the project were a wide-ranging coalition of merchants in fishing communities, the fishing industry itself and its support services, churches, native, youth, environmental and anti-Free Trade citizen groups as well as many municipal councils. The Fraser River is one of the most important salmon producing rivers in the world and protecting this resource for commercial, recreational, and environmental reasons is important in many communities throughout B.C.

Cross: So what did your coalition do? How did you approach the government?

Burrows: Initially, the UFAWU and other coalition members spent a great deal of time trying to convince the government to examine the social, environmental and economic consequences of Kemano on the entire province, not just the local area recommended by Rankin. We met with the government. We lobbied them. But in the end, the government ignored our concerns and designated the B.C. Utilities Commission (BCUC), a provincial body that usually deals with hydro-electricity projects to review Kemano II. Through the terms of reference it set, the Harcourt government forced the commission to assume that the project would proceed; the commission's job would be to recommend methods of mitigating the negative impacts of Kemano II — how to "fix" the project, in other words.

Most insulting for the fishing community was that the only people and the only fish to be considered were those that lived or spawned in the Nechako and Kemano watersheds. The shoreworkers who can Nechako-bound salmon in Prince Rupert, for example, the fishers who fish near Comox, Steveston and New Westminster would be outside the commission's terms of reference and thus ignored. As Harcourt said in one of his letters to the Coalition, only those "most directly affected" would be considered in the Commission's cost-benefit analysis. Conveniently left out of the equation were the fishing industry and fishing communities which would be directly affected by the project, no question.

The government said that Alcan had the right, by contract, to proceed with the project and that's as far as it went in its analysis. In response, a number of coalitions sprang up along the coast, in the lower Mainland, and in the Prince George and Nechako areas resisting Kemano and arguing for a broader mandate to the BCUC hearings. In particular, that a proper environmental assessment needs to be done, and that BCUC is not the proper body to undertake this task.

Cross: How did your community, and the coalitions react?

Burrows: The UFAWU decided to take on the government. Even though Alcan's Public Relations strategy was to claim that Kemano II was necessary to maintain smelting jobs, it was clear that its real motivation was to sell power to BC Hydro to boost profits for its international shareholders. We say they can't do that at the expense of a sustainable fishery, especially without undergoing the scrutiny required of all independent power producers. In June 1994, the UFAWU filed a petition in B.C. Supreme Court asking the court to order the government to require Alcan to undergo an Energy Certificate Review, since Kemano II is a major energy production project. That would require socio-economic and environmental assessments. The government could stonewall and limit the mandate of that assessment, too, but that is not likely because the union and the other coalition members have been building strong positive support against the project. Despite Alcan's financial resources and its ability to control the media agenda, on this one, the "little guys" are winning the battle for the public's hearts and minds.

Cross: What's the major lesson you have learned from the Kemano II experience?

Burrows: The actions of the NDP government in the Kemano II affair are evidence that citizen groups need to stand up to this government as they have to other governments, and make the NDP aware of the right thing for it to do for the long-term sustainability of the province — not to look only after the interests and rights of the major corporations nor be totally concerned about the threat of capital as represented by Alcan.

This is happening in the context of a fishing industry being shut down in Washington and Oregon states, largely as a result of dams and waster diversions built on every major river there. Meanwhile, the B.C. government seems prepared to let Alcan complete its project for the sole purpose of earning revenues selling electricity while the fishing industry at home languishes.

That brings up the issue of trust. We're wondering how collusive the government is being in trying to raise revenues from its Hydro sales at the cost of a sustainable fishing industry.

Cross: What would you expect from the government in a case like this? Do you think your expectations are too high? That you're asking too much from average folks elected to government? What alternatives do you have?

Burrows: The NDP's primary concern should be a sustainable industry that continues generation after generation. Selling hydropower doesn't produce jobs although it may produce revenue. We needed the Members of the Legislative Assembly to work with us to resist a looming environmental disaster; instead, they parrot Alcan's threats. We can't obtain the answers we need from government, which is definitely not working with the citizen groups on this issue. The answer is grassroots organizing.

Government politicians argue that "certainly we were elected on the principles and policies of the New Democratic Party, but now that we are in government, we don't represent those interests any more, we have to represent all interests."

The problem with that is they are not representing our interests, and most of all, they are not representing the principles on which they were elected. Their message in opposition was long-term sustainability for both jobs and the environment. So what we have to do now is our grassroots organizing around the issues, so that we can build a public will and perception to give the government the poll results it needs — since apparently it won't do anything without the right numbers — so it will do what is right. The government should have done the right thing and followed its principles from the beginning. We are still hopeful that there will be a turn-around in the government's position and that it will take a stand against this Tory-inspired deal and protect the interests of B.C. communities.

Cross: Is this typical of your experiences with all governments, local governments? What do you see as the root of this problem?

Burrows: The New Democrat government's record on Kemano II is typical of the experiences we have had with grassroots organizing and dealing with government officials — full of frustration. Politicians I worked with before the election have become isolated and insulated from their constituents at the grassroots level by their spin-doctors, pollsters and bureaucrats. They won the election using the strategies and tactics of polling and media manipulation, but this approach is not sustainable — it has cut them off from their communities. The result is that, as in the Kemano II affair, we end up having to fight the very people we worked hard to elect. The same principle applies for issues at the local level.

Cross: I have heard community organizers in the past talk about the strength that can often be won at a local level, dealing with local politicians, who were often, themselves, neighbourhood activists brought to office by coalition and community organizing efforts. You're saying that's not the case, that's not your experience. Can you talk about that more?

Burrows: There are now more NDP politicians than ever before elected to municipal councils, but we still have to fight them tooth and nail. We are involved with the Save Georgia Strait Alliance on a clean-water campaign to prevent further pollution of the Georgia Strait and the Fraser River, and to force municipalities, regional districts and the provincial governments to mend their polluting ways.

One big issue we've been fighting is the lack of adequate sewage treatment from major municipalities such as Victoria and regional districts, such as the Greater Vancouver Regional District, that dump virtually untreated sewage — billions and billions of litres every year — into the Fraser River, Burrard Inlet and the Straight of Georgia: the main thoroughfares for millions of salmon and other species of fish. The provincial government has taken a commendable stand on this issue, both in terms of setting deadlines for municipalities to get their sewage treatment facilities into place, and in participating in joint federal provincial funding for facilities. What we've run into with municipal politicians is the NIMTOO phenomenon.

Cross: I've heard of NIMBY — Not In My Back Yard — but what's NIMTOO?

Burrows: "Not In My Term of Office," squawk the politicians, "am I going to raise taxes so that I become unpopular and get voted out of office." The consequence for us is that the politicians have done little to improve and upgrade sewage treatment for decades, which is part of the reason treatment costs are so astronomical today. Now the bills are coming due — sewage plants rupturing — and they are very high. Politicians have to be hounded to do the right thing.

In fact, some followed a more disgusting route this year and feeding into a "citizen" tax revolt. The politicians felt that citizens wouldn't pay for sewage upgrading. Save Georgia Strait found that this was not true — people were saying, "I'm willing to see my tax dollars go for things like sewage treatment so that we don't continue to dump billions of litres of toxic chemicals and untreated domestic sewage into our costal waters and leave the bills for the next generation."

Once again, politicians didn't take the lead, it was citizen groups that brought the issue to a public head. Citizens said they would pay and the politicians, who were elected to lead, are now rushing to catch up with the people.

Cross: What strategies, tactics did you use to reset the stage?

Burrows: It didn't come easy. To get the attention of the politicians and the media, Save Georgia Strait, the Suzuki Foundation, the Union and the Serria Legal Defence Fund filed charges against the Greater Vancouver Regional District alleging it was in violation of the federal Fisheries Act, by dumping deleterious substances into waters inhabited by fish. So it took the threat of a court case to make the politicians realize that what they were doing was wrong. There is now some movement, with federal and provincial money being promised for sewage treatment. It's only secondary treatment, and we have many concerns with that kind of treatment, but it's a start. But it took a lot of citizen action to get the ball rolling. This is a key message: it is citizens who have to take the lead in environmental matters.

Cross: Do you have other examples, other stories of how citizen action has made a concrete difference, changed the course of decision-making?

Burrows: A second instance was the issue of how to maintain the quality of drinking water. The regional politicians have allowed logging of Vancouver's watershed where drinking water is stored, resulting in frequent murkiness in the water. Plus, with explosive growth — another issue local politicians are loathe to take on since their focus is still on the old paradigm of unblocked development — water quality was visibly deteriorating.

Cross: You mentioned this paradigm before, and have spoken about the jobs vs. environment paradigm blocking choices, limiting the discussion and development of sustainability as a concept. I take it this example describes what you mean. . .

Burrows: The politicians would look at only two options for purifying water. Now, when politicians and bureaucrats tell you there are only two options available, you know something is missing and you are being manipulated. That is clearly how the issue came across to the community.

The choices were: very expensive chlorine treatment or less expensive treatment by a chemical called chloramine. What were omitted were two effective and less environmentally damaging, although expensive in the short term, processes — ozonization and biological filtration.

Cross: What was wrong with the cheaper option? Why was it unsound?

Burrows: Chloramine may be cheaper, but it is lethal to fish. It binds to their oxygen-exchange cells and kills fish instantly. Any kind of spill

— and we have very old pipes in Vancouver so there will be breaks, and there have been breaks in the past — would immediately lead to a fish kill. This was not acceptable; citizens were outraged by the way the issue was presented to them. Considerable citizen action and coalition building took place. The result was that the politicians and the bureaucrats eventually acknowledged there were other choices available and chloramine was taken off the agenda. That's a clear victory.

The politicians are still planning to use the chlorine, but they are being forced to experiment with ozonization and biological filtration. That is where they should have started in the first place.

Cross: Why wasn't it a first choice to try new methods?

Burrows: It wasn't the first choice because the politicians felt they had to offer the taxpayers the cheapest choice possible. Citizens said, "No, we want the best choice, best in the long term, the solution that is sustainable. Not just the cheaper choice."

The politicians were also led by the bureaucrats, many of whom received their training in the 1950s and their solutions reflect this engineering mentality and technological approach of those times. They are not familiar or comfortable with the newer, more holistic and organic approaches of today. It's a very hard sell to force these bureaucrats with their engineering rings to widen their perspectives and look at things like solar-aquatic-based wastewater-recovery systems. These are not the technological solutions involving large mega-facilities and mountains of concrete so beloved by the civil engineers of the 1950s who have risen to the top of the bureaucratic ladder. I must note that this mentality is not consistent throughout the bureaucracy; there are progressive bureaucrats to be found in the fish/food/agriculture and environment ministries, for example. But there is a problem of entrenched, old-guard bureaucrats who still influence the agenda.

Cross: What do you see as a partial solution, a mechanism that gets around NIMTOO and old-style decision-making?

Burrows: We want real consultation at the initial question-setting stage, but often we're asked to participate in rubber-stamping pre-set processes, or asked to participate in processes which do not really make the decisions.

I learned a lot about so-called consultation processes in the past year in relation to CORE — the Commission on Resources and the Environment, established by the NDP government and headed by former Ombudsman Stephen Owen.

Cross: What was CORE like for you and others involved? What did you learn from that experience?

Burrows: What CORE has meant for us as an organization is that we have had to sit in multi-stakeholder meetings two or three full days a month for over a year. That is a tremendous amount of volunteer time in order to give the government "input" into what we wanted to see happening with forest practices in various regions of B.C.

Some people say that CORE was an attempt to democratize decision-making. Others say CORE was a good way to keep people off the streets and out of the forests and out of the government's face for a year while it did it's polling, ran its focus groups and tested its market strategies. Still others say that CORE was an effective way for the government to not have to make decisions about logging, that it was a stall tactic for a full year. Many participants expressed the opinion that CORE was a very elaborate and covert gap analysis for both government and corporate sectors bent on uncovering the strategies and interests of the other participants. Some felt the company and government players were using the meetings to assess the strengths and weaknesses that were played out later in the campaign to influence public opinion.

It's hard to say what CORE really was, but for us it was a costly exercise were we sat with 21 people at the Vancouver Island CORE table — including multinational forest companies, forestry workers, environmentalists and tourism people, talking about what kinds of logging practices on Vancouver Island we wanted to see. At the end of the day we were supposed to arrive at a consensus on what we wanted. The problem is that the process didn't work. I think most people recognize that.

Cross: So if it's not consultation, what do you think is shaping policy at the provincial level?

Burrows: What seems to be shaping government policy are its public-opinion polling and a successful campaign waged by unhappy loggers. What we saw was government polling to find what the citizenry in general wanted. Second, the logging sector embarked on a very high-profile campaign — to sway the media and the government. The campaign was spearheaded by northern Vancouver Island logging companies and loggers who were very annoyed at the CORE recommendations because they saw too much erosion in the access to the forest resource that they had traditionally enjoyed.

So that exercise certainly taught me something about where to put my energy. I should go to some of the meetings, to keep a finger on the pulse of the discussion, but I will not take them as seriously as other efforts, such as attempting to change public opinion, and the direction of public debate. Public opinion will affect polling results, which is what government decisions are based on. No more sitting politely in government-sponsored meetings.

Cross: So where are you headed, where do you see your time being spent?

Burrows: There have been many good initiatives by this government, but often citizens have had to lead the way. Come election time, who knows what I'll do. Perhaps by then the government will stand up to Alcan and challenge the poor deal handed to it by the Mulroney government. Perhaps there won't be any choice but to vote NDP.

But as one fisherman, a 20-year NDP activist who is thoroughly frustrated by the government's stand on Kemano II said to me, "They'll probably get my vote, but they won't get my 100 hours of volunteer time to help get them elected again. Alcan can pull the vote this time."

Of Canola, Cargill and International Capital

by Kathy Baylis

Farmers possess tremendous potential for power. They produce a commodity essential for life itself. Still, they have been conditioned over the years to accept exploitation as a legitimate and essential part of farm economics.

Stuart Thiesson, Executive Secretary of the
National Farmers Union, 1969

Uncle Alwyn leaned up against the fence, one foot propped up on the bottom rung, arms slung over the top. A Holstein eyed him warily from the hay feeder.

"Nice looking herd."

Aunt Amy stood silently next to her brother, regarding her heifers with thought. "Yes, they are. I just hope we can keep them."

Alwyn disengaged his foot from the fence and started back towards the house. Amy lengthened her stride to keep up, "I guess you'd be affected by the GATT too."

"Humph. The GATT, the federal government, Cargill, take your pick," he responded. "What's worse is the groups that should be there fighting for the farmer are either busy fighting for their own survival or are acting just like the enemy." He turned towards Amy. "But I guess you would know what that's like."

"Yes, it's hard to know which side our marketing boards are on sometimes," she sighed.

They stopped at Amy's vegetable garden. The squash, as always, looked like it was about to take over. The tomatoes were surviving, but would probably fare better without the odd interference from the neighbourhood bush rabbits.

"Garden looks good, but you could use a fence," commented Alwyn.

"I know, but there's never enough time, between cows and cropping . . . How's your crop coming?" asked Amy.

"Well, there's lots of weeds with the wet spring, and we sure could use a couple of good, hot days. But the crop's coming up nice."

At the door, they both struggled with their boots. Alwyn tried to knock off the chaff, grain and other sundry out of the cuff of his jeans. Amy, like their mother, got perturbed when her house started to resemble a grain bin.

"What did you seed this year?" Amy asked. She held open the door as Alwyn regained his balance.

"Wheat, mostly. Figured no one else was growing it so we might as well."

They stepped in, and headed for the kitchen.

"Don't know if I told you, but last year we had a couple of fields seeded to canary seed. Somehow it's ironic that we can get more for bird seed than we can get for human food. The price was at nine bucks per bushel for the longest time. Then it started to rise. It sat at 11 dollars for a while. That's when I sold. Figured that was as high as she would get. Besides, I needed the cash flow." He took the proffered cup of coffee. "Any idea where the price was a month later?"

Amy shook her head.

"Over $40. I can't believe it. And there are still some of my young neighbours that think we can do without the Wheat Board. I think all grains should go under it. The guys with canola got caught with the same thing. Anyone who had the money to be able to hold onto their crop, has the time to watch the markets, and is exceptionally lucky, can make some money. The rest of us have to take the price we're given."

Amy smiled into her coffee. Even though it had some faults, the cost-of-production formula shared by supply managed farmers afforded a bit of security.

"Now everybody's seeding canary seed. Sometimes I don't know what they're thinking. Unless there's a massive crop failure somewhere, they're going to flood the market and no one is going to get a decent price."

Alwyn downed the coffee and held out the cup for a refill.

"I suppose I shouldn't complain too much, we're still surviving. How are you and Hal doing? Any decisions yet?"

Amy and her husband had been trying to decide whether to keep their dairy herd. It wasn't small by Canadian standards, but by U.S. standards it was tiny. They were not sure if it would continue to be viable in the post-GATT era.

"Well, I still figure that 30 cows are plenty to deal with first thing in the morning. The idea of expanding our operation five or ten-fold in order to be 'competitive' is just not realistic for us."

"Three hundred cows are quite a bit of milking."

"There are neighbours that have over one hundred cows. Frankly, more power to them, and as long as we have supply management, we can both survive. What gets me is the idiot down the road who says that he is just waiting for quota prices to go down, so that he can hurry up and milk several hundred cows. I guess he figures he can compete with the several thousand head herds in the southern states."

"Well, out west, we've got some young farmers, not many of them mind you, who figure the best way to survive is to buy their neighbour's farm as cheap as possible. Some of them are looking at other ways of surviving." Alwyn got up and poured them both another coffee. "Some other younger farmers are now banding together to set up what they call 'inland grain terminals.' They don't seem to mind that it might mean the shut down of small elevators, and more rail lines being pulled out. They say they are doing it because they want an alternative to selling through our local co-operative."

Amy looked up from her cup to watch her brother wear out the kitchen tiles, pacing. "That sounds a bit strange. They're setting up a co-operative as an alternative to a co-operative?"

"Yep." Alwyn sat down. "But do you know who one community has running their new huge 'locally-controlled' grain terminal?"

Amy raised an eyebrow

"Cargill! It's plain nuts."

"Watch, you'll spill your coffee."

Alwyn looked chastised, and set his cup down. "Well, I admit that I can sort of understand where they're coming from. Our original co-operative grain handler wants to turn my equity in that corporation into shares that can be traded on the open market."

"Wouldn't there be a problem with a large business just taking over the co-op?" asked Amy.

"That's what I'm worried about, although they're talking about caps on the number of shares any one investor can own. But who knows what my equity will be worth 10 years down the road? It doesn't have a thing to do with how the corporation is doing, it has to do with how many people or businesses want to buy shares. Plus, here's a co-operative who is supposedly working for farmers. Say they bought my oats for a low price, turned around and sold them for a decent amount. Up until now, that profit was turned around and given back to the farmer. Now it will be shared between the farmer, and whoever else owns shares in the corporation. It will no longer be in their best interest to give me a decent price for my crop."

They both sat for a while, quietly sipping from their cups. Amy finally looked up at her brother. "You know, sometimes it feels like we're fighting the same issues as we did years ago."

Alwyn harumphed an agreement.

"For our industry, we got supply management 25 years ago, although it did not come without one big fight. But since then it's allowed family farmers to continue to farm. Now we're fighting to keep it."

"For our part," Alwyn rocked softly in his chair, "we got the Crow rate years ago, and have fought to keep it and now we're fighting to keep its weak offspring, the Crow benefit. Back in the 40s farmers fought to get the Canadian Wheat Board, and now we're fighting to keep it alive," said Alwyn.

"We'll probably be fighting the same fights next century," said Amy.

"Well, I suppose that's better than there just not being any farmers left to fight."

In 1994, the National Farmers Union celebrates its twenty-fifth year of existence. Depending on who you talk to, and the mood they're in at the time, things have either changed drastically over the past twenty-five years, or they've remained the same. Multi-nationals have mutated into transnationals. As a nation, we are now tied into several international trade deals, which hamper our ability, as a nation-state, to control the flow of capital. The general public is more skeptical of economic alternatives. Yet the biggest irony of the last 25 years is that the issues we are fighting for are often the same.

Fighting for livable farm income has been the major issue for farmers and farm organizations. This involves numerous ways of trying to mitigate the power of corporations who want to lower their input costs — which in our case is the raw food. All farmers would like to see a livable income from their product. Through organized and co-operative marketing systems like supply management, and orderly marketing, which are both forms of horizontal integration, a certain amount of stability in farm income has been achieved.

Transportation is an essential part of marketing and distribution, and a key to farm income. The Crow rate, later changed to the WGTA subsidy (Crow benefit), is constantly under attack. Because you cannot move the main agricultural input — land — we as farmers are forced to find a way to get our products to the consumer, without hampering farmers that happen to be situated further away from the market.

Therefore farmers need a system to subsidize the movement of their goods to market.

This article starts with the premise that control of the production of food should be in the hands of farmers. If consumers want a safe reliable source of inexpensive food, farm families are the best conduits for that production.

Food safety and quality is best brought to the consumer by a producer who is growing food, and is receiving a decent income. This leads to production which does not cut corners, or depends upon more intensive agricultural methods which generally involve increased chemical applications.

Because farm families want to keep farming over the long term, they are more likely to adapt sustainable methods of agriculture. Thus they have an interest to conserve topsoil and not to deplete organic matter.

Any consumer should also be concerned about rural development and land use. Farmers when farming, are not a drain on the social safety nets, and are often employers. They create demand for goods and services at a community level.

Massive corporate farms are not conducive to building and sustaining rural communities. A few rich, often absentee landowners who depend on poorly-paid, seasonal help, are not likely to concern themselves with wider issues — schools, proper health care, recreation and cultural facilities even as they press for services such as water, roads, lines and maintenance from local governments.

The present trend toward 'industrialized food production', i.e. monoculture, is not environmentally sustainable. Nor is it developmentally sustainable. Yet the alternatives are less and less economically sustainable for a family farm. In Ontario, we see corporations like ConAgri buying huge tracts of land from family farmers, and hiring some of the ex-farmers to work it. The irony is that this corporate farming cannot last in the long run. The land will be exploited, and the population will end up on urban welfare rolls.

We, as a nation, are continuing to hand over our food security to transnational corporations like ADM and Cargill. Is this desirable? Is it sustainable?

Through the desire to keep family farmers farming, alternatives have been set up such as the Canadian Wheat Board, The Co-operative Prairie Pool system, supply management, etc. But slowly those alternatives have come under attack, both from corporate interests and from some farmers. Like all other sectors, agriculture is seeing the move toward deregulation and privatization. Historically, the agriculture and farm movement has been an area where collective action and democratization has been put into practice. To now see these ideas come under attack from "competitiveness" and "globalization" should concern everyone who would like to keep economic alternatives alive in both theory and practice.

Roy Atkinson, the first National Farmers Union (NFU) president, said the NFU worked to mitigate the excesses of the current economic system in largely three ways: education and agitation; legislative and legal; and through use of our market power. These tactics are not new. The first western farm organizations used them, from the Territorial Grain Growers Association at the beginning of this century, and since.

Western farmers faced great vertical integration of the storage, transportation and marketing system. They developed alternatives, like the Wheat Pool, a co-operative to handle and store grain, a transportation rate schedule to give farmers constant rail rates, and the Canadian Wheat Board, a government legislated agency, to market grain for farmers. Supply management came along later to deal with many of these same difficulties experienced by other agricultural sectors.

The Grain Growers Association started by taking the rails to court. They pressed to give the farmer the right to load a producer car. Up until then, railway companies not only had the right to choose where they picked up grain, they had the power to dictate where communities were located, where elevators were located, and who ran those elevators. They would often play with the grade of the grain. As a first step in mitigating the rail companies' control, the Grain Growers won the right to let a farmer load a producer car.

The Grain Growers worked with their collective selling power. They wanted to be able to sell directly on the Winnipeg Commodity Exchange, as opposed to going through, and losing money to, a grain trader. They found that a true co-operative could not, legally, sell on the exchange. So they formed a corporation with a two-tier share system; voting shares for members (farmers) and non-voting shares for others. This ended up becoming the United Grain Growers Corporation (UGG). Anyone who knows UGG today, knows they do not resemble their original co-operative parent. Immediately after they became a corporation, they started to show signs of leaving their progressive roots. Their publicist was fired because he was spreading too much "propaganda" which might have upset their commodity exchange colleagues. Ironically, this is similar to the system being investigated by the Saskatchewan Wheat Pool (SWP) today, in order for the pool to get more investment capital.

The statutory rates for rail freight were originally put in place in part to keep the country together. It was recognized that the heart of Canada's grain growing region was 3,500 km from the Atlantic and 1,700 from the Pacific. Because Canada is not aligned along economic geography, it is cheaper to ship goods south rather than east-west. When the Crow rate was implemented there was a concern for community and political development integrated into policy. The government has changed a system of rail rates for farmers transporting grain. At the turn of the century, the Crows Nest Pass Rates set down specific freight rates for the producer. In the 1980s the railway companies argued that they could no longer afford to give farmers a set rate, so the government complied and established a compensatory rate schedule under the Western Grain Transportation Act (WGTA). This formula increases the amount farmers have to pay in freight every year. At the time, the rails agreed that they could be penalized if they did not fulfill their duty to ship grain. The government has never used this provision. This year, the present Minister of Transportation has suggested that he will end the subsidy altogether.

The farm movement has consistently fought any move to deregulate transportation. If farmers lose this Crow Benefit, it will mean the average grain farmer in western Canada will lose $5,000 net income (out of an average net of about $15,000). Many farmers in eastern Saskatchewan, Manitoba and the northern prairies will be forced out of the grain export industry. Yet rural development is not seen to be a priority by the government.

The first version of the Canadian Wheat Board (CWB) was set up during the First World War. This was after lobbying from the Winnipeg Grain Exchange which had earlier been forced to suspend trading as traders were getting caught short selling wheat. What farmers noticed is that this marketing system also had a stabilizing effect on prices. The Board was dismantled in 1920. Producers responded by demanding that the board be reinstated.

The government decided to establish a 'voluntary' system in 1935. The newly-elected Liberals ensured that farmers would have to sell to the Wheat Board when prices were low, and sell to the grain traders when prices were high. There was no question that the real beneficiaries of this system were the grain traders who were now basically ensured a profit. Farmers and farm groups continued to push for a mandatory system.

The Mackenzie King government began to experience some of the problem with its 'dual' wheat marketing system. In 1938—1939, the government offered an initial price, basically, a price guarantee, that ended up exceeding the actual end market price, which had fallen dramatically through the year. The government ended up $61.5 million short. In 1943, the U.S. had a shortage of wheat, and world prices were increasing rapidly. The Canadian government had entered into agreement with the U.K. and Russia, ensuring to sell its allies a set amount of wheat. But producers saw the lucrative market to the south as a better buyer. Thus the government could not get the supply it needed. Only then did the government make it mandatory for farmers to sell western Canadian wheat to the Wheat Board.

Presently, the CWB acts as a "single-desk" marketer. That means that everyone who sells through the board gets the same price for the same grade of product. The Wheat Board then acts as a marketer for that grain trying to get the best price for farmers. The whole point of single-desk selling is to pool the product and the returns, so that the board can get the best price, and return that price equitably to farmers. Because prices fluctuate so much during a crop year, the board can hold onto the wheat and sell it when the price is high, ensuring a better return for all farmers. But if farmers are only selling to the Wheat Board when the prices are low, the returns are not going to be particularly great. The Wheat Board can not pre-determine how much wheat it will have to sell, so some of the more lucrative, large-scale deals it can make — with a foreign country, for example — are undermined because it cannot ensure supply.

Many farmers are now frustrated with the CWB for a variety of reasons. Many are once again pushing for a "voluntary" system. There is a sense that the Wheat Board is not doing all it can to sell producers' wheat. There have also been some structural difficulties with the shipping of the product. Thus some farmers, with the backing of groups like the UGG, the Alberta government etc., are working to end the single desk selling and price pooling of the CWB. They couch it in terms of giving farmers a 'choice,' but there is no recognition that the choice they propose fundamentally undermines one of the options.

Supply management is a system that works to match domestic demand for a product with domestic supply. This way, producers are not producing a surplus which serves to drive the price down. There is a Cost of Production formula that averages out the real cost of all farmers to produce that product, including farmers' labour and return on investment. The CoP formula gives a supply managed producer what amounts to somewhat less than that average.

Supply management is now under attack from within. Some farmers feel they could compete in the "open" North American market without the dairy, poultry or egg board. In provinces where quotas have been allowed to be traded openly, their price is high to the point where it acts as a real deterrent for young farmers trying to get into production. Yet both with the CWB and supply management, there is not the realization that these structures can be changed for the better (everyone has seen them being changed for the worse). Instead, some farmers want these structures destroyed so they can pursue other alternatives.

Farmers who have been around since the time before supply management know that the death of this system that allows 30 cow herds to survive, will spell disaster for the vast majority of Canadian dairy, poultry and egg farmers. There are farms in the southwestern United States that are milking several thousand cows. They do not keep them past one lactation cycle. They are willing to burn out the cows, get as much milk as they can from them in that year, and then sell them as beef. (The disposable society meets agriculture.) These farms do not promote rural development. In fact, you will not see rural communities around them. They are worked by cheap labour, often illegal immigrants. They are not environmentally sustainable, producing huge amounts of manure that is not worth the owner's time to put into the land. They use huge amounts of subsidized water. Yet the government seems to see them as a progressive move.

The chicken industry in the U.S. is vertically integrated and is owned by three large agri-food industries. Tyson Foods is one. They contract out their chicken production to farmers, who are forced to buy their chicks and feed through Tyson (vaguely reminiscent of the old company-owned mining towns). They often have to turn around batches so quickly, that they do not have time to properly clean their facilities. The amount they receive for these birds is a pittance. Basically, it allows the farmer to remain on the farm, and the spouse is expected to bring in enough off-farm income to support the family. That is what the "free market" means to price takers like farmers in a vertically-integrated system.

Supply management has acted to help keep family farmers farming, and producing milk throughout the country. If one removed supply management for dairy production, especially its pooling of transportation costs, the farmers furthest away from the major urban center markets would cease to produce. Thus, supply management has greatly contributed to community development.

The Saskatchewan Wheat Pool (SWP) is celebrating its 70th anniversary in 1994. It was an attempt, like the earlier one of the Grain Growers, to create a co-operative to handle and ship grain. Generally it, and the other Prairie Pools (Manitoba and Alberta Pools) have been a real asset to the prairie economy. The Pools mitigated the grade and price gouging experienced by grain farmers when loading their product at the terminals. The Pools work by ensuring that any profit made from the buying and selling of non-Wheat Board Grains (thus things like oilseeds, oats, rye, mustard seed, etc.) is returned to the farmer-members as a "patronage dividend" in the form of cash or equity. The equity can be cashed in when the farmer retires. Many farmers use this as a sort of pension; it can end up being a sizable sum of money, in the thousands of dollars.

The SWP is looking at the option of going public. They want to change their equity in shares. They are concerned about there being a drain on their capital reserves as their early members start to retire. Others claim that the real reason SWP is doing this is to raise capital to build a large number of concrete elevators, as they proceed to "rationalize" their terminal system. They have proposed closing down a number of smaller, older wooden elevators, and putting up fewer, larger concrete elevators in more central locations. Another option the Pool has to deal with the possible cash flow shortage is to either divest itself of some of its secondary processing (it owns a chunk of Robins Doughnuts) or to offer their secondary processing industries to the stock market. But transferring equity to shares has an accounting bonus. Equity which is listed as a liability is transformed into shares which are "assets."

The interesting thing is that during the debate, many Pool delegates are arguing that the only way for the SWP to survive is as a Prairie-based transnational. They therefore do not see divesting assets as an option. It seems that the popular impression of a viable alternative to Cargill, is to develop a Cargill clone.

The irony is that farmers, whether they know this or not, are trying once again to develop progressive alternatives to their former progressive alternatives. The big push in Saskatchewan today is setting up large grain terminals. There are two already underway, and a third in its formative stages. Groups of farmers are selling shares to their neighbours in these new giant elevators in order to have a grain shipping point that they control. At least one of these terminals will be run by Cargill. Now the SWP is shutting down its small community elevators in order to build the large cement elevators, which will be further apart. Thus, farmers will have to truck their grain further and CN and CP will have further excuses to abandon more rail lines.

Another alternative some farmers are practicing, in order to decrease their dependence on transnationals, is organic farming. Organic production allows farmers to cut back on their purchase of inputs from large corporations. They are fighting the same fight that others fought years ago: the right to orderly marketing. Not all organic farmers want to avoid the orderly marketing structures. Not all of our orderly marketing structures are willing to change to accept a separate pool for organic produce. If they do not, they are in the end signing their death warrant. Organic farmers are no different in that they need affordable and efficient transportation, single desk selling, price pooling and some sort of quality regulation, etc. There is an international group that has developed a set of standards to identify what is "organic," although they are not recognized in an official legislative capacity as yet. Once again, we have the people leading the government. And once again, if the government and orderly marketing structures do not catch up soon, they will continue to lose power, which will end up in the hands of transnationals. Everyone has noticed that the distributors of "green" products are making a great deal of profit from excessive mark up. Obviously the market can "bear" quite a bit when it comes to sustainable products. It would be nice if some of this could get to the producer. But meanwhile, some producers have become discouraged with the Wheat Board and the Supply Management Boards for their inability and lack of interest in handling organic produce. These farmers are now looking at ways of circumventing these structures which will only result in the demise of these former economic alternatives. Lower non-organic produce prices will not help, and will likely drive down the farm gate prices for the organic producer.

"Past attempts to organize farmers have tended to keep farmers isolated from each other in little interest groups," said Roy Atkinson in 1969. We are now seeing this phenomenon again. Although these small groups are often organized, by commodity or region for all the best reasons, they can often act to undermine national action. This is rarely intentional, usually by default. In working to further community development, or a commodity interest, the collective agricultural interest is overlooked.

Often these community and commodity projects and structures can either be undermined or overtaken by interests of international capital. An example is the attempt by organic potato producers in PEI to develop a marketing co-operative which failed. Irving decreased the costs of their chemical inputs, and increased the price spread between the organically-produced product and the traditionally-produced potatoes. Thus "education and agitation" on a large level is often needed to support activities that use market power.

Often the farm movement falls into the trap of solely addressing national and international issues, in some ways "disempowering" its members by default. It is much more difficult to keep members involved in "big picture" struggles, when they cannot see how it affects them. We leave many of those whom we purport to represent on the sidelines watching what looks to them like Don Quixote tilting against a windmill. Like many of Canada's labour unions, the farm movement has to strive to be able to give its members a tangible benefit and work on a national and international level to be able to sustain that benefit. For farmers the direct economic benefit can be either information of local economic alternatives, collective bargaining for inputs, help with farm financial crises, etc. Farmers and their organizations have to act on a nation state, and now international level, to allow those local developments to succeed.

Agriculture is an area where the economic concept of "scarcity" is foreboding. If scarcity exists in agriculture, it means that people are going hungry. Yet the concept of scarcity is fundamental to the workings of the "free market." Thus, in the past, some economists were willing to allow some "tampering" with the free market to "mitigate the excesses of the capitalist system" in agriculture. These alternatives have worked in the past. They may need some modification to include new groups, and return to their original principles. But in an era where so many economic alternatives are touted as failures, it is important that farmers and consumers work to preserve those alternatives that are and have been a success.

> *Our movement is based upon a foundation of understanding. It is an understanding that highlights the positive concepts and needs that will unite us as farmers; for understanding follows learning, and we are learning that as farmers we hold a common stake in the welfare of one another and our nation. We are learning that the society in which we live and toil is exploitive in nature and the power of abundance we possess is widely subjected to economic exploitation to our disadvantage.*

> *The common hope and aspiration of us all is that the creative power farmers possess may be a blessing to all humanity and not a curse. It is our hope and aspiration that our families may live in dignity and prosperity — that we may, as farmers, live in harmony with one another and that all the world's people may live in peace and prosperity.*

National Farmers Union Statement of Purpose, 1969

Kathy Baylis is an activist working inside and outside the NDP. Currently, she works as the NFU Communications Director.

Organizing for Change

. . . While it is indeed understandable that we some-times turn away from confrontation, we must inevitably agitate for the right to define ourselves. To have no agenda is to be captive to someone else's agenda . . .

Michael Darnell
Storm Over Erie: *The Great Lakes Fishermen and Allied Workers' Struggle for Recognition*

Essex Windsor Makes Its Own History

by Victoria Cross

S ave Our Station," chanted families, church groups, autoworkers, artists, lawyers. Bands played. Union banners waved. Hundreds of artist-produced, cardboard Maple Leaf emblems saying CBC-Windsor Yes! were held aloft by demonstrating students, children, nurses, teachers.

On December 16, 1990, over 8,000 people from Windsor and Essex County were on the march to demand a return of funding for local news at the Canadian Broadcasting Corporation affiliate in Windsor, CBET-TV.

It was the largest demonstration in the area's history. Marchers poured from Dieppe Gardens at the foot of Ouellette Avenue to head down Riverside Drive and gather at the lawn in front of the CBC television centre for a series of speeches. "We're sick and tired of being shoved around!" shouted then-Mayor John Millson into the microphone. The crowd roared.

Organizers marveled at the sight of so many on a winter's Sunday. Some were struck by the irony of 8000 real, live people ready to fight to protect the flickering images of television.

Misty-eyed union old-timers chuckled at the traffic jam that rivaled the history-book 1945 demonstration, when the United Auto Workers blocked the streets to prevent police and scabs from entering the old Ford plant on Riverside Drive. That action helped win the landmark Rand formula, the backbone of union dues "check-off" in Canada.

The turn-out at the rally represented the effect of an all-out effort by community members, elected officials at all levels, and an unprecedented level of national media attention.

All around them, pundits and predictors spoke of a national political malaise and the alienation of ordinary people from politics. What made

Windsor-area people so committed to action, so ready to fight, so polit-ically motivated?

The fight to save CBET-TV was never solely about television. It was more than a battle to preserve a local outlet of a key cultural institution, and more than a battle for political control, though it was also both those things. It was, of course, extremely political, but it was not about politics as generally portrayed even on Canada's national network.

Windsor and Essex County people were once again fighting for national recognition, for a place as a key part of Canada, for their own identity against both a hostile, outside elite in Toronto and Ottawa, and the looming presence of the United States.

In the battle, and in the resulting victory, the Windsor-area labour/left played a key, even decisive role. Elected New Democrats and their staff members, working in concert with area community action group and labour leadership figures were able to effectively operate an inside/outside strategy for change on both the local and national level. The intense period of activity could have resulted in a permanent change in how labour/left forces in the Windsor-area oper-ated. Unfortunately, though the lessons remain, other political factors intervened to undermine many of the gains made in the CBC fight.

Realpolitik and Real Politics — Parliament and the People

A seat in Parliament is like Teddy Roosevelt's Presidency — a "bully pulpit" from which to advocate and agitate. For those on the left, hav-ing members who view their role as such is an invaluable asset. Yet, there is a higher level of action possible. A constituency office, replete with telephones, facsimile machines, photocopying capabilities and a computer makes for an instant organizing centre, as well as a servicing centre. Having the freedom of movement, access to information, and ability to marshal parliamentary resources were key to organizing the Save Our Station demonstration: essential to restoring CBET-TV.

Our role in that fight was also a conscious part of a wider plan of community organizing.

Steven Langdon's election marked a shift in the electoral patterns of Windsor and Essex County. It had taken three tries, and some breaks on the national scene, but the 1984 election of two New Democrats in the Windsor area represented a significant shift in how Essex County and Windsor people were prepared to do politics from then on. Far from viewing electoral success as the end of the story, we viewed the Langdon win as the start of a whole new era for the community.

In our office, we handled an inordinate case load, sometimes as many as 250 major cases per month. We were not content to work on a case-by-case basis. We wanted to engage in collective action and help others to do so, too. From the outset, we decided the "real politics" of the office were to create the base for the kinds of economic change and social policy in which we believed. I called it creating "a circle of real power." That meant we consciously sought out and — if necessary, established — the community groups and activists to help devise and propel our larger agenda.

This was not a totally top-down effort, but it was a very conscious one. We centred it in what we viewed as the strategic elements essential to building a democratic left coalition — the labour movement, women, small communities and farm families, and social justice advocates working through religious groups or other community organizations. For us, our job was to represent "The Other Essex Windsor," the world of factories and farms; the folks barely hanging on to their homes, health or dreams. More, we wanted to help people speak and act for themselves.

We were very open about our plans and point of view, and annoyed others by joining in the usual power structure activities only as a means to reach our goals.

Groups and issues emerged in a rather chicken-and-egg way — sometimes it was impossible to determine what came first. There were even times when we decided to create organizations out of the thin air simply because we believed they were needed to reach a larger goal. Inside the office, however, we used to chuckle about how three phone calls on anything made a committee, five an organization, and 10 a demonstration. In addition to the CBC efforts recounted here, for example, we helped establish or worked closely with the Third World Resource Centre, the Windsor Occupational Safety and Health group, the AIDS Committee of Windsor, the North American Black Historical Museum, the National Farmers Union, Maidstone Against Dumping, Essex County Citizens Against Fermi II, the Clean Water Alliance, the Train Noise Committee, the Coalition for Peace (against the Gulf War), tenants' rights organizations and various union organizing, contract and shut-down battles.

We called it our inside/outside strategy. The role of the MP *inside* Parliament was enhanced, strengthened — even changed — by actions taking place *outside* Parliament. We applied the inside/outside strategy to all levels of government, ensuring that we spent more time "with the people" than we did with local, provincial or federal officialdom. As time wore on, we became increasingly identified as a centre of area democratic-left organizing. People came to us for tips and hints; ideas and advice. The office was a sea of paper, a jangle of ringing telephones, a backroom filled with picket signs and leaflets and newsletters in progress. We'd be visited by self-appointed "moles" operating under assumed names, field anonymous tips, and find "brown-paper envelopes" on our desks or dropped for us at a nearby coffeeshop. We followed up on everything.

As we engaged in each battle, more phone calls and "blind" visits would follow, asking for help on some other issue. Newspeople knew we almost always had a story to tell, facts to back up our arguments, and "real" people ready to interview. We were limited only by the hours in the day and the need for some small amounts of personal time.   In the last two years, the phone calls started coming from right across the country. In the end, we could have used a staff of 10.

The circle of activity and relationship to the MP was fundamentally altered from that of other community group/MP relationships I have seen. Far from having to "lobby" us, we would often work out activities with group leaders, carefully establishing different roles as we went along. The groups were enhanced by a strong relationship with an MP who helped create the viewpoint he carried forward.

We chose to work in a variety of ways, borrowing tactics from a variety of sources. Sometimes we were very conventional, other times Saul Alinsky-like, at various times agit-prop or Popular Front. Sometimes, the groups took on their own life and agenda, but the relationship with Steven and the rest of us generally remained strong. Always, we viewed the role of the labour movement, particularly but not exclusively, the Canadian Auto Workers, as central to our strategies, and took it upon ourselves to assist in building relationships between, say, environmental activists and CAW leaders.

The strategy was time-consuming and often frustrating. Sometimes groups weren't prepared to move as fast as we liked; other times we found them swerving off into directions with which we were not so comfortable. Occasionally internal stress in groups would be created by people who were consciously representing the views of another political party, or by those intent on keeping an MP and staff around solely as "go-fers."

At times when it worked the best, we were able to move forward with a sense of conviction and the knowledge that a small army of conscious leaders were alongside us. *We were not captives of "special interests" nor were the groups captive to us.* Instead, we were acting with others to bring forward alternatives for change and the organized base ready to act in support of such change. As the real politics became more vital, the House of Commons-caucus-committee-question-period grind transformed into an element of the various battles, a set of high cards to be used to benefit others' hands. The House was not the sole goal of the effort in which we engaged but a place where some small victories might be won, a marking point of how we had developed our point of view or brought an issue to national attention. The organizing, the base activities became our real focus. The diverse voices of "The Other Essex Windsor" were being heard in a glorious cacophony of sound. Essex Windsor's big-hearted spirit was on the nation's front pages.

For us, that was real politics, as well as *Realpolitik*. For Langdon, it meant his actions were rooted firmly at the grassroots, and there was a set of both formal and informal advisors unafraid to speak their minds, argue or push him in fresh directions as we too, pushed and shaped the local debate. It was democracy — engaged democracy — because there was a sincere dialogue between the parliamentary representative and the community.

In the end, it meant that we could not be ignored by an entrenched power structure, even though our alternative view of politics was seldom appreciated by other elected officials — even New Democrats. The most narrow criticism was that our actions were aimed at headlines, designed solely to raise Steven Langdon's profile. The most frightening criticism for me as a democratic-socialist was that some, even when we explained our analysis and strategy, flat out rejected it as a proper role for an MP or elected New Democrat. Sadly, that rejection left us carrying forward the strategy on our own — only to dream of the geometric progression in real people power that might have occurred if other elected officials had joined us in our work.

We probably should have realized we were on an inevitable course of conflict with people in our own party who had chosen a different path, and saw a different role for elected representatives, the party and the legislative arena. Nonetheless, when times got rough, that "circle of real power" gave us a sense of deep political certainty and security. When times got downright mean, that circle was a source of essential personal strength to carry on.

It was also tiring, taxing on creativity and required a constant commitment to meetings and start-from-scratch organizing efforts. It meant I had to learn the hard way how to say "I don't know what to do right now. What do you think?" — and hope like hell I'd get an answer we could act on. There were many sleepless nights as I gained an ever-deepening trust for people, and they for our work.

When Essex Windsor was lost, the deep, aching sadness I felt was in part because this period of engaged, heightened struggle was temporarily derailed by factors beyond our control, by the actions of people who could not see that ours was a strategy that made politics more than an electoral footrace, and the legislature more than a global outpost of middle-management for international bond marketeers. We had tried to offer a blue-print, a path, for the future.

After years of organizing in this vein, we were in a perfect position to move when the CBC cutbacks were announced. The CBC fight could have easily slipped into a city-directed plea for maintaining federal patronage or a nationalist arts-and-culture appeal spoken in a language irrelevant to a working-class community. Worse, angry Windsor-area people might have chosen to ditch CBC altogether deciding a privatized station was better than no station or an insensitive, weak national one.

We Do Disdain The Men With Powdered Hair

Nestled south of Detroit at the base of Michigan's mitten, the fiercely proud people of Windsor and Essex County have always felt the sting of isolation from the rest of the nation, even though the area has been the home of valiant Canadian fighters.

Some of that isolation is self-imposed. Since the first days of ill-funded settlement at the turn of the 18th century, area residents have exhibited a deeply-rooted skepticism of all those in power and a wilful need to go their own way. Francophones have held on to a sense of community in the face of real pressure. The area Black community is rich with the history of staunch freedom-fighters and seekers who have extracted a measure of control from the white power structure. The labour movement has always found rich ground in Essex County. Prior to confederation, the Bricklayers and Masons organized the area's first union local. They were followed by the shoemakers' Knights of St. Crispin, the Society of the General Union and the radical (for the times) Knights of Labor (U.S.-based group) who promised to organize workers "without respect to colour, creed and nationality." In 1887, the Windsor area held six chapters of the Knights. Carpenters successfully struck for a nine-and-a-half hour day in 1899, and the first-ever sit-down strike in Canada took place in Windsor in 1936.

Canadian nationalist singer/songwriter Stan Rogers captured the Windsor area's mistrust for the powerful and wealthy and its independent spirit in his only song referring to an Essex County site, "The Nancy." During the War of 1812, the schooner *The Nancy* heads for Amherstburg, Ontario. Warned by friendly Wyandot that Amherstburg fell and an ambush awaited, an on-board British officer orders immediate surrender. *The Nancy*'s crew refuses to give up the ship. As the British officers display their cowardice, *The Nancy*'s crew of nine ordinary sailors fire on the U.S. force of 50 or more, winning the day.

The belligerent lyric found in Rogers' song is sung in the voice of *The Nancy*'s captain. It is also the loud and populist voice of Essex County: *I do disdain men who are vain, the men with powdered hair.*

Like Captain MacIntosh and the crew, when pushed by circumstance or the stupidity of those in power, Windsor area people will take on tough odds and engage in drastic action to win their points. Equally, they will fight hard to prove their deep loyalty to Canada.

The 1500-car traffic block-up of the 1945 Ford/Rand strike is one example of such creative and decisive energy. So is Windsor Medical Insurance, a precursor to national health care. Strong Windsor-area locals played a decisive role in the creation of the Canadian Auto Workers union in the "split" from the U.S.-based United Auto Workers. The top national officers of the CAW, and many staffers, come from Windsor and Essex County.

More recently, on January 2, 1988, thousands of labour and community activists had stormed over the Ambassador Bridge to protest the U.S.-Canada Free Trade Agreement in a demonstration of both nationalist zeal and the need to protect Canadian jobs. The marchers were greeted by Detroit Police assembled in full riot gear. Though the demonstrators didn't invade the U.S. that day, activists, including Steven Langdon and the Labour Council President, were sued for their participation in that demonstration by an angry bridge company determined to restore lost revenue.

Fort CBET-TV — The Final Frontier

The Windsor-area media market is dominated by a market 50 times its size — Detroit. U.S. network and drive-time radio wars are legendary in the industry. The Canadian Radio-television and Telecommunications Commission (CRTC) always recognized the complexities of surviving in this vicious media atmosphere. For radio, they have relaxed Canadian content requirements, adjusted standards. When taking over the TV station from private operators in 1975, CBC inherited a substantial debt, but the move was made to ensure local, Canadian content to news and programming.

Since its inception, the station had never made enough from advertising to offset production and salary costs, and always stayed in the red. The corporation supported the Windsor station, ostensibly, on the basis that CBET-TV was the last outpost of Canadian culture.

The location of the broadcast centre in Windsor is an inadvertent reminder of this pioneer perspective. Poised on prime riverfront real-estate, the building faces a postcard-perfect view of the Detroit sky-line, a stone's-throw across the Detroit River. The Maple Leaf and CBC flags are like wind-whipped standards at a modern-day fort signalling to those on the other side of the river that Canada Starts Here. In that spirit, CBET provided a Windsor-based picture of Canada to the Detroit-area U.S. market. It also acted as a Canadian window on the U.S., covering major events centred in Detroit.

For newsies, Windsor is a key part of Canada's manufacturing and farm communities, a power-centre for the young, scrappy, news-mak-ing Canadian Auto Workers, home of leading figures in Liberal and New Democrat political circles, and near enough to Detroit to dabble in U.S. stories. Though considered a "local" station, CBET-TV had many staff committed to making a career in the area. One could raise a family in a mid-size city, keep (for the most part) out of the cold and snow, and still file occasional national and international stories.

The station maintained its strong community relations through solid local coverage and support of local events and fundraising drives, but also because many staff developed deep local ties. Windsor and Essex County people are informal by nature and suspect of celebrity as well as power. Windsorites remained on a first-name basis with on-air per-sonnel, who participated either directly, as individuals, or indirectly, through family members, in local activities.

Cutbacks and Context

The Mulroney government and the CBC could never have cut fund-ing to CBET without a fight — it was too much a part of the communi-ty for there to be a lackadaisical response to such a blunder. It remains mind-boggling that CBC's best bureaucratic minds could have miscal-culated the potential level of public outcry in Windsor to such a degree. When the cuts came in December 1990, they could not have picked a better time to galvanize a battered community.

Nationally, CBC reeled from the 1989 decision made by then-Finance Minister Michael Wilson to cut $140 million from CBC's operating bud-get, and from the decision to build a massive new state-of-the art studio in Toronto, where a real estate boom had pushed land and construction costs into the stratosphere. The corporation responded to the pressure from Mulroney's government by attacking the local news and produc-tion component, announcing that a total of 1,200 people nation-wide would be laid off as a result of the decision.

The announcement of CBC cutbacks came as Windsor's unemploy-ment level soared, as the U.S./Canada Free Trade Agreement took effect and as Gulf War fever built in the U.S. The unemployment level for October 1990 was set at 8.8 per cent, Windsor was "officially" at 9 per cent, but area activists placed it at about 15 per cent— and climbing. Nationally, business bankruptcies were up 141 per cent over the previous year. In Windsor, the year had seen a continuous round of announcements of layoffs at area auto plants and shutdowns in the auto parts industry. Thirty plants had closed, some with little warning. The area's downtown core, long-dependent on U.S. customers, eroded. Shops and offices were closing, buildings were boarded up. As the year ended, evidence mounted that the area was in the worst recession since the Dirty Thirties.

When December began, Windsor-area labour leaders and community activists were near exhaustion. The fight against the Free Trade Agreement, the mounting recession, Mulroney government actions and a hastily-called provincial election had forced a grueling year's gantlet of shut-down bargaining, fundraising, committee meetings, intervention efforts, canvassing and coalition building. This was, of course, in addition to the daily work of providing service to members and constituents.

Though many people were near burn-out, the period of intense work, both in organization and agitation, also meant that groundwork for a massive action had already taken place. Networks and phone trees had been established, an informal team of spokespeople and leaders were ready, and a superior sense of camaraderie developed among those activists due to a history of shared work.

That summer, Canadian Truckers Fighting Back had protested deregulation of the trucking industry by blockading traffic on the Ambassador Bridge that links Windsor to Detroit and serves as the main artery of north-south transportation. Though not articulating a careful set of demands, the truckers had received an overwhelming level of community support for their actions.

In September, the Windsor-area labour/left coalition had finally broken through to victory in the provincial election, gaining four of five area seats, losing one county seat by just over 200 votes. Some thought the landslide area-wide vote for the NDP a strange "fluke," especially since one winner and the one near-miss were virtual unknowns. Others maintain that working-class voters perceived, long before media pundits declared it to be so, that Ontario was at the start of a devastating economic period, and chose at last to elect New Democrats in hopes their interests would be defended.

For a year, a coalition of labour and business leaders had organized to fight the Mulroney government's Goods and Services Tax. Throughout the time period, there had been street theatre, community meetings and letter writing campaigns. On December 3, as the Senate debated the tax, hundreds of Windsor residents had packed the City Council chambers to demand that Windsor be declared a GST-free zone. Charging the crowd with inappropriate behaviour, councillors defeated the motion sponsored by both labour and business organizations 7-2. An ugly shouting match ensued, as labour and community activists made open threats of defeat for Team Windsor in the next year's municipal contests. City council members, conducting the meeting in the absence of Mayor John Millson, were visibly shaken at the palpable anger in the crowd crammed into Council Chambers and spilling out on the street.

The next day, on December 4, 1990, a stunned Eric Sorenson was handed a late-breaking newswire report revealing the next day's official announcement of the planned cuts. On air, Sorenson read out information that was, effectively, his own lay-off notice. The cuts would include Windsor's CBET.

Sorenson's face displayed a shocked expression no different than that of the thousands of blue-collar workers who had recently faced similar experiences. The abrupt passing of the news release on-air was identical to harsh announcements occurring in other workplaces. But this time, thousands saw it happen first-hand. The action stripped away social and class differences viewers assign on-air television personnel and helped struggling factory workers identify with the so-called elite CBC workers.

Worse, except for a brief statement prior to the next day's regional broadcast, CBET staffers, community ties or not, weren't allowed a last on-air farewell. "They didn't even let us say good-bye, just like that, the lights were out," said reporter Percy Hatfield, snapping his fingers.

The method of the announcement angered CBC staff to the point that some became willing (yet background) participants in strategy and planning discussions, breaking down the newsperson's arm's length relationship to ordinary people, citizen activists and elected officials.

Area Members of Parliament were bombarded with phone calls from outraged residents. Essex Windsor's constituency office logged over 120 phone calls in the morning, as we desperately tried to keep an outgoing line free to conduct research on the announcement, plan House of Commons strategies, develop a unified community response, and keep in touch with insiders at CBC and the local newspaper, the *Windsor Star*. No other issue had received such a response.

The community buzzed, and after expressing general outrage, the activist Mayor's office called a hasty meeting, even though then-Mayor Millson was out of town. Millson struck media gold. The day the news broke he was held up in Montréal due to a snowstorm. He was able to scoop news coverage on his way home by attending the announcement in Ottawa at the urging of MP Herb Gray. While there, Millson met with area MPs, and got an agreement they would work together in the House of Commons "for the good of Windsor." Fast on his feet on TV, tight with MP Herb Gray, Millson was clearly going to need a close watch due to his shoot-from-the-lip style of policy setting.

From the first day of CBC's so-called "regional news" format, Windsor's sense of rejection from the centre was glaringly evident. After the cutbacks hit, the Toronto-based news format did nothing to ameliorate the situation. When the city lost a highly respected former mayor, Bert Weeks, the regional broadcast refused to run a feature story on Weeks'' considerable contribution to the area, despite political reporter-turned-bureau-reporter Percy Hatfield's pressing appeals. He says they told him Weeks' death would be of no interest in the Toronto market. Word of the obvious oversight on the news, and Toronto's response spread throughout Windsor and Essex County. Any fence-sitters on the issue of the need for a local station were won over by that foolish act, and it helped fuel the turn out at the demonstration. Unfortunately, while the action helped bring people to the December 16 rally, that action contributed to hostilities toward the network, slowing the building of an all-out, pro-CBC response.

Committees, Committees and More Committees — The "Official" Strategy

In what is a typical Windsor-area move, the Mayor's office organized a special task force meeting to determine the community response and usurp a leadership role. Elected in 1988 on a good-news platform promising to end council in-fighting and transform Windsor to a "world-class" city, the Mayor's staff had taken a broad brush approach in assembling the Windsor-area faithful for the discussion. The community elite gathered in the council chambers included both labour and Chamber of Commerce representatives, those intent on restoring CBC's presence and those ready to demand the return of the CBC license so a private station might enter the market. After the acrimonious council meeting of the previous Monday, the Mayor's Task Force meeting had all the trappings of a revival meeting. Team Windsor was back in place, and its goal was to save area TV coverage.

The Mayor and prominent Liberals spoke of court cases and public hearings.

Stunned local Tories, led by former Windsor-St. Clair candidate Bruck Easton were also there. Easton was genuinely upset. As the "point man" for the Mulroney government in Windsor, he had just been battered as a part of the GST fight a few days before, survived through the free trade arguments with his skin intact, and now saw any shred of Tory support in Windsor slashed along with the CBC cuts. He retreated into his Windsor roots, and promised faithfully to intercede with the Mulroney government to make the City's case in Ottawa. Later Easton would also make the case for a privatized solution, helped along by CBC's own blunders, such as the insulting response to Bert Weeks' death.

Business people worried about a lack of affordable local advertising, and the inability to pitch Windsor as a world-class city if it didn't have television — any television. Representatives from private broadcasters offered to "help" Windsor and bring their station(s) to the area.

Not able to act in a way that was openly hostile to area New Democrats, the Mayor and council were dominated by the Liberals, who spoke dramatically of a need for a "non-political, non-partisan" approach to organizing efforts. While they recognized the need to push for the greatest level of political outcry, this non-partisan approach also served as an attempt to prevent tying the group to any coherent agenda, or list of specific demands.

This Liberal tactic is common in Windsor, a community whose recent political history has been a struggle between New Democrat and Liberal forces for control at all levels of government. This struggle is deeply rooted in the area's political and labour history, reaching back to the 1945 provincial/federal elections. Then, a Liberal/Labour alliance devastated the fortunes of the New Democrats' predecessor party, the Cooperative Commonwealth Federation (CCF), and set in motion a Liberal political dynasty in the Windsor area, centred around the late Paul Martin. Solicitor-General Herb Gray remains as that dynasty's direct beneficiary/inheritor and its current warlord.

In 1990, area Liberals reeled under the recent decisive sweep of area Provincial Parliament seats by New Democrats. After wresting the federal seats of Essex Windsor and Windsor-Walkerville (St. Clair) in the 1984 elections, and keeping those seats in the 1988 election, it appeared as if the last remnants of the Liberal/Labour alliance had been eliminated. The area Liberals needed to be seen as key in the fight back on CBC, and were prepared to pull out all the stops to do so.

Given the status of holding two of four federal seats, and four of five provincial seats, New Democrats were invited — but few were allowed to sit at the main table discussion. We were cautioned by the Mayor's office to let "the people, not the politicians" deal with this highly-charged issue. Attempts to keep a "non-political" approach are a skilful public technique for stickhandling open New Democrats and their sympathetic labour allies. In public, labour and other left wing leaders are used to ensure community outreach efforts are successful, yet those activists are kept busy and away from the significant informal decision-making process which, in the CBC case, was intended to centre around the Mayor's office and the Liberal caucus in Ottawa.

Once watered-down decisions are made, those very same community activists are prevailed upon to defend the decisions on the basis that they were partners in the group making them. This frustrates the left wing in three significant ways:

1. The left is not part of the real decision-making process; the left ends up ratifying weak — or bad — decisions.

2. Absorbed into "official" activity, the labour/left loses control over its own work. Worse, it loses public credit for its ideas and actions, and success ends up ascribed to others.

3. When speaking to their base, labour/left leaders must choose between keeping their public relationship with the elite and separating themselves from their base or representing the interests of their base and limiting communication with the decision-makers.

Often, Windsor's left has chosen to accommodate communication rather than harm it.

This time, the labour movement and New Democrats did not give in to the crocodile tears of "non-partisan" appeals.

The Mayor announced a list of committees, including an "Other Options" committee originally designed to explore privatization. Labour representatives and New Democrats were urged to sit on the "Outreach" committee. Worried that the Mayor's Task Force would take a weak approach on CBC given the strong statements from the business community and the appeals from Liberals for a legalistic approach, and a list of committees which retained strategy in the Mayor's office, New Democrats responded swiftly.

As the official meeting ensued, empowered New Democrats and their allies in the labour movement held a hurry-up caucus. Communicating with each other through hand signals and whispers, New Democrats volunteered for both the Outreach committee and the Other Options committee. In a stroke of serendipity, the Mayor's office had invited recently-arrived former Manitoba premier Howard Pawley to the meeting. With only the barest consultation, New Democrats in the room (some introducing themselves to Pawley for the first time) requested Pawley co-chair that committee. Pawley was pleased to oblige — and given his status, Pawley was a choice the Mayor's office could not criticize.   Liberals suggested area "red" Liberal rainmaker Charles Clark, as "their" co-chair. The Other Options committee quickly loaded up with representatives from every political stripe and community interest.

The next morning a group of labour/left activists, community group and union leaders met at the CAW Local 195 Hall, ostensibly to distribute petitions.

In reality, as Langdon's staff rep, I had decided even control of the decisive Mayor's committee was inadequate. The Mayor's Task Force lacked the distinctive presence of people from farming areas of the county, and did not include members of citizen action groups, students or the arts community. Without some quick maneuvering, those key groups would be left out of the fight — and so would much of the farm/labour/community base we'd been trying to build. After mapping out a plan with Langdon, I wanted assent that this would be a key fight for all of us, support for a tough approach and the widest possible mandate to ensure the greatest possible room for maneouvre both inside the House of Commons for Steven, and outside the House for the rest of us.

A New Course is Set

The meeting at the CAW hall lasted a scant two hours, but during it, the strains and differences within the labour/activist community were clear. Some leaders were certain the Mayor's Task Force offered ample opportunity to fight the CBC cutbacks, and were content to operate through it. Others, smarting from past "non-partisan" efforts, felt a fully separate strategy should develop, and Windsor's left should play a role in the national fight. A few expressed acceptance that if CBC were leaving, the primary goal of any group should be to get some TV, any TV, to Windsor. Still others saw the CBC fight as a key step in ensuring a sharply focused community-wide fight back campaign, and that the role of the labour/left should be to ensure the widest possible participation in what could be a decisive anti-Mulroney campaign.

The meeting showed signs of breaking down, as one after another, activists spoke of their genuine need to enjoy a holiday break and prepare for what looked to be a horrible year ahead. "What more can we do?" said one. "We've promised help on petitions. We can't afford any more money from our treasuries — our membership is dropping."

At the urging of NDP/community activist Len Wallace, Larry Bauer, then Vice-president of the powerful CAW Local 444, made a motion that led to the creation of the Coalition to Preserve Public Broadcasting, a group that would work with The Mayor's Task Force, yet retain a separate identity in case sharper action was required. Larry spoke of anchoring the Mayor's Committee for labour, maintaining tactical freedom and the need to keep some independence in reaching 444's membership. Once Larry spoke, the decison was made. Bauer's action that day signalled the real development in the approach to labour/left organizing in Windsor. It also clarified how he would see his decisive role in area activities until his untimely death in 1994.

The newly-born Coalition to Preserve Public Broadcasting was invited to make a further presentation at Labour Council. Hastily, Geoff Coupland, an Anglican priest from the wealthy St. James parish in South Windsor, agreed to co-chair the organization with me. Geoff's presence offered the perfect sense of establishment-level reason to counter-balance what could be baited as an "ultra-left" group in the Windsor context. He knew that was his role and relished it.

In the Mayor's Outreach committee meeting chaired by City Councillor Sheila Wisdom, the core group in the Coalition to Preserve Public Broadcasting pressed the Task Force committee to broaden its plan. Pressed from the floor, the Mayor's people agreed to incorporate County residents, allow the presence of "unofficial" banners, signs and protests, find a role for the arts community, and agreed to set up fundraising and petition collection points outside of the City offices. The door had opened to make the December 16 demonstration a "bottom-up" event, rather than an elite stage-show.

The following Tuesday's Labour Council meeting focussed heavily on CBC. There, worries were gently expressed about the Mayor's commitment to preserving the CBC, and the announcement of the citizen coalition encompassing the labour movement, church activists, farmers and community groups was announced to the press. Labour Council President Gary Parent made it absolutely clear that a private television station would not be an acceptable option for Windsor's labour community.

In a "spontaneous" collection, the Labour Council financed a banner for the upcoming demonstration, and saw to it that petitions from labour and community sources would be collected by the unions, Labour Council, area New Democrats and community groups. In short order, the labour movement was able to claim ownership over its own work and a share of public credit for the massive December 16 rally turnout. According to press statements, CAW local 444 collected over 10,000 petition signatures, and in total the labour/left efforts netted about two thirds of the 57,000 signatures. Labour/left activities provided the opening for the Windsor area to participate, however nominally, in the national 100 Days of Action fight-back strategy.

100 Days of Action

The Coalition to Preserve Public Broadcasting walked a fine line between supporting the mayor, and keeping pro-CBC public interest alive. One of the important benefits of such a creation was that local newspeople had to "balance" reports on the Mayor's activities with comments from the Coalition to Preserve Public Broadcasting.

Ultimately, the labour/left Coalition to Preserve Public Broadcasting kept the Mayor publicly anchored in the CBC camp. Mayor Millson expressed in private that he was not concerned with the whole of CBC — just Windsor. Millson was also not-so-subtly hostile to the Coalition to Preserve Public Broadcasting, regularly making it clear that he felt dual organizing was a waste of time.

Millson was not alone in this point of view. One New Democrat Member of Parliament also said it. Nonetheless, thanks to the existence of a left anchor, and much negotiation, the Mayor agreed to participate in the 100 Days of Action Coalition events held nationally and locally. Even though suspicious of the Coalition's motives, and mildly hostile to those who were not cheerleading behind him, but working energetically alongside him in a parallel strategy, Millson had been out-manouevered. In the end, he was forced to participate in joint activities, including a news conference announcing the formulation of the national committee and portray — at least for television cameras — the Coalition to Preserve Public Broadcasting as an equal partner.

100 Days of Action was drawn together from Canada-wide nationalist liberal-left and arts groups. National unions helped pay the bills, and the Canadian Union of Public Employees co-ordinated activities through its broadcast division. In addition to media work, and as part of the 100 Days of Action campaign, the Coalition sponsored a discussion regarding the CBC featuring Judy Darcy, president of the Canadian Union of Public Employees, conducted a very successful video letter campaign in union halls and churches, and sent a representative to the national March 27 lobby day in Ottawa.

Continually, Windsor area activists attempted to clarify why "CBC, Not Just Any TV" was important. At a specially co-ordinated national lobby day, the Labour Council's president, Gary Parent, represented the Mayor's Task force, and I represented the Coalition, giving Windsor a doubled presence in Ottawa. Gary and I used a "Mutt and Jeff" approach. As the official Mayor's representative, Gary was reasonable and kindly. As the Coaliton's representative, I was more abrasive and theatrical. An old trade-union trick, it allowed Gary to point out that one could see just how angry the community would remain by my "pushy" actions, and that perhaps the Tories should listen.

Other Options

In public, the Mayor's Other Options committee took a benign, arm's length view of its role. Windsor quickly found that beneath Howard Pawley's conciliatory, mild-mannered approach, there lurked a crafty advocate pleased to play out his role as elder statesman with as much clout as possible. At the first meeting, the NDP-stacked committee determined the primary goal of the "Other Options" committee was to *see to it CBC was restored* — despite a strong case made for exploring private options made by Tory Easton.

Clued in prior to the meeting, Pawley put in a Gemini-winning performance in assuring tub-thumping New Democrats that the committee would not make a move to undermine CBC.

Pawley and his co-chair decided to make a careful exploration of all —even remotely possible — options before presenting its gathered knowlege to the Mayor. The list was very long, extremely detailed and quite time-consuming. Again, those committed to blocking the privatization option provided helpful lists and ideas to Pawley, whose eyes sparkled with every fresh addition to his list.

Former premier Pawley had a title, a telephone and the ability to reach just about any one he wished. Charles Clark had deep red-Liberal roots and the freedom earned from a lifetime of lawyering. Committee members were kept occupied researching employee buyouts, co-ops, community run stations and TVOntario as well as the briefs provided by eager private broadcasters. As leaders of the Other Options committee, Pawley and Clark "free-agented" nicely in the stratospheric regions of the bureaucracy of the CBC, the Province of Ontario, New Democrat and Liberal Parties, and the CRTC. Pawley kept in regular contact with New Democrats, just as Clark most certainly kept counsel with Liberals. The duo determined that CBC was not prepared to give up the license to operate the station at any rate, and enjoyed — conciously or unconsciously — stalling off the private broadcasters without rebuffing them completely. When pressed, they could point to the potential hard-core reactions of others on the committee.

Once general assent had been reached on the goal to save CBC, the full committee met infrequently. Likely, the co-chairs rightly realized that to meet often would invite wrangling.

Let's Seize Fort CBC

Far from a wild-eyed threat, the seizure of the TV station was an "other option" seriously entertained by the labour/left community. As CBC geared up to move out the equipment, there was discussion of a station take over —so much so that the speculation reached reporters, who started inquiring about it.

A Southam News reporter had read minutes of the January 5 founding meeting of the 100 Days of Action committee, where that option had been discussed. The national group issued a news release clarifying that they would urge legal protest only.

It is generally conceded that most Windsor-area people would have supported such a move, though "official" Windsor would have cringed and decried the action in public. The Mayor's office issued sharp behind-the-scenes warnings "not to try such a stunt."

Still, local leaders did to explore the feasibility of a takeover or "pirate" broadcasts from the station. In the end, the station's workers decided not to risk accrued pension benefits and recall rights with such an action, and union leaders decided the proposed move had been telegraphed too much so the idea was discarded. Some Windsor area labour leaders still wish it had happened. There was no doubt that if the workers had chosen to do so, Free CBC Windsor would have been on-air. The perceived ability to successfully complete such a tactical move may have been as important as actually undertaking it.

Does Anybody Out There Hear Us?

Though the home of many "firsts," national political figures, and an economic powerhouse, the Windsor area is often considered an anomaly — even in the broad-brush Canadian nationalist liberal-left. Too far away from Toronto's intelligensia, too distant from Ottawa for a daily feed to the bureaucracy except through forceful politicians or old bureaucratic hands, the Windsor area remains isolated from the decision making within both the left and in the centres of power, except, of course, in the CAW, which in turn plays an important part in national issue and coalition debates.

Even so, the Windsor area is frequently ignored completely in wider labour/left debate. During the CBC fight, it was somewhat different. Acting in my joint capacity as a staffer for a high-profile MP and as the co-chair of the Coalition to Preserve Public Broadcasting tied so closely to the labour movement, my calls were, at least, returned.

Repeatedly, we made attempts to have Windsor a special focus in the national fight to save CBC funding. We also felt that our approach would assist in the national strategy. In Windsor, Ontario, the usual cultural/nationalist "arts" arguments were not the arguments that motivated the response on CBC. The issues were local identity, the ability to participate in the hard-core news of the nation, and the need to declare, one more time, that southwestern-most Ontario wanted local control. We felt those were the very arguments that would work in Calgary or Corner Brook. Those were the arguments used in Rimouski, Québec, the only other jurisdiction in which a demonstration brought forward over 5,000 people.

We felt Windsor could represent most fully the English-Canadian case for a national network, by its very proximity to the U.S. Since back-room intelligence had informed us that CBC deeply regretted its Windsor decision very shortly after it was announced, we suggested that Windsor might be a useful example that could bring down the entire batch of cut-backs, when later lobbying efforts ensued, by pressing the issue of local control, local content, over the sheer nationalist rhetoric of some other coalition participants. The national group was not convinced — I'm still not sure why.

Perhaps it was because all national strategy meetings were held either in Toronto or Ottawa, and Windsor remained in contact only by phone. Meetings were often called on short notice when a trip to the meeting would take two full days away from home, at a time when my office-mate and I were also knee-deep in organizing against the Gulf War.

Upon reflection, one wonders if the national groupings were, themselves, caught off-guard by such a heated interest in the CBC coming from what is seen as a working-class town, led, essentially, by a working-class institution, and uncertain of how to relate to people who were not elected officials or part of the usual "artsy left" crowd. We hope that's not the case.

Another explanation might be that the national 100 Days of Action coalition chose the strategy of lobbying who they perceived to be "weak" Tories to force emergency CBC funding. The closest Tory to Windsor was in Sarnia, and our intelligence, gleaned through both former Tory Geoff Coupland and Bruck Easton, indicated that no such strategy would work. The Tories were determined to meet budget targets and the back bench relished slashing the CBC, since they regarded it as such a left wing institution. Their utter contempt for the institution was demonstrated by the appointment of right wing, continentalist John Crispo to CBC's Board of Directors. But even within that context, the Windsor example made Tories squirm. Unfortunately, perhaps our sharing of the back-room information helped 100 Days of Action partners conclude that Windsor would get a deal, so the emphasis should be placed elsewhere.

The CRTC

For us, the Canadian Radio-television and Telecommunications Commission (CRTC) became a battlefield for Windsor only as a tactical move to keep the fight alive and on the national stage. Early on, the CRTC had made it clear that it could not intervene to stop the decisions to cut local programming, though due to House of Commons pressure, the CRTC had agreed to hold hearings on the cuts. The Mayor's Task Force chose to use the CRTC as a place to make another emotional appeal about Windsor's need for a station and to back up legal arguments. The Coalition to Preserve Public Broadcasting chose, through a presentation by Steven Langdon, to place the blame for cutbacks on the Tory government in Ottawa and defend the Corporation regardless of its foolish action in Windsor. In his remarks, Langdon spoke quietly of the communities of Essex County, and how proud they were to show themselves to fellow Canadians through a CBC which recognized the key part local programming played in its historic mandate. The Mayor's emotional appeal gathered the most coverage. Langdon's speech gained the most information.

A surprised Gérard Vielleux thanked Langdon for his careful remarks and told him CBC was "trying to find a way out."

A negotiated way out would take over two years to come.

The End

The recession had deepened dramatically in Windsor in the three months of intensive organizing around the CBC. The CBC fight had clarified to everyone in the area where the enemy lay — 24 Sussex Drive. Fundamentally, Windsor-area people had made up their minds — there would be TV again, but there would be no TV until the Tories were out of office. Eight thousand strong, Windsor had made it clear that in this geography, Tories would be dumped again.

Precious energy reserves were needed to deal with other issues. The labour/left moved on to try and stop the haemorrhaging of jobs, and confront increasing family poverty and local cutbacks. Sadly, many labour/left activists were also drawn off in attempts to ameliorate the blunders of the inexperienced Rae government. In the Langdon office, we would spend the spring fighting the Rae government's announced community school closings and transfers that placed real stress on the left/labour coalition in Essex County, and reopened generations-deep wounds between Catholics and Protestants. Then, both city and county ratepayers added Bob Rae's face to picket-sign caricatures of Brian

Mulroney. Even though area residents won their points with help from Steven and my colleague, Suzie Sulaiman, they did not forget the crisis the Ontario government moves had wrought in their lives. There was little room for forgiveness when the 1993 budget and the devastating social contract rolled around.

Meanwhile, inside the CBC, remaining staff members and union leaders continually reminded the brass that while the community had held off from demanding return of the CBC license for use by a private station from the CRTC before, upcoming licencing hearings would not be so pleasant unless some action was taken.

In August 1993, the federal election campaign heated up along with summer's dog days. A phone call came announcing CBC would reveal a "pilot" project to begin in Windsor. The "pilot" project would teach new ways of gathering and presenting the news. It would re-establish the CBET local news and programming, but require a breakdown of jurisdictional lines between on-air and craft personnel. After years of quiet internal negotiation between brass and the unions "a way out" was found for Windsor.

The announcement was too late to save any Tory vote in Windsor.

It was also too late to preserve the area New Democrats who had worked so hard to save the station. The labour/left coalition that had grown during the anti-free trade fight, and peaked in the fight to preserve CBC, had collapsed in the face of provincial NDP government mistakes and weak federal NDP leadership in Ottawa. Union members who had marched proudly beside New Democrats in the winter of 1990-91, slammed their doors in disgust at New Democrats who came canvassing in 1993. Working people and their families felt as isolated from New Democrats as they did from Tories.

On October 3, 1994, CBET-TV debuted its half-hour local news shows.

After One Torch Fizzles

For a few months in Windsor, Ontario, the labour/left demonstrated how it could act in a consciously strategic, cohesive manner. The left wing elements represented the full range of the democratic-socialist coalition — workers, farmers, academics, church groups, community organizations — and did so with the full support, encouragement and advice of their MP, whose office acted as a clearing house for information and a nerve centre of activity. The labour/left had tapped in to the community's deepest feelings of identity.

The fight-back on CBC strengthened existing labour/left ties, and marked a step forward in political organizing in the community, a step that matched the potential power of new political circumstances originating from the strength of the new CAW, previous public organizing efforts on the Free Trade Agreement, the GST and 1990 Provincial election. The CBC fight forcefully demonstrated the power of unified action inside and outside "official" structures at the local, provincial and federal levels.

Activists planned together, acted to preserve a precious Canadian institution and expressed fully the spirit of the community they sought to represent. That spirit found its expression in a full range of tactics, from petitions to the very real threat of a station take over — and in increased expectations of left wing activists.

Labour/left coalition members acted inside all levels of government, but retained their strength, ability to operate and their independence from official decision-making, by choosing to create a body they could control. They also exerted a measure of real control over traditional lobbying/political action forms. They worked well with "official" organizations at home and in Ottawa and attempted to keep them on track with the most progressive agenda possible.

Activists fed each other information, kept lines of communication open and were in a constant state of ready alert. Individuals acted to their own strengths — for example, Pawley as a perceived conciliator in Mayor's committee meetings, or Gary Parent and me in "Mutt and Jeff" mode during Ottawa lobbying.

The CBET-TV fight demonstrates that ordinary people will fight hard to defend a national institution as long as that institution can be seen as essential to the community — even in periods of economic crisis. It showed the role of the left in ensuring the broadest possible arguments are made so those institutions are defended.

If all other factors had remained equal the CBC fight in Windsor would be remembered as the first public activity of a newly-empowered political force. Instead, that fight remains as an isolated, useful example of how people can organize through conscious political action and temporary coalition to a productive end.

*Victoria Cross is a freelance writer. Her political commentary, columns and articles have appeared in the **Globe and Mail**, the **Windsor Star**, **Our Times**, **Canadian Dimension**, and the **Mystery Review**. Her work also appears in **Far and Wide**, a collection of recent Canadian essays. She is one of the co-founders of Windsor Works Publications.*

Facing a Multinational:
Choices and Challenges

by Michael McLister and Maureen Curtis

On October 15, 1993, Windsor's Wyeth, Ltd. closed its doors for the last time after over 60 years of operation, at a cost of 219 jobs to the community. This article will discuss the reasons for this closure, how the workers, labour movement and community reacted, and the ramifications for the people involved.

Wyeth, Ltd., a wholly owned subsidiary of American Home Products, was, and is in its new corporate guise, one of the major international pharmaceutical manufacturers. American Home Products is one of the most profitable U.S.-based multinationals. The conglomerate has a range of labels and products in the food, drug, and beverage industries. The Windsor plant shutdown did not represent the action of a corporation in trouble. Nor was the Windsor plant a drain on the corporation. During the struggle over the shutdown, documents were discovered that showed the Windsor pharmaceutical plant was itself highly profitable to the corporation. The Windsor plant earned some $30 million in net profits in the 1992-93 fiscal year.

The Windsor operation primarily focused on contraceptive production, in particular the Triphasil birth control strip. As well the operation produced angina tablets, penicillin, and tranquilizers. Though, with the exception of penicillin, unit profit for these had gone into steep decline in recent years because of competition from generic clones. Local 368 of the Communications, Energy and Paperworkers (CEP) had represented plant workers in the operation, in various forms since 1947, when it originated as a local of the Oil, Chemical & Atomic Workers (OCAW). It had a tradition of activism in the health and safety field since the mid-1970s, winning a number of precedent setting cases in the fields of health and safety and compensation of chemical exposures. This activism resulted in a substantially cleaned up plant. In recent years, however, new technical processes were raising concerns about noise and repetitive strain injuries.

Wyeth, because of its general immunity to the ups and downs of the Canadian economy, relatively good wages and conditions, and largely female workforce was considered one of the best employers for unskilled women workers in Windsor. As well, younger women hired in the 70s, having had secure, long-term employment, found themselves during the 80s well positioned to take advantage of seniority provisions in the collective agreement and advances in human rights legislation. As older male workers retired they were by and large replaced by women workers, who, by the time of the closure dominated every department but the skilled trades. Some belated wage improvements resulted for historically female classifications came about as a result of the Pay Equity Legislation. The generally small wage differentials already existing, as a result of the union's long term commitment to addressing this problem, meant that they had little effect on women's paychecks. However, they did result in the elimination of various intermediate job classifications which expedited the movement of women into previously male preserves.

Despite a number of organizing drives, the office and clerical workers remained unorganized at the time of closure.

Rumours

In mid-March, about two weeks prior to the announcement of the closure, rumours began to circulate that the plant was going to be closed. Rumours of closure were not unusual. However, this time the rumours were persistent and coming from management personnel.

The rumour's substance was confirmed in our minds by a rather amusing incident. The Joint Health and Safety Committee was asked by the Ministry of Labour's Health and Safety Branch to participate in a pilot project whereby the initial task was to agree on some future goals for our joint committee, and shared methods of achieving them. During the discussion, one of the union committee members suggested a good place to start would be to have the company make the same kind of financial commitment to eliminating workplace injuries as it does to appealing Workers Compensation Board (WCB) awards.

The Director of Plant Operations, a man who raised cynicism to high art, was noted for utilizing these joint committee meeting opportunities to engage in a diatribe on the sloth, malingering, tendency to prevaricate, and overall delinquency of the typical Wyeth employee.

Understandably, the worker representatives practically fell out of their chairs when he said " . . . of course such an approach should be taken because to do otherwise would be immoral." After recovering from shock, we realized this change of heart was because there would never be time to initiate these changes anyway.

The union's concern heightened as the company failed to take action to address the rumours. By this time, rumours had reached such a fever-pitch the plant credit union was officially urging employees to defer new loans until such a time as our situation was clarified. Calls were made to the national union and to other American Home plants but no information was forthcoming.

The Announcement

A retirement party for outgoing Wyeth president Paul Bilodeau was used as a cover for gathering company officials in Windsor for the announcement. The cat slipped out of the bag prior to the meeting with plant employees when it was reported on the morning of the announcement that Wyeth and Ayerst had "merged" in Canada and that the Montréal operation would be expanded by some 90 jobs.

At about 1:30 p.m. on March 30, 1993, members of the bargaining committee were told to go to the conference room. As we entered we could see this was it. Nicholas Papson, Administrative Vice-President of American Home Products, the company negotiator was present along with Bryan VanRassel, National Representative for the Communications, Energy and Paperworkers Union. The tension in the room was thick as Nick informed us of the Corporation's intention to move Wyeth's Windsor operations to Montréal. As we tried to fight back tears, we asked all of the immediately obvious questions about AHPC's intentions on closure agreements, transfers and if there were any way to reverse this decision. We were told we would be treated fairly, that the decision was final and we had to immediately go to the packaging floor because the rest of the workforce was assembled waiting to be told the news by Paul Bilodeau, President of the Canadian Wyeth division.

Mr. Bilodeau gave a pitiful, almost inaudible speech, stating he was sorry to have to "inconvenience" us, but in order to remain profitable and competitive they were heading to Montréal. The workers reacted in a variety of ways, from open sobbing to extreme anger. Before Mr. Bilodeau subjected himself to this array of emotions he divided the group. We were told to meet in specific locations throughout the plant, based on where our surnames fell in the alphabet. The workers, believing they would be given more specific information, found their way, with each other's support to the designated locations. What they believed would happen was a far cry from what did happen. We found ourselves confronted by strangers who informed us they were with a firm called Drake, Beam and Morin (DBM). These smartly-dressed young men and women were going to help us find new jobs. Now the workers reacted with anger (just as Mr. Bilodeau suspected they would if he stuck around). They began questioning who these people were and where they were from. We found out they were not from our city. We felt they were not in a position to carry out their task. This feeling was confirmed when we met them in a classroom session later.

A woman who was approaching 50 expressed concern regarding her ability to find work for similar pay at her age. She went on quite tearfully to say she would be unable to meet her financial obligations if she had to take a cut in pay. The DBMer told her perhaps she would have to take two jobs at half the pay. This was not a good solution for a single mother who had worked hard all her life. At that moment, it was clear we had to rid the plant of the DBM staff, and take control of job search and training services ourselves if those services were going to provide any real assistance.

As the days passed, production continued much as usual, although people crying and consoling each other became an all too familiar scene. What also became routine was the sudden bonding between bargaining and non-bargaining employees. Until then we dealt with each other with polite respect for each other's obvious differences. The differences became less obvious and our similarity of situation was now evident. Moreover, the non-bargaining workers had all been given a closure package on the day of the announcement, while the union was now in the process of negotiating a closure agreement. The salaried workers wanted to be kept informed of the progress of our bargaining and fretted as though they had an official stake in the negotiating process. They finally realized we had been negotiating their benefits and wages for years.

These negotiations were not going well. The union felt they owed the workers more than a decent severance cheque. We felt they deserved to have benefits paid while they looked for work and training money if they needed to improve their education level or simply wanted to improve their career options. We also wanted to run our own committee to help our members find work and dump the DBMers once and for all.

From the first day, the union leadership was in contact with Steven

Langdon's office, working to develop a strategy to deal with the crisis. Throughout, they said their goal was to provide us with the most information possible, and to assist in ensuring that the community and the workers had a wide array of options in dealing with American Home Products and Wyeth. They also worked closely with a group of workers and managers outside the bargaining unit. With Langdon's help we were able to access the House of Commons, hold regular press conferences and rally the public for support. After Steven spoke of our case on the Canadian Broadcasting Corporation's "The Nation's Business," we received calls of support from across Canada. A meeting was arranged with the Ontario's Labour Minister, to ask him to intervene in negotiations because the clout present during normal negotiations was certainly gone out the window. The clout we now had was an extremely sympathetic public and complete access to them via Steven and the media. Labour Council also lobbied on our behalf and indeed were ready to take the plant over and promote a full scale boycott if we gave them the nod.

The Grants

Langdon's research staff discovered the Canadian government had given American Home Products grants and loans. These agreements were significant for two reasons. In effect, they allowed the Wyeth Windsor facility to be closed without any cost to the American Home operation. The grants were of benefit to AHP, but they also were a rallying tool for the mobilization of the community and the workers.

In September of 1984, the Montréal facility, Ayerst, McKenna & Harrison, entered into a contract with the Canadian government. The contract's purpose was for the government to contribute $4.1 million to expand this other American Home Products facility.

At the same time American Home Products Corporation was making plans to shut down the Windsor facility the federal government, along with the Province of Manitoba, announced interest-free loans to expand their Brandon, Manitoba facility.

The grants were more than a little disturbing to the 219 employees. We found ourselves out of a job, and not eligible for unemployment insurance benefits because of our severance package. Meanwhile, a wealthy foreign pharmaceutical company was given $4.1 million dollars and interest-free expansion loans as a gift.

The Montréal news release claimed 90 new jobs would be created in St. Laurent. 219 jobs were lost in Windsor. Even if the company did offer 90 jobs to Windsor workers (to date they have not) it still amounts to the loss of 129 jobs. Repeatedly, we were told, "It is a business decision."

We believe that statement is equivalent to: "It was greed that made us do it."

The workers could understand and expect that from a foreign-owned pharmaceutical giant. What bothered them most was the financial assistance AHP received from our government to carry out this greedy task. As the details of federal grants became known, workers at Wyeth became angrier, more ready to fight back.

The effect was similar on the community. In a city devastated by plant closures resulting from the auto industry downturn, it was maddening to see the elimination of a profitable, non-auto related industry with the assistance of government largesse handed to industry with no return guarantees. We told Wyeth-Ayerst "We want our money back." $4.1 million would have made a real difference in the lives of the 219 workers.

The Negotiations — The First Round

We entered closure negotiations with certain advantages. They included: a banding together of bargaining and non-bargaining unit employees, a sympathetic community, active support from local politicians at all levels, good relations with the press, an enraged labour community, tremendous shows of solidarity from our fraternal locals in the community and a negotiating partner with deep pockets that all knew could afford a lucrative settlement. As well, we could draw on the experiences of a closure of a sister plant in Elkhardt, Indiana, where the OCAW had conducted a corporate campaign of considerable intensity. The campaign lasted for over two years and finally resulted in a ground-breaking settlement.

Some discussion of the Elkhardt closure is warranted at this point, because of its effect on the subsequent union strategy. The Elkhardt closure had caused OCAW, our former parent international, and a negotiating partner in our bargaining with American Home Products, to institute a corporate campaign. OCAW had thrown the entire weight of the union behind the campaign. This involved an extensive publicity effort, boycotts of AHP goods, and a U.S. legal suit under the Racketeering Act (RICO). The union also undertook Congressional lobbying, and other legal cases centred around the issues of plant closure legislation. They sought to limit the ability of companies to close plants when moving operations to Puerto Rico and end U.S. tax loopholes which encouraged such steps. After a period of two years and several court victories concerning the plant closure legislation, and numerous creative and vocal demonstrations, American Home opted to settle this dispute with a generous agreement.

The Elkhardt agreement was used by the union negotiators as a benchmark to determine the efficacy of its own efforts. Indeed, many of the points of our closure agreement were lifted almost wholly from the Elkhardt one. However, it was also pointed out to the leadership that any breakthrough agreement would take more than the courage and determination of the local membership and an enraged community. We needed a strong legal handle (which we tried vainly to build out of the $4.1 million grant agreement's default provisions), and the backing and resources (both financial and expert) that only a large organization dedicated to our purposes could provide. Discussions with national union leadership on the issue left us with little hope that such resources would be provided. In the national leadership's defence, the Wyeth situation was only one of many unfortunate closures during this period, and all were happening at a time when the national staff was in disarray because of the recent merger/creation of the Communications, Energy, and Paperworkers Union (CEP).

Overnight, our negotiating committee had to develop a strategy that could utilize assets in a situation of uncertainty and intense pressure. The initial strategy we developed was carried out as consistently as possible. It included building the unity of the local employees by never at any point criticizing local management in any of our statements to the press. In carrying out this activity we tried to focus attention on the (readily apparent) greed and corporate irresponsibility of American Home Products for closing a highly profitable plant that was so deeply rooted in the community. We also tried to expose, where possible, the political ramifications of this closure.

Make no mistake about it, this closure was a political pay-off to the Conservative government for its passage of the Patent Drug legislation and was financed by grants provided to the corporation from the Canadian taxpayer. Throughout the negotiations, we took the position that the corporation should spend a minimum of $4.1 million on the closure agreement, which was the amount received by American Home Products in Montréal for the expansion of its operations there. The negotiating committee of course realized this demand was unlikely to be met, but we also felt that we owed it to the community, our supporters, and our membership to raise it.

Union President Michael McLister first made the accusation that the closure was a political payoff to the press on the day of the closure. As time went on, it became more and more clear that we were correct.

As the date for the initial round of negotiations neared, and to carry out the union's strategy of building community support and maintaining unity, the leadership worked with Steven Langdon. We engaged in a series of joint news conferences and addressed a number of events and rallies. Our goal was to have all of Windsor up-in-arms about Wyeth.

The response was an overwhelming outpouring of support from both the labour and the general community. However, as much as this was appreciated, it was creating a dilemma for the negotiating team. Membership expectations for the outcome of the negotiations rose exponentially. This was further fuelled by unfounded reports that the sister plant in Elkhardt, Indiana, had received double what was being offered in severance to the non-bargaining unit employees, which the union was using as a floor as it entered negotiations. Rumours of a plant occupation were widespread. We worried there might be some spontaneous actions.

In counterpoint, the company threatened a premature closure of the operation. An incident had occurred, and though resolved, increased management's concern about the potential for sabotage. Suspicions that the closure was a ruse to eliminate a relatively highly paid work-force arose early.

A leaked corporate memo discussed the potential market for a generic oral contraceptive which would be marketed under the brand name of WyPharma, utilizing the existing Windsor facilities. The negotiating team took this memo very seriously.

As the first round of negotiations neared, the negotiating team was concerned the gap between management's willingness to settle and the membership's expectations was becoming unbridgeable. The likelihood of an agreement being reached without third party intervention appeared to be diminishing rapidly. When Steven Langdon suggested he arrange a meeting with Ontario Labour Minister Bob Mackenzie, we responded gladly.

We did not expect any real commitment on the Minister's part. The union saw the Ministry as a wild card, in that management would not be aware of any closed-door discussions that we might have had with Mackenzie. However, the Minister clearly was more than willing to provide real support, loaning us the use of his personal staff, in particular Brendan Morgan, and he promised a top mediator would be assigned if the union should seek to mediate an agreement as provided for under the recent changes to the Labour Relations Act. This intervention by the Minister strengthened the determination of the negotiating team as it entered its first set of meetings with the company.

The first round of meetings were both short and frustrating.

Wyeth's position was that it would provide the union members the same package provided non-union employees. The corporation maintained there were simply a number of technical questions to be ironed out, for instance, what the moving allowance would be for those who wished to transfer to Montréal. This package, which might be considered reasonable in a situation where the company was facing financial difficulty, was taken as an insult by the bargaining committee. The offer, while providing some protection for the older long-term workers, provided little to the bulk of the workforce. In a tense session, the union presented its demand that the corporation take the $4.1 million into consideration and that it was going to exercise its rights under the Labour Relations Act. Negotiations then broke off with most of the real issues not even discussed: pension supplements, training allowances, extension of benefits, etc.

Attempts to Keep The Plant Operating

The negotiating committee was further burdened with the difficulty of considering whether potential existed for an employee buyout or whether it could find alternative investors to keep the plant in operation. The corporation was contacted about the possibility of selling its operation and expressed no willingness to do so. The position expressed by President Paul Bilodeau was that the building and property were for sale, but equipment and licenses were not.

Despite this discouragement, contacts were made with the provincial government in terms of investigating possibilities of an employee takeover. As well, private investors were contacted. The idea under consideration was to use the facilities to follow the plans to create a generic company producing birth control pills.

This plan eventually floundered. While it appeared that the capital might have been raised, most scenarios envisioned a start-up period of up to two years as licenses and equipment were purchased and put into place. It was also premised on maintaining basically whole the skills and talents of the entire workforce. However, with the long lead times envisioned, the technical people increasingly opted to take alternative employment and the plan had to be abandoned.

The Second Round of Negotiations

Following the collapse of the first set of talks, tensions in the plant escalated. In particular, workers nearing retirement became disgruntled with the union's stance. They felt that they would obtain few benefits from the package the union was arguing for over the company's offer. In this, of course, they were correct, the main thrust of the union's plan was to *increase the number of workers* sheltered under the umbrella of the benefit package and pensions. As well, the union was pushing hard for training monies to be allocated, severance provisions for those that opted to transfer to Montréal, and extension of benefits for those that would be seeking work. None of these improvements would have significant impact on employees close to retirement. More importantly, the company spread the rumour that the employees' benefits and pensions would be held in abeyance if an agreement was not reached.

On the other side, many younger workers were becoming increasingly frustrated. They were pushing for more militant action by the executive. The potential for plant occupation, sabotage, and work stoppages heightened as workers and supervisors were brought in from the Montréal facilities to observe plant operations.

To its credit, despite the intense pressure, and with sporadic exceptions, the negotiating committee managed to maintain a consensus and present a united front.

Two days of negotiations opened on June 17th, with everyone clear that we were in the crunch. The first day ended with the parties hopelessly deadlocked. The company failed to move on a single issue of contention. The day was spent in endless costing of hypothetical scenarios, but with the company making no commitments. At 10:00 p.m., negotiations broke for the evening with no progress.

This being said, it was with some surprise and trepidation that the union learned that the company had asked for a closed meeting with the provincial mediator, Al Heritage, at 8:00 a.m. the next morning.

The company and the mediator met for less than an hour and called us into the room. There had been a complete change in the company's attitude. They agreed to most of the union's demands with a certain amount of modification. By noon, the tentative agreement was transmitted to New York to be typed.

The company requested that the union schedule an in-plant employee meeting to ratify the agreement. This was scheduled for 3:00 p.m. The union spent the time frantically contacting laid off and afternoon shift employees.

When the appointed time came for the meeting, the agreement still had not arrived and half of the negotiating committee was sent to the plant to calm the membership. The agreement came about 3:30 and we set to proofreading it. Much to the union's consternation, there was one major change in the proposal.

The collective agreement provided workers a transfer rights option to other Wyeth operations. The company proposal that appeared suddenly read:

> *The selection of employees will be made at the discretion of management of the facility of the affiliate of AHPC where the employee has bid.*

Clearly, the union could not agree to forego the right to transfer for one that placed transfers at management's discretion. Discussion continued for another hour with the company and union compromising on the company's wording — with the inclusion that the decision be done in accordance with the collective agreement. The union interpreted this as no different than what was already in the agreement.

The negotiating team, with its not-quite-completed agreement, rushed across the city to the plant. In a brief but emotion-charged and tear-filled meeting the agreement was ratified unanimously by the membership.

In looking back over this set of negotiations, our own feeling is that the government mediator may have been the key. However, as is the way of all negotiations, it is only speculation. Our suspicions are that the negotiator correctly read the union team. While we were by no means confident that we could win an extended battle, we were, if necessary, prepared to reject what the company had previously offered, regardless of the consequences. While the company may have survived the Elkhardt closure, it was most likely not an experience they relished repeating. Further, the negotiator may well have "leaked" the union's willingness to fight and to involve the community and the labour movement in fighting the closure by whatever means possible. The company's chief negotiator did mention off the record that he had to seek approval for the agreement from the CEO of American Home. That was very unusual — even for American Home. Preventing an explosive situation from developing further was, therefore, probably viewed as worth the extra costs incurred in the settlement.

Post Closure

An adjustment committee that had been put in place and funded through the industrial adjustment program was now in full operation. Initially it was located in the plant but was required to find office space shortly after the closure. The committee's mandate was to help the displaced workers find either training or a new position.

Around the time of the closure Chrysler geared up for a third shift. Most of the plant workers and a large percentage of the office workers applied for the new positions. Approximately 12 per cent of the unionized employees found positions due to the new Chrysler third shift. A few of the non-bargaining workers also went to work at Chrysler although we have no accurate numbers available. This third shift also created spin-off openings at other plants due to these plants losing workers who went to work at Chrysler.

We would be remiss if we did not express our gratitude to the late president of CAW Local 444 for his wisdom in negotiating the third shift at Chrysler. We are aware this was a controversial issue, in view of the fact that it would cut overtime hours for some Chrysler workers. Larry Bauer convinced his members a third shift was the right choice when so many people in the city were unemployed. The members of CAW Local 444 expressed their approval by voting him back into office just a few weeks before his untimely death, May 28, 1994.

People found work in various industries, plastics, machining, smaller pharmaceutical plants, school boards, social services, sales, and of course, at the new casino.

Although this sounds like good news with workers adjusting to their new surroundings, it was indeed difficult for most. This was not due to any particular flaws in the workplaces where they went. It was due to the emotional upheaval they had experienced. Many workers likened the effects of this closure to the grieving process one goes through when a family member dies.

To date, there are still nearly 30 people who have not found employment or enroled in a training program. In some cases, getting into a training program was as difficult as securing employment. This is due to the large number of people out of work and the limited program seats available.

The adjustment committee's contract expired at the end of June, 1994. An extension of six months was requested, but only a one month extension was granted, even though the money set aside by the company was not used up.

It is clear to us that the committee had not exhausted its usefulness. The people who entered training will not have support when they are ready to work and those that have not found work or training will feel abandoned once again.

Conclusions

As we review the events surrounding the closure certain points become apparent. Many of the obstacles faced by the union could have been avoided if we had given greater priority to the possibility of plant closure during normal negotiations. This topic is often discussed in seminars on negotiating contracts, but it is a principle that is rarely adhered to in practice. The local's language on plant closure was probably no worse than the majority of local contracts, that is to say, dismal. While we urge readers who are in a position to deal with this to address this situation, we suspect few will take positive action. Those who have attempted to do so in the past understand our pessimism, for those who haven't, we have some advice.

In the good times, when a negotiating team tells you that it's holding out for better language on job security, consider what the company's dollar offer is going to be worth if your job disappears. We say this because it is our experience that negotiating teams tend to feel intense pressure to drop language items when the money is on the table and strike deadlines are pressing.

The second area that needs addressing is firmer plant closings legislation. While some improvement was made in the latest round of changes to the Ontario Labour Relations Act, the language is still far from adequate. While the Act does require that the parties negotiate a closure agreement, noticeably absent is a requirement that the parties actually *reach* an agreement.

We cannot overstate the weakness of unions in a closure situation. A union's power rests on its ability to impact production. If the company is no longer interested in a plant's productive capacity, this power becomes meaningless.

A legal requirement to reach an agreement would do two things. First, it would address the power imbalance between unions and companies to some extent. It would make plant closures more expensive and it would therefore also become a consideration in a corporation's willingness to relocate the operation for spurious reasons.

On the positive side, the experience showed that an aroused community can have an impact on negotiations in even small operations of major transnational corporations. It was clear that throughout the struggle, the company was keeping a close watch on the mood of the local population. More importantly, the community provided a significant morale boost to the individuals affected, and increased the union's confidence that they could take a stand even though "objective" analysis of the forces arrayed against it would indicate otherwise.

The primary point to be kept in consideration is that community support is a factor that should be actively weighed when determining how media and other organizations should be addressed. Community support must be fostered consciously by seeking out the media and forums which would not be addressed in "normal" situations. Messages, where possible, should be tailored to the intended audience, showing what is at stake for each constituency. Especially in high tension situations, energy must be expended on ensuring that actions taken appear responsible and in the interests of the whole community as well as the group involved.

Last, trust yourselves. While there were many instances of pettiness, by and large we were unceasingly amazed by the unswerving courage, support, and selflessness of those involved in this struggle.

Mike McLister is now participating in a retraining programme. Maureen Curtis currently works for Labour Programmes at United Way of Windsor as an Associate. They dedicate this article to the memory of Raymond Hokansson, a Wyeth worker and Local 368 member since 1966. Ray lost his valiant struggle with cancer just weeks before the closure.

A Griot's Tale:
Dedicated to Black Pioneers

by Elise Harding-Davis
Curator/Administrator
North American Black Historical Museum, Inc.

The North American Black Historical Museum and Cultural Centre, Inc., located in Amherstburg, Ontario, is dedicated to the preservation and promotion of Black heritage from African origins to present day development. There is a focus on the Underground Railroad Movement and Black settlement in Southwestern Ontario.

This mandate makes the Museum a unique place on the North American continent. Most museums and heritage sites are dedicated to a person, a place, or a specific topic. Our institution encompasses the history of an entire race of people and their activities.

As the Curator/Administrator of the North American Black Historical Museum, I have witnessed a phenomenal growth of our activities and functions in the last two years. We have increased in awareness, recognition and credibility. We have had visitors from all over the world, such places as Australia, Japan, Sweden, Africa and Great Britain. Bus tours have been booked by diverse, interested groups from most of the United States and many of our provinces. Individual visitors of varied cultural backgrounds and ethnic roots have been drawn to this museum to learn about a proud, courageous race who have suffered much and accomplished much through the centuries. The National Film Board of Canada and production companies from around the world have used our resources to produce more factual portrayals of Black heritage.

In order to account for what has occurred, the history of our facility must be examined. In fact, the very history of museums has to be examined. Let me explain.

Traditionally, museums have been formulated by the rich to display personal collections in order to showcase a way of life beyond the reach of the average person, or to perpetuate a particular slant on history that aggrandizes a Euro-centric point of view. Museums have exhibited artifacts and disseminated information in an exclusionary fashion, showing the trials and tribulations and the prowess, successes and progress of mainly white Anglo-Saxons.

"He who controls history controls the world." This phrase leads us to yet another fact — history has generally glorified men, exhibiting gender bias.

In spite of these irregularities, museums have served a positive purpose. The history of the given world has been preserved for us to view and examine at our leisure, to educate us, enrich our lives and to find the pattern to include every heritage in its rightful place.

Follow the Drinking Gourd

As a young child, my parents exposed my siblings and me to culture and heritage. Our own family heritage was discussed and emphasised. I was given dance and piano lessons from age three. We were taken to theatrical performances. Weekly family outings to the movies were the norm.

Star-gazing with Grandpa, we learned to locate the Big Dipper and the North Star which slaves followed north to freedom. Often, the Big Dipper was called "The Drinking Gourd" by slaves.

"Follow the Drinking Gourd" was one of many songs slaves used to share information and inspiration about the road to freedom.

Field trips with Grandma enlightened us on what plants and herbs could be used to heal, or to augment our diet. Travel took us through North America, all the way to the east coast of the United States.

Wherever we went, we were sure to visit the local museums and heritage sites. My childhood was exciting, adventurous, and very secure — to a point. While all the world's wonders unfolded before my young eyes in all these sacrosanct places, my own history, the history of Black people was nowhere to be seen. That was my real point of insecurity.

Fortunately, we viewed these exclusionary bits of history with Mom and Dad. They filled us in on what people of African origins had contributed as these different events took place.

I remember questioning my father as to why our historic presence was ignored. I can also vividly remember Dad telling me, "This is for you to correct, Elise. This is for you to do. If you want the history of coloured people to be dignified, you will have to do it yourself. The history of our family and people is great. You know this because your mama and I have made it our business to make sure you were told. Make sure you tell your children. Make sure you inform the whole world. That is what you are here for."

My father was right. Within the Black community, I have always held a curious place. Older folks would take the time to tell me things about our race and caution me to remember what I was being told. I actually knew a woman who was born a slave. We called her Granny Jenkins. She used to tell stories about her childhood as I sat and listened. An ancient tradition was being carried out. The age-old custom of handing down our heritage through oral tradition was taking place once again. I was being trained as a "Griot." In certain locations in Africa, Griots have acted as the keepers of the history, the tellers of the tales. Griots repeat history orally and make sure it is preserved generation after generation.

So I became a Griot for my people. But where could I tell my tales? Where could I legitimize the golden heritage of the Black race?

Dreams to Brick and Mortar

It is true that if a need exists, in its proper time a solution presents itself. The solution to my dilemma was the creation of the North American Black Historical Museum and Cultural Centre, Inc., which was the brainchild of Melvin T. Simpson.

"Mac" as he was affectionately known, along with his wife, Betty, were the co-founders of the museum. The ability to dream and the sheer force of character made their dreams a reality.

Melvin T. Simpson was born and raised in Amherstburg, Ontario. He was steeped in pride for his people, the Black Race. Stories of daring escapes from slavery and accounts of heroism by people of colour fed that pride. The fact that Black people had been in Canada since 1605 was known by very few among us.

When Mac retired in the late 1960s after working as a florist in the city of Windsor, he returned to Amherstburg, his birthplace. The stories of his youth remained with him. No one else seemed to remember or care about this part of history. Mac felt the only way to address the apathy he witnessed was to establish a museum dedicated solely to the promotion and preservation of the Black Race, a monumental task!

This dream fuelled a desire that ignited similar flames in just about everyone Mac encountered. He began collecting artifacts, soliciting help and funds and exhibiting displays on Black history where he could. The dream of housing this precious material was always foremost in his mind.

Convinced he had hit upon a solution, Deacon Mac Simpson persuaded the last seven members of the Nazery African Methodist Episcopal Church to erect an annex to the structure to house a museum. The Nazery A.M.E. Church is one of the oldest remaining refugee structures in Canada. It was built from the ground up by refugees from slavery who had followed the North Star to freedom. In 1975, the annex became the first North American Black Historical Museum. It was done!

Melvin T. Simpson's dream was a reality — but not for long. According to some law, museums cannot be attached to functioning churches. What a disappointment.

But Mac, armed only with the knowledge that it could be done, and the desire to make it happen, was more determined than ever to open a true and proper museum. His vision had to become a reality. It wasn't easy. During the trying times, his wife, Betty Simpson, helped and supported Mac in an enthusiastic way that only a loving spouse can. Her belief and trust carried Mac's dream forward. Her warm embrace and a willingness to share sacrifices were what made the difference.

The result was that two ordinary, everyday people, if they can be so called, founded a museum like no other in North America. Their personal struggles are a story in themselves.

I knew and respected Mr. Simpson. When I heard about his dream of building a Black Museum I knew that he had to succeed. Moreover, I knew that he and Betty would succeed. I must confess my belief was based on the knowledge that the majority of our community, Black and white, supported his efforts. How could such a widely encouraged endeavour fail? The collective dream of dignifying our culture was about to be realized. My God, those were exciting times!

A sense of multicultural community exploded. The hidden pride of local people of colour burst through the invisible restraints that had enslaved so many of us far too long. Black business and professional people joined with the larger community to pool resources of every kind to build an edifice worthy of housing one of the world's most important and interesting histories. Credit must be given to Blacks and whites alike who worked side by side to achieve this wonderful goal. Even the detractors and non-believers should be thanked. They steeled the determination of the faithful.

Opening Day

The North American Black Historical Museum and Cultural Centre, Inc. opened its doors on September 20, 1981. It was a soft, gentle, sunny Sunday afternoon. Hundreds of dreamers attended the ceremonies. Four generations of my family were present. My eldest daughter was a Tour Guide on that glorious and triumphant day. Throngs of misty-eyed people from all walks of life filled King Street buzzing with wonder and pride.

Mac was subdued that day. He mingled with dignitaries, common folk, relatives, friends and supporters alike showing a quiet, humble satisfaction. The dream, the vision was a reality at long last.

My joy that day was boundless. I have attended other openings and dedications in my lifetime but none to compare with the ceremonies and celebrations for this one. Everyone who came realized the importance and magnitude of that event! From the oldest to the youngest, pride shone forth. We were all witnessing something unique and fantastic. We were watching history unfolding before our very eyes. We absorbed every detail so that we could recount them to the generations in the years to come.

Our museum was set up and equipped just like any other museum except the exhibits housed in our museum reflected my face. The contents displayed a fascinating and vital race of people. The guides told the tales of proud and defiant women, men, and children. The significant difference was and still is that the North American Black Historical Museum promotes and preserves Black heritage by telling Black history from our point of view and invites the world to see through our eyes. This was a homecoming like no other.

In January of 1982, Mister Melvin T. Simpson went to meet his maker. I believe he died contented. His dream was a reality, those left would surely carry on.

I have never lost the supreme sense of boundless joy experienced that sunny Sunday afternoon. The sheer satisfaction and the feeling of total rightness I inherited has stayed with me. Every time I open the exhibit doors, or answer the phone, or speak about this marvellous facility, truthfully, whenever I think about our unique museum, tears mist my eyes. My heart and mind fill with a pride that is beyond simple description.

One of the worst things that can happen to an individual in terms of personal validation and self esteem is to be made to suffer invisibility. To walk the earth having no face and no legitimate history is devastating. Seldom seeing or hearing of yourself while having to emulate and acknowledge another culture is cruel and very dehumanizing. My people have been subjected to this fate time and time again. The only part of our history that has ever been given any credence is our time of slavery. That small portion of our history has also been taught from a Euro-centric point of view, not mine. Our entire heritage has been systemically ignored. The history of the Black race has been treated casually at best. Our subjugation has been romanticized and sanitized. The exclusion of the rich heritage of people of African origins, the deliberate re-assignment of our accomplishments and the constant discrediting of our heroes has seriously damaged the positive self-image of Black people.

The embodiment of so many secret dreams in the form of a museum, a sacrosanct place of our own, instantly changed the self-image of every Black person who was present at the opening. I believe it also heightened the self-esteem of every ethnic group who helped and were there that day. Best of all, a truer understanding and appreciation of our cultural similarities and differences began to emerge.

With the opening of the museum, what has always been referred to as myth, legend or stories, took its rightful place as fact in our physical monument to truth about the world-building efforts of people of African origins. After all was said and done, a beautiful three building complex was completed.

Climbing Jacob's Ladder — Our Structures; Our Dreams

The Nazery African Methodist Episcopal Church is the right arm of the complex. Constructed in 1848 by former slaves, Nazery was a "station" on the Underground Railroad. Black refugees escaped from the oppression of cruel masters in a foreign country. They found shelter in this "safe house" upon reaching freedom on the Canadian shores at Amherstburg. Untold numbers of weary, frightened souls found comfort at this terminus point after having the courage to flee the horrors of slavery. Here, they were welcomed, fed, clothed and housed until they could find ways to support themselves in a new land, a land of opportunity.

The work ethic amongst Black people, contrary to some beliefs, has always been strong. Our forefathers and mothers took inferior jobs, earned meagre wages and lived on land useless to others — and still they prospered. Still they helped others.

Nazery was used as a church on Sundays and a school during the week. There, many a former slave learned to read and write. Social graces and political savvy developed and a strong Black community arose within its walls. What more fitting place could there be to house the first North American Black Historical Museum?

The second building, the left arm of our complex, is the Taylor Log Cabin. It is named for Mr. George Taylor, a former slave and Civil War veteran who became a shop owner after finding a new life in Canada. The building he called home began life as a shed at Fort Malden, the British military installation, after the war of 1812. Around 1848, the log structure was dismantled and moved to King Street by a French family who turned it into a home. Mr. Taylor took up residency there in the late 1870s. With help from former slaves, the upper level was added by 1900.

Members of the Taylor family occupied the house until 1971, when the last seven faithful parishioners of the Nazery A.M.E. church purchased the property to establish a museum site.

Once again, the cabin was dismantled and relocated to adjoin the newly constructed museum. Now it stands as an exhibit demonstrating how Black families might have lived in 1855, when the bulk of refugees seized freedom in Canada.

The ironic parallel between an old shed finding new uses as a home and former pieces of property becoming free, independent human beings is strikingly gratifying to me.

The third part of the complex is a splendid three-storey building which consists of a lower level of offices, work spaces and archival storage area. The main floor houses what is termed the permanent exhibit. The display only changes by the addition of information. So little is known about Black heritage that we feel people should be able to view it over and over again to truly absorb the wealth of factual material that is presented. Many visitors return, proving our theory correct.

The second floor houses the Cultural Centre, where various community oriented functions are held. Black artists are given a rare opportunity to showcase their paintings, crafts, photographs. Videos with Black-related themes are shown. Lectures and book signings are typical. This space is available to rent by other community organizations.

This third building is the heart and nerve centre of the entire complex. Embraced by its simple historic arms, the structure and its natural sheetrock facade nestles quietly into the surrounding neighbourhood.

Thousands of people visit yearly. Many ask if the museum is a converted house because they say it is so home-like in atmosphere and appearance. What these visitors actually sense is the open-hearted welcome of the souls of millions of people of African origins who have finally found a resting place, secure in the knowledge that their miserable existences were not lived in vain. Love and hope and pride emanate from every corner. The energy thriving within our walls is generating the light of truth around the world.

A Griot At Last

I have been involved with the museum since the early years in every capacity imaginable. I served on the Board of Directors, designed and installed exhibits, scrubbed floors and spent many sleepless nights worrying about the fate of the museum. I have taken museology courses at my own expense in order to better understand the workings of such an institution and entreated others to do the same.

My love of history led me on a marvellous journey over the centuries throughout the world on paper, searching for tiny fragments of Black heritage. When I volunteered, I would sit behind the front desk studying volumes, from scholarly work to comic books which related to my culture. I would walk around the building studying the space, conjuring up images of Black-oriented displays. All the while, I would be anxiously waiting for the telephone to ring — someone inquiring about our open hours. I waited impatiently for visitors to arrive.

I wanted to be the Griot I had been raised to be and guide people through our facility educating them as they listened to the history of my people flow from the well-protected recesses within me. My memory banks were primed!

Some days the chance to share my knowledge with others did not present itself. Ah, but there were days when I would exhaust myself with the sharing. Unless you have experienced this type of exhilaration you cannot possibly understand when I say it is one of the most satisfying emotional sensations one can feel. I desperately wanted to carry Mac's dream forward.

Until 1988, I balanced my work-load to include the museum, to be honest, perhaps leaning more towards the museum. Just around that time I set my dreaming aside for awhile to deal with the reality of aging parents and fledgling young adults leaving the nest. I kept in touch with Betty lending comfort and support whenever possible, humbly advising her on ways to cope with the difficulties and successes the museum was experiencing.

In 1989, with the help of a grant from the Ontario History Society, I installed an agricultural exhibit dedicated to Black Pioneers at the International Plowing Match, held in Maidstone Township. The idea came about through my father-in-law, one of our region's best farmers.

Dad took us to the Plowing Match each year for over 20 years. There was never any evidence of the significant contributions made by Black agriculturalists. As usual, the family made plans to attend, excited about the news that Dad was entering the Seniors Plowing Competition. Sadly, Dad passed away. I determined to finish the exhibit in his memory. My own father aided in collecting information and he provided mountains of encouragement.

Three days before the exhibit was installed, my father was buried. The display dedicated to Black pioneers did great honour to two of the biggest dreamers I have ever known.

In 1992, I resumed my dreaming and accepted the curatorship of my beloved museum. The sustaining qualities of so many people who believed in Mac's dream and Betty Simpson's custodial nature kept the doors open. They helped the museum progress to a stage that allowed me to further our goals with confidence. There can never be enough praise given for their tireless efforts.

On The Map, Our Role and Projects

Since my return, our museum has made huge strides in being recognized and accepted as an educational facility. Scholars, researchers, the every day seeker of truth and knowledge and those who simply love heritage sites have sought us out to help fill in some of the gray areas and blank spots that our history can make clear. We've been involved in a tourism program since 1991, partnering with five other Black heritage sites in Southwestern Ontario called "The Road That Led To Freedom, An African-American Tour." Through sponsorship from the Ministry of Culture, Tourism and Recreation and the Windsor, Essex and Pelee Island Convention and Visitors Bureau and the Chatham and Kent Convention and Visitors bureau, this tourism initiative has become one of the most popular on the North American continent. Through this program, the number of visitors to our site has increased 40 per cent. Coupled with our other ongoing activities, booked tours have increased by over 100 per cent each of the last two years. As the spokesperson for the Canadian Black Heritage group made up of representatives from all six sites, I have been privileged to speak in several cities in the United States and Ontario promoting our familial saga.

Interested groups in places like Chicago, Detroit and Toronto, have heard me tell of our proud Black Canadian culture. I have done radio and television interviews for dozens of stations including CNN and CBC. Over $3 million in free advertising has been generated through this program. Our combined sites have hosted media from all over North America. Reporters have written inspired articles after they have had the opportunity to tour our sites. Tours resulting from these articles come to Amherstburg to see the wonder of our hidden riches for themselves. They in turn send others.

The Museum is also partnered with the Niagara Falls region, the city of Detroit, Michigan and Lorain County, Ohio in successful Heritage Tour Programs. We have helped with the identification and preservation of Underground Railroad sites throughout North America in conjunction with the Smithsonian Institute in Washington D.C. and the U.S. National Park system. The museum has helped institute a one credit curriculum course in Black studies in a local high school which is being viewed as a potential pilot program in other regions. Our facility sponsors a project through an Anti-Racism Secretariat grant that has serviced Essex, Kent and Lambton counties by sending staff to schools in this tri-county area to set up workshops on racism, aiding students in realizing how ugly and harmful prejudice can be in our society. A brochure on racism has resulted from this same project and it is available at our museum.

Additionally, our institution is actively partnering with the town of Amherstburg and its other heritage sites to promote ourselves as a multicultural heritage tourist designation. Travellers will spend a few leisurely days experiencing the several different cultures represented here. They will be able to shop in a pleasant small town atmosphere and enjoy walks through our Navy Yard Park, one of the safest and most beautiful recreational walkways on either side of the Detroit River.

In 1993, our museum and cultural centre received the prestigious Phoenix Award for cultural and heritage preservation on the North American continent. An international group, the Society of American Travel Writers, based in Washington, D.C., chose our museum along with five other recipients out of a field of one thousand nominees. We are the seventh Canadian recipient in this group's 38 year history to receive this distinction. Proudly, we are the first Black Canadian organization ever to be given such a singular honour.

The evening of the Phoenix Award Ceremony, the representative for the Ministry of Culture, Tourism and Recreation gifted the museum and its partners on "The Road That Led To Freedom" with a grant to erect signage. The signs feature the North Star and the phrase "The African Canadian Heritage Tour to herald the Underground Railroad Sites in Southwestern Ontario." Yet another dream come true.

TVOntario has similarly honoured us by producing a three minute vignette on the museum. It can be seen on CBC.

With modest amounts of formal funding from the Ontario Museum Association and the Town of Amherstburg, we are making steady inroads in once only dreamed of worlds. We sustain ourselves through bingos and by donations at the door.

Other creative fundraising events are held. Each year, we hold Emancipation Celebrations to commemorate the abolition of slavery. The law that ended slavery in all the British Commonwealth was enacted August 1, 1834. So each August 1, that civic holiday so many of us enjoy is really to celebrate the emancipation of slaves. Our museum's remembrance of this significant, world-altering event is one of a very few held throughout the world.

Our institution is busy collecting family histories. We have taped oral histories and published a booklet with the help of the Ministry of Culture, Tourism and Recreation. Genealogical material of 180 local family names and 3,000 single names has been computerized with the help of the Church of Jesus Christ Latter Day Saints joining us to one of the world's best genealogical data bases in Salt Lake City, Utah. Members continue to build these files by sending the museum family charts.

More Rivers To Cross

It would seem to me through their own ideologies and co-operative initiatives unions and special interest groups could provide wonderful opportunities to further cross-cultural understanding and to enrich the lives of their members by supporting educational facilities like the North American Black Historical Museum. The more aware people are of their surroundings and the more they value the diverse cultures represented in our great nation the better we will be able to address the ills, inadequacies and long standing prejudices that impede our progress.

Third World countries are reshaping our destiny. South Africa has recently taken steps to redefine political and cultural polarities. The onus is on us, the workers and every day people of Canada, to protect and arm ourselves intellectually so that we do not slip farther in our world standing through ignorance and apathy. Multicultural education and understanding is a very important key.

Our museum — yes, it belongs to everyone — is a magic place where history is being made every day. The role of the North American Black Historical Museum and Cultural Centre, Inc. is growing to fit the name Melvin T. Simpson gave it at a fantastic rate. All of

North America is becoming more aware of our museum's existence and its precious contents. Here, the true history of all the people of African origins is held out to the entire world by Black hands!

The future of the North American Black Historical Museum looks bright. Countless believers are dreaming new and loftier dreams. The Board of Directors of this facility is working on a fundraising initiative to raise $2 million. These funds will enable us to restore the Nazery A.M.E. Church to its former glory. It must be saved, for Nazery is an irreplaceable national treasure. The Taylor Log Cabin will also be finished according to Mac's original plans. The museum proper will expand to twice its present size in order to better serve the thousands upon thousands of seekers of truth and knowledge we expect to come in the not-too-distant future.

So many of my dreams have come true. Many more are on the verge of being realized. The help and support of the greater community is the only way this can happen. Just as in the beginning — dreamers are needed!

Elise Harding-Davis is a seventh-generation Canadian residing in Harrow, Ontario. With her spouse, Garland Davis, she's sucessfully mothered three grown women and continues to use her relentless energy to develop the North American Black Historical Museum, Inc.

◇

Nazery A.M.E. 1848-?

Letter to Nazery African Methodist Episcopal Church, Amherstburg, Ontario
On the site of The North American Black Historical Museum and Cultural Centre

What will become of you?
Many people have entered your doors,
sought refuge
comfort
home, for a while.

Then, as fast as they came,
the people left — their needs met
stomachs filled
spirits mended,
housed for brief transition in the wood and mortar
that made you strong,
that crumbles now:
a history in decay
memories that fade.

My ears remember
the hollow echo of voices in your walls,
strong singing from grandpa's gut

Mary's delicate fingers travelling across the old, upright piano
notes that seemed slightly out of tune.

My heart remembers
the warmth of grandma's lap,
the taste of sugar-coated this-and-that
pulled from the huge overflowing cavity of her purse,
that endless depth of sweets
to pacify my restless dancer-body.

Whether spinning tops on your cold kitchen floor
with friends, cousins, and my brother,
or painting in Saturday art classes
I never dreamed you were
such a special place
an ancestral gift
built from the earth by the hands and backs of fugitive slaves,
a place to be welcomed from the chains of bondage
that wrecked the bodies and spirits
of their brothers and sisters.

Nazery, you were
a hearth of refuge
when the daily toil of survival
in a world of snow
and cold people
became too huge a burden.

For our children
and children's children
and their children
will the descendants of your builders
forget the crumbling dreams of the past
left standing on its last leg to rot and melt

Maybe the earth will welcome your death,
Nazery,
but my ears and heart will never forget.

janisse browning, 1993

The North American Black Historical Museum and Cultural Centre, in Amherstburg, Ontario, has embarked on a special fundraising drive to preserve Nazery A.M.E. Church. As part of the effort, janisse browning has given her poem to the Museum, where copies are available to visitors for a donation.

Small Town Ontario Environmental Activism: *Review and Reflections on Essex County Citizens Against Fermi II*

By Paul Hertel

T he mouth of the Detroit River has been the location of many historic moments in the annals of colonial North American history. In the days of New France's glory, LaSalle explored the area on *The Griffon,* as he headed toward Lake Huron.

It was a passage for the traditional Great Lakes Aboriginal tribes as well. Tecumseh knew it well in his last, desperate struggles to defend a traditional homeland in the Ohio Valley during the War of 1812.

The battles of early history included the ill-fated British naval venture into Lake Erie under Barclay in 1813 against Perry. The Battle of Lake Erie established Perry's reputation, and the Treaty of Ghent divided the Detroit River and the Great Lakes for all time.

The British, first stationed in Detroit, moved to Amherstburg in 1796. Fort Malden became a defence against an aggressive new neighbour up to the 1837 Rebellion and beyond.

On the U.S. side of Lake Erie, Monroe, Michigan, is the infamous George Custer's hometown, and the River Raisin flows through this community today. At the edge of Monroe is Frenchtown Township, the site of an international controversy for environmentalists since the mid-1980s. Map borders won't stop radiation.

Against this background of historic challenges between Canada and the United States, the recent conflict over the viability and safety of an American commercial nuclear reactor, Fermi II, tested the will and energies of local citizens to stand on guard for Canadians.

Amherstburg, Ontario, is a town of some 9000 residents. It claims "Historic Amherstburg, an Old World Town with New World Charm," as its theme. Amherstburg has always been a frontier town with strong links to the Great Lakes military and merchant marine history. Since 1987, it has also been home to a new generation of defenders in the environmental movement, the Essex County Citizens Against Fermi II (ECCAF II).

Fermi II and the origins of ECCAF II

The development of an American commercial nuclear energy industry has its origins in the privatization history of the 1950s. In the state of Michigan, the drive towards nuclear energy was led by the Detroit Edison company. This story has been chronicled more fully in the 1966 book, *The Day We Almost Lost Detroit.* That book describes the near-meltdown of the Fermi I nuclear generating station. Undeterred by near-disaster, the Detroit Edison company remained bullish on nuclear power, immediately beginning the design and construction of the Fermi II plant.

Parallel to this nightmare story, a Michigan anti-nuclear and environmental movement grew. In 1987, a unique juncture in time, the Michigan group spread its story across the river/border to Amherstburg, Windsor and Essex County.

In 1987, the Essex-Windsor border region was intensely involved with debate around the Free Trade Agreement, because of its historic, uneasy economic relationship with the U.S. Great Lakes region. A series of water pollution incidents along the Detroit River to the St. Clair River system had increased public awareness of cross-border environmental problems.

In May 1987, then-MP Steven Langdon held a series of public meetings in the Essex Windsor constituency. During the Amherstburg meeting, one of the items which arose was the issue of Detroit Edison's nuclear power plant. Its twin-towers were visible from certain parts of Amherstburg's shoreline, and people in Amherstburg were aware the utility company had requested permission from the U.S. Nuclear Regulatory Commission (NRC) to move to 100 per cent (full power) production at the plant. Langdon's staff had contacted the Safe Energy Coalition of Michigan (SECOM). Members of the Michigan group present at the Amherstburg meeting outlined alleged design flaws, management mishaps and accidents. As the meeting concluded, local citizens realized that a Canadian citizens' environmental group had to be created to tackle the problems of the Monroe-based plant.

By mid-July, public meetings had been held, and the emergence of a formal group — ECCAF II — occurred at the Canadian Auto Workers' (CAW) Local 89 union hall. To assist the group's start-up, Langdon had used constituency budget dollars to hire a student to compile an extensive dossier on Edison, nuclear power in general, and the history of the Fermi II plant, and loaned other staff time to the group.

A fledgling executive, led by Amherstburg area citizens, began a struggle which today is no nearer resolution. In hindsight, the seven-year struggle of this small group may be seen as just as courageous as any of the continental outcomes of the frontier battles of the Seven Years' War — which also occurred along this frontier.

The Citizen Volunteers

ECCAF II's steering committee was a collection of grassroots people committed to a common cause. They agreed on a mission: shutdown the Fermi II nuclear power plant.

Lynwood Martin, of Malden Township, became the leading spokesperson of the executive. He brought years of experience in hydro plant operations to the group. Martin was also a strong environmental health and safety representative for the CAW, working in the Amherstburg General Chemical plant.

Joe and Mary Thrasher are a retired, community-minded couple, and brought deep knowledge of the town to the group, as did June and Jim Skinner. Gord Taylor, another CAW health and safety activist from CAW local 1973, representing General Motors' workers, joined the executive. I also served on the executive, bringing my experience as a secondary school teacher and former town councillor and deputy reeve.

Over the next two years, further contributors to this grassroots committee included Bob Martin, a University of Windsor law student, and Bill Hutchinson, a McGill Ph.D. candidate, native to Kingsville, Ontario. Rolly Marentette and Rick Coranado, both active in the CAW environmental committee that emerged from the Clean Water Alliance, provided help and advice to ECCAF II.

Together, this diverse group educated themselves and the community. They developed a plan to include political action, public education and "watchdog" strategies. Close contact was maintained with all area Members of Parliament. But on-going contact and assistance from MP Steven Langdon (representing Amherstburg) and help from staff members Victoria Cross and Suzie Sulaiman became an essential plus for the new group.

Over the past seven years, ECCAF II has gone through significant phases in its development. The highlights of each should be addressed next.

1987-1989 A Time of Community Consciousness-Raising

With ECCAF II's executive in place, the program to shut down Fermi II began.

Aided by backfiles from SECOM's spokesperson, Mike Keegan, and materials from a dormant Windsor-based predecessor organization, Downwind Alliance for a Safe Energy Future, and Langdon's file drawer full of fresh research, the paper trail of the plant's past had taken shape. We agreed it was "an accident waiting to happen" and decided we would take that message to area people. What emerged was a need to educate citizens immediately.

Between the fall of 1987 and the spring of 1988, three feisty public meetings were held in Amherstburg and Windsor. Experts exposed the issues of nuclear energy production, safety issues, and health issues. Sister Barbara Bacci, a member of the Immaculate Heart of Mary, an order of nuns engaging in extensive intervention actions as Detroit Edison stockholders, spoke to a good-sized crowd in Amherstburg on the economic and safety issues at Fermi II, as did Irene Koch from Ontario's Nuclear Awareness Project. Mary Sinclair of Michigan and Judith Johnsrud, a Pennsylvanian deeply involved in the Three Mile Island nuclear plant controversies, addressed overflowing crowds at the University of Windsor's Law Faculty Moot Court.

These educational events were demonstrations, too. Music, leaflets, picket signs were all features of the events. A strong media following developed. U.S. TV stations jammed the Moot Court foyer at the February meeting, held just prior to the U.S. NRC's approval of Detroit Edison's application for full power production. Our U.S. friends, who were used to fighting a sometimes lonely battle, were amazed at the number of people turning up at meetings.

On a second front, MP Steven Langdon co-ordinated a joint meeting of area municipal leaders in Amherstburg, and the townships of Anderdon and Malden with all the southwestern Ontario federal members of Parliament. An all-party agreement was hammered out to raise the international issues of safety and third-party independent monitoring of the plant. The MPs filed a "brief" with the U.S. NRC, outlining Canadians' concerns with the plant. Our Michigan friends were also confounded at our ability to work with press operatives on both sides of the border, and the powerful effect of timed questions, letters and news conferences put forward by Langdon and other area MPs. While then-External Affairs Minister Joe Clark recognised the issue and promised to pass on the issue to the U.S. federal government, no further long-term action was taken by the Mulroney government — much to our chagrin.

Looking locally for more action, ECCAF II started a dialogue with local officials for the establishment of a tough nuclear safety emergency plan for the tri-communities of Amherstburg, Anderdon and Malden. A complicated municipal and government approach to safety plans involved both municipal and county levels at this time. ECCAF's immediate purpose was to demand a better, more realistic and updated plan which dealt specifically with the evacuation procedures needed for a response to an accident at Fermi II.

To force the upgrading, ECCAF II also brought pressure to bear on the Ontario Peterson government, specifically on the Solicitor General's Ministry, responsible for Ontario's nuclear plant safety plans. The high profile activities of the group pushed area Member of Provincial Parliament Remo Mancini to arrange a meeting with then-Minister Joan Smith.

In a two-hour meeting, we presented a full, documented brief on the plant's perceived design flaws, safety problems and a picture file of citizen actions. ECCAF II requested an epidemiological and base-line health survey of the area to determine the cancer-related impacts of low-level radiation.

No formal response was received from the minister but the process of building a better safety plan had begun.

By the summer of 1989, the three-pronged strategy of education, three-level government lobbying and group development had reached a first stage of success. The Detroit Edison plant had even become a featured election issue during the 1988 federal election.

1989-1991: Vigilance and Counter Attacks

Over the next two years, the executive members of ECCAF II developed its educational profile, continued with strong contact with the media and took opportunities to strengthen its contact with Michigan environmentalists at conferences.

Steven Langdon and his staff continued to press External Affairs to act "government to government" with modest, yet significant, success. Then Langdon applied his "bottom-up" strategy to approach to that department and move the issues surrounding Fermi II into the polite world of international diplomacy. He and his staff built a strong, cordial relationship with a new Canadian Consul General in Detroit, Anne Charles. Charles was not the old-school-tie variety of diplomat. Her style was just right for expressing the personality of our southwestern Ontario communities — friendly and relaxed, yet efficient. Charles' staff placed a high priority on the nuclear plant. Firm inquiries from that office regarding delicate questions were a key counterpoint to other organizing activities, and a further example of the complex role an MP can have developing and working within a citizen-action strategy.

A federal environment ministry grant application assisted in the educational and information costs of our group's activities. Newsletters and were used for distribution locally, constituency news and mailings came from Langdon's office, and regional and labour newspapers carried much copy of our activities.

During this time, Detroit Edison's public relations profile changed. A more aggressive campaign was observed in the Canadian media in this region — every news outlet appeared to be on their release list. U.S. NRC reports on the plant became the basis for our on-going criticisms, and yet no true new pressure level against the corporation's enterprise was reached.

A major public relations success for Detroit Edison occurred when it donated a "Hawk Observation Tower" to the Essex Region Conservation Authority for installation at the former Holiday Beach Provincial Park. This gift was likely an indirect response to a modestly successful ECCAF II "tag day" at the Point Pelee National Park during the height of the spring bird-watching season. Point Pelee is an internationally known birding site, and with the co-operation of a Michigan chapter of the Audubon society, ECCAF II had asked bird-watchers to write letters protesting the plant. Ironically, the gift from the "land of the eagle" designed for hawk-viewing could also be used to see the twin cooling towers of the nuclear plant.

Another challenge faced ECCAF II's grassroots organizers during this phase: the monitoring of the emerging safety plans for the Amherstburg area. The need for a safety plan for a chemical spill emergency at the General Chemical plant at the town's north boundary forced the local council to seek an integrated emergency evacuation plan and to seek money for new sirens for early warning. By the end of 1991, and at the latest, in the spring of 1992, most of the local safety plan changes had been made. Even testing had begun, starting with elementary school bus run escapes to a designated safety depot.

1991-1993 Transitions

From late 1991, to the fall of 1993, ECCAF II found itself in a period of transition. With a new safety plan in place, and with Detroit Edison NRC report cards showing improvements in management, safety, and operation, no visible target existed on which to focus. Had we done our job? Had we won? Had we taken the community as far as it would go?

With a new provincial NDP government in place, the environmental community had initial high expectations. The "go-slow" nuclear energy platform was attractive, and we felt there might be a carry-over into the on-going monitoring of the safety issues at Fermi II.

Even with the expected federal election sometime in 1993, it was felt that Fermi II would continue to be on the agenda. Steven Langdon continued to work closely with ECCAF II and SECOM, joining the investigation of the sale and use of Thermo-lag, an insulating material which failed tests and yet remained at Fermi II and other plants. He assisted in other efforts regarding nuclear power and nuclear waste storage issues in the Great Lakes basin. During the 1993 election campaign, Langdon pressed the International Joint Commission (IJC), an international body responsible for co-operative environmental clean-up issues in the Great Lakes area, to include nuclear power and waste storage in its mandate.

Just as a lazy, hot and humid afternoon in southwestern Ontario takes the breeze away and leaves one tired and retiring, so did the presence of positive public relations reports take the momentum from our group. There seemed to be no issue that grabbed public awareness, helped us organize. We talked of disbanding the group, and transferred our small bank account to a Windsor environment group to help them. ECCAF II was all but ended. However, both Lynwood and I were loathe to make any public announcement, take any vote — just in case something happened.

In October 1993, Steven Langdon was defeated.

And then the accident happened.

1994: A Time for New Initiatives

The ground was cold, temperatures freezing, but the sunny Christmas Day morning held a serious crisis for the personnel on hand at the Fermi II nuclear power plant. Turbines ruptured, pipes burst, a fire was in progress. Radioactive water collected in the basement. Sensors detected powerful trembling in the building — equivalent to the standards for earthquakes in the region. A major emergency was declared in the turbine building.

The technical details of the December 25 accident were sufficient for the NRC to condemn Detroit Edison's record — the same record it had marked "improved". The accident initiated a new round of action for both U.S. and Canadian anti-nuclear activists.

Christmas 1993 fell on a Saturday. The first local reports of the plant accident came in the December 27 edition of the *Windsor Star*. In the story, no Canadian official was cited, indicating that carefully drawn emergency plans had not worked. Outraged, I made inquiries.

Here was the classic "holiday scenario" to test all the components of the nuclear emergency plan, including its political leadership at the local level. As it turned out, Malden Reeve Carl Gibb acknowledged that a need for better public communication existed. But did the rest of the plan pass the test? Out of this issue emerged the broader need to reactivate ECCAF II and its relationship with the Michigan environmental groups fighting Fermi II.

Our goal now had to switch to pushing Edison to start decommissioning the plant, instead of leaving the plant in an extended, yet temporary shut-down.

January through March, the major shut down of Fermi II was detailed by the press, as was the local emergency plan evaluation. ECCAF II made presentations at Amherstburg's town hall, and attended an NRC-sponsored public meeting where the interim report on the accident was discussed.

A major issue for environmentalists on both sides of the border was the disposal of millions of gallons of low-level radioactive water in the plant. The water had to be removed before any full on-site investigation could proceed. Yet, there were few options for the disposal of the "slightly heavy" water. Edison announced it would release the water into Lake Erie. The issue emerged just as the IJC produced its biannual report in which, for the first time, a recommendation was made to keep the Great Lakes free from low-level radio-nucleids!

Detroit Edison held a meeting to show that dumping the "clean water" was safe. This event initiated further hostilities and some overnight arrests of protesting environmentalists by U.S. police. ECCAF II members attended the meetings, but were not arrested in the U.S.

Further ECCAF II energy was spent in trying to engage the newly-elected MP Susan Whelan and MPP Bruce Crozier. Finally, in March and April, both expressed concerns on the water-disposal issue, as did Environment Minister Sheila Copps. There is some hope the current federal government will act on the IJC recommendations.

Since spring of 1994, ECCAF II has held further public meetings, and strengthened ties with other groups. Thanks to the continued support of CAW Local 89, the union hall in Amherstburg is once again filled with concerned citizens to hear about the new issues in the Fermi II fight. I have spoken where and when invited, and it shows how deeply imbedded in the community ECCAF II has become. I've spoken at both Earth Day rallies and Rotary Club meetings.

In September and October of 1994, ECCAF II, endorsed by the Windsor and District Labour Council, participated in an extended, international two weeks of public activity and organizing to force the end of Fermi II.

Personal Reflections on the Future of the Struggle

After seven or more years of on-going struggle to a encourage a consistent, honest, community-minded monitoring of a serious environmental issue — in this case a U.S. nuclear power plant — one needs to examine how to improve on ECCAF II's record, and to gather the enthusiasm to fight "burn-out."

The alliances and personal friendships continue to play a strong role for ECCAF II members. I find no small sense of satisfaction in our record but I realize the public has a hard time keeping a sense of readiness. We're bombarded with cross-border media and issue after issue. It seems many people are motivated only when large-scale events affect them directly.

December 25, 1993 was the biggest "reality check" event. The challenges of organizing further integrated action are also shaped by our personal lives, the people who represent us in public life, and the shifting sands of public opinion. I believe there is a need to build anew a political youth movement based on environmental issues which can help shape organizations such as ECCAF II.

For provincial and federal political parties, renewal is a constant theme. Perhaps it's all the more important for the left, as the New Democrats press forward to sort out their role in the political scene. For me, the redefinition of a moral base of personal action is inherent to the search for meaningful economic and environmental goals. There must be a sense of "the movement" within the structures of a party. That's what also faces ECCAF II — reaffirmation of community action toward economic and environmental goals.

Paul Hertel has made his home in Amherstburg since 1971. Originally from Hespeler, Ontario, Hertel is a secondary school history and social sciences teacher. He is active in union, political and community arts and museum organizations. Hertel has served as an Amherstburg town councillor and deputy reeve.

Storm Over Erie:
The Great Lakes Fishermen and Allied Workers' Struggle for Recognition

by Michael Darnell

J ohn Rodrigues[1] was worried. As captain of a commercial fishing vessel on Lake Erie, he was ultimately responsible for both the productivity *and the safety* of his crew. In this case, the crew included his son. Therein lay his dilemma. He had recently informed the fish company boat's owners of the vessel's deteriorating condition. Rodrigues' greatest worry was the boat's alarming dependence on the back-up pumping system to clear the vessel of water. The regular pumping system couldn't deal with the increased demand placed upon it, and it seemed to Rodrigues that the back-up pumps were overworked, too. The company's response had not been unexpected. "We're in the middle of the season, keep an eye out and we'll get to it in the winter," the owners had said.

Rodrigues had discussed his fears with his wife, and had already made one decision: he asked his son to leave the vessel's crew, for his own safety. Informed of his father's decision, John Jr. was adamant. He declared he would not leave the boat unless his father also left it.

But if John Sr. stepped down as captain, he would lose his captain's bonus, (a larger financial share in the catch) as well as jeopardize his standing with the company. Rodrigues worried some more. And then he decided — his son was right. They would both leave the boat. The company assigned both men to deck hand positions on another of their vessels, and assigned a new crew member and captain to the first boat.

Approximately two months later, while pulling nets within sight of Point Pelee, the fishing boat Rodrigues had worried about lurched — and sunk. Three crewmen, including the new captain, drowned.

The boat was never raised, and the subsequent investigation of the incident found no blame.

Cristina Copa had immigrated to Canada from Portugal just four years before. She worked hard, long hours at her job as a fish filleter. Her knife flashed through the fish that came from the boats working Lake Erie, and Cristina was proud of her skill.

Yet, Cristina Copa was certain she and the other commercial fish filleters she worked with were being cheated. Unlike some of the women she worked with, Cristina had rapidly learned to speak, read, and write English. The government pamphlet Cristina had obtained *seemed* clear. It said that after 44 hours' work, she and the other women she worked with were entitled to overtime pay. Cristina went to her boss, pamphlet in hand. He deflected her inquiries. "Normally, you would be right, Cristina," he said. "But the fishing industry is exempt from provincial employment standards."

Frustrated, Copa gathered her courage and called the provincial government's Employment Standards Branch. She told the man who answered the phone of the long hours, low pay, and tough conditions she and her friends endured. The man listened as she put away her pride and asked for help. *Then the man told her the company was right. He said there was nothing he could do.*

Cristina and John would not give up.

The Seagull Flew

John Rodrigues and Cristina Copa are symbolic of the several hundred Portuguese fish industry workers who immigrated to Canada in the early 70s to catch and process perch, pickerel, whitefish and other fish species which were gaining increasing popularity in the market place. Their stories are true of what the fish industry workers faced. These workers had been actively recruited to come to Ontario. Yet, they faced dangerous working conditions and unfair bosses without the same protection other workers in Ontario enjoyed.

For about one hundred years commercial fishing on Lake Erie had provided a sparse living of sorts to numerous communities on both the U.S. and Canadian sides of the international boundary which runs through the lake's centre. Work was arduous, prices were poor, and finding individuals dedicated to the fishery was difficult.

As North America's diet changed, demand for fish increased. This, coupled with the close proximity of Lake Erie to the U.S. eastern seaboard provided the objective conditions for a growing and lucrative fishery. The rapid expansion of the industry during the early 70s caused the newly-formed fishing ventures to look "offshore" for the skills and tenacity required to mount a serious commercial industry. A source was found in Portugal.

Originally populated by the Phoenicians, the villages of Nazaré, Peniche and Aveiro had long supplied the world's fisheries with skilled seamen. For over 500 years, this area of Portugal had sent fishermen to all parts of the globe. Initially a trickle, greater number of Portuguese fishermen and skilled fish cutters — the men's wives and daughters — sought relief from the fascist government of Portugal's Salazar dictatorship and the grinding poverty of his fifty-three year rule. Commercial fishing in Canada provided a tangible alternative to pre-1975 Portugal's oppressive political climate which was wracked by domestic strife and a mounting resentment of debilitating colonial wars in Mozambique, Angola, Guinea, and Timor. The mandatory draft of 16 year old boys was the last straw for many families.

Initially, labour contracts were the vehicle of entry into Canada. This arrangement provided the employer with greater than usual control over many facets of employees' lives. Exploitation was intense. For filleters and other process workers, adherence to employment standards as set in Ontario was non-existent. Overtime provisions were ignored by many, if not most employers. Some plants employed children as young as 11 years of age. Their pay was added to the cheques of their parents. Fishermen were paid arbitrarily. Complaints could result in immediate dismissal and subsequent deportation.

In at least one case, a crew of Portuguese fishermen were compensated at a lower rate than "Canadian crewmen." In a hearing against one firm, the taped proceedings note for posterity this exchange between an employer and myself as the crew's representative:

> "So why doesn't the rest of the crew share in the bonus? Why is it just your family who gets the bonus, yourself and your brother?"
>
> "Because we don't like the Portuguese."
>
> "When you say, 'We don't like the Portuguese', is that something you and your family have decided on?"
>
> "Yes."

By the late 80s, the fishery had developed a profound dependency on the Portuguese "factor". Simultaneously, the people in this sector of the workforce had arrived at that confluence of human emotion wherein their anger at their situation now exceeded their fear of reprisal. John Rodrigues, Cristina Copa and others were ready to act.

In the spring of 1986, community-wide discussions became serious, moving beyond complaining and taking on an organized form. Formal meetings were held. Leaders emerged. Inevitably, a decision was made. A union was the only logical defense against the entrenched exploitation.

This decision, taken in early April of 1986 by the community of fishers and allied workers in and around Leamington, Ontario, was to end up changing the legal standing of commercial fishermen from coast to coast. Many of the founding members of the fledgling "Great Lakes Fishermen and Allied Workers Union" were to suffer serious financial and social dislocation. For some, like Armindo Ferreira and his wife, Sao, their mutual desire for unionization and equity would demand a profound price.

How I Came To Leamington

On May 5, 1986, the United Fishermen and Allied Workers Union President, Jack Nichol, asked me to talk to him regarding an "organizational" matter. As the top officer of British Columbia's militant "fisherman's union," Nichol had initially used his 6'3" frame in the "ice house" for one of the primary fish processing companies on British Columbia's coast. Nichol's physical attributes were augmented by a quick and fluid intellect, which saw him rise to the leading position in the province's commercial fishing trade union.

As an organizer and operative for the UFAWU, I was aware that Nichol's request to see me on a typical cloudy coastal Sunday was likely not a social invitation. The union was in receipt of a carefully worded written request for organizational help to form a trade union in the growing Great Lakes commercial fishing industry. While much too far away to seriously consider as an "eastern wing" of the UFAWU, Nichol felt that the sincerity and enthusiasm expressed in written correspondence was genuine and deserved a response.

"I'd like you to consider going out for three months or so and see what can be done. Come home at your discretion. Don't promise them the moon. Just see what can be done to help them," he had instructed. For ten years, similar directives had been given me by Nichol's predecessor, the mercurial and somewhat legendary Homer Stevens.

Through the years, instructions to "See what you can do" had taken me to northern British Columbia, Saskatchewan, Manitoba, the Northwest Territories.

I left for Ontario on May 9, 1986, driving my own vehicle. The several thousand kilometre journey provided ample time to meld my feelings of both enthusiasm and apprehension — which, for me, always precede an organizing drive — into a working strategy prior to my arrival in Leamington, Ontario.

Leamington is a picturesque town of 14,000. It is located on the shores of Lake Erie, and just on the periphery of Point Pelee National Park. The park and the surrounding agricultural activity has resulted in attracting a vibrant collage of British Empire Loyalists, German, Italian, Lebanese, and Portuguese immigrants who are the source of an exciting and diverse cultural and social dynamic and, in my own view, the foundation of the quintessential Canadian riding.

What was about to change was the acquiescence of the Portuguese fishing community to conditions they now universally agreed were intolerable. Upon my arrival, on May 17th, a meeting of all interested fish processing workers and fishermen was convened at the Leamington Public High School. Approximately 500 individuals were in attendance. Whole families turned out to meet me, listen to the discussion, participate in the arguments. There was mass consensus that a union should be formed and on that basis we began the process of signing workers to a collective bargaining unit.

Jack Nichol had said to "See what you can do." Clearly, these people were already organized. My job would turn out to be to help them *stay* organized — and to change Canadian labour laws forever.

Reprisals

Retaliation to the organizing drive was swift and immediate. Within a 14-day period, 57 of the original 376 union applicants were fired. No work-related reasons were given. In most cases, those who were fired were told the truth, "You have turned on the company. We would like you to leave." The firings involved individuals of varying seniority, from one to twelve years.

The common factor was that all had been "seen" to sign union cards, and all were Portuguese. One creative group of fish boat owners representing five vessels combined together and fired one worker per vessel. The prerequisite was consistent. The individual would have the highest seniority, and again, would be Portuguese. This outrageous action caused a furious response in the Portuguese community.

A meeting was called. At this juncture, we had yet to make application for union status before the Ontario Labour Relations Board. Protection for the new unionists under the relevant sections of the Act was still non-existent. Further complicating matters was the question of which jurisdiction — federal or provincial — exercised primacy over the labour relations in the fish industry. It was becoming a legal nightmare.

Most workers had several hundred years of historical connection to commercial fishing. Transferable skills were few, and language was an impediment for most. A failure to be employed in the industry meant dependence on others. It meant possible blacklisting and inevitably the necessity of moving from the area and/or returning to Portugal. For most the only choice was to fight the companies. The alternatives were not tenable.

The fish companies, some townspeople, other workers failed to grasp an important point. Most unionists were from one town, Nazaré. Most were related by blood, marriage, geography. Firing one fisherman or plant worker had the immediate effect of enraging twenty of his or her relatives and close friends. By firing 57 workers in less than two weeks, the companies had galvanized and mobilized the workers into a high state of collective activity that would last until the battles were resolved.

Forward Now, For Freedom

At 3:00 a.m., on a warm, foggy morning, in the beginning of June, approximately 20 fishermen and I went down to the docks to deal with the arbitrary worker-firings. As the captains arrived to crew the vessels, they were stopped and told that the vessels would not sail without the fired crewmen. The captains initially could not believe the seriousness of the delegation blocking access to their boats.

When it became evident that they would be unable to reach their vessels, police were called. Seven or eight members of the local force attended the scene with their captain, Ardell McIntyre. McIntyre was blunt, "You will have them move immediately, or we will have to take serious measures to do so, Mike."

I went back to the group blocking access to the boats and through an interpreter explained the situation. The response was simply put. The workers told me, "If we allow the companies to fire us now, we are finished here. We have to take the consequences."

I explained the decision to McIntyre. We could not leave or allow access to the men's boats until the fired workers were re-employed.

As I proceeded to leave and rejoin the group, McIntyre restated his position that things would get "very serious, very quickly." I have had many dealings with Ardell McIntyre in the subsequent years, in extremely tense situations. I found him to be a man of integrity, his word and rationale were sound and I believe that he never acted in a manner which I found vindictive or unprofessional.

As news of the blockade spread through town, we were joined by wives and process workers as well as other fishermen. It was evident to McIntyre that he did not have the personnel to adequately deal with the growing number of unionists on the dock. The decision was made to call the Ontario Provincial Police. At about 10:00 a.m., 30 officers arrived with their gear. Mace, shields, helmets, visors and other required tools of the trade. I was again requested to cross "No Man's Land" and discuss the situation with the new officer in charge. He restated the position, "You will move or people will be hurt."

I responded that there appeared to be no course of action other than each side doing what "it had to do." Upon returning to the group, which now numbered about 60 unionists, family and supporters, the workers linked arms and began to sing "Gaivota."

This song, written by the great Portuguese songwriter, poet, and patriot, Jose Afonso, had been banned by the fascist Salazar government. It is a testament to freedom. Roughly translated, the words declare, "With our freedom, we will not return to the old ways again."

As the police marshalled themselves into two line columns, those of us in the front lines joined arms. I remember I was linked to Jack Meca on my left. To my right was Cristina Copa, eight months pregnant, and singing as loudly as the rest. I could only mouth the words. I knew no Portuguese and to be candid, it's difficult to sing when fear constricts the voice box.

The police began to move in lock step, at slow march. They beat out a cadence on their plexiglass shields. Jack Meca, who would become president of the union and whose arm I was now crushing in mine, asked, "Mike, what the hell is going to happen?"

I said, "Jack, I've never seen anyone beat up a man who has a gun, a club, and a shield, using only his bare hands. In two minutes you and I will be lying on this dock, out cold."

Jack turned to me, and shook my hand and said, "Boa viage." (Have a good journey.)

Meca proved on this occasion and many others that he had the courage to lead from the front, as did Cristina Copa. The OPP marched to within 10 feet of the front line. The officer in command stopped his contingent. He raised his visor, looked at a clearly pregnant Cristina Copa and said, "Ma'am, I don't want to hurt you. Why don't you step out of the line?"

Copa's courageous response was heard by everyone on the dock. "Why don't you hit me first?" she said, "And then I won't be in the line."

That finished it. The officer turned to the thirty men behind him and told them to leave the dock. He then turned to me and said, "Mike, you can have the goddamn dock today. Tomorrow we'll be back and you won't have it by tomorrow night."

There was cheering from the workers and on that day those boats did not sail. At that night's hastily called meeting, many workers demanded we return immediately to the docks and confront the larger contingent coming in the next morning. I spoke against this. I believed that the police would not back down twice. People would be badly hurt. I said we should appeal to the Labour Board for relief. Finally, after hours of debate, this advice was heeded. The next day the offending boat captains were escorted to their vessels by 70 OPP officers. The little town of Wheatley, Ontario (population 1500) looked like a military zone. I was convinced we had made the right decision. We would now avail ourselves of the legal remedy.

Jurisdiction

While Canada has engaged in commercial fishing for over 400 years, one question has always been outstanding. Were fishers and their civil rights as workers a matter of provincial or federal jurisdiction? Through the OLRB, the companies quickly combined to insist that the jurisdiction was federal. A ruling of this nature would have been the end. It may have required us to resign the entire membership. All of those fired may have ended up without legal recourse through the provincial board. This was not acceptable — we had to fight them. It was also a case of national and constitutional proportions that would cost tens of thousands of dollars to mount. We had no money, yet without legal assistance we were surely sunk.

Dick Barry, President of the hard-fighting United Electrical Workers union (now part of the CAW), heard of the situation in Leamington. Dick's organization was no stranger to struggle. UE, along with other unions, had been expelled from the Canadian Labour Congress for failing to rid themselves of the "communists" in their ranks. This action did little to stifle progressive action by the UE and other expelled unions. In my view, this particular period was a sad and tragic chapter in the history of Canada's working people and their organizations. Many worthy and talented activists were hounded from union office at the behest of international union leaders and their allies in the corporate sector.

Barry called the Toronto legal firm of Pollit and Arnold. The firm had a long relationship with the union movement. He asked the firm to render some assistance to the small group of workers on the shores of Lake Erie and they agreed.

Laurence Arnold is a man who approaches a hopeless cause in the same way others get a glass of water. From the outset, he and Paul Falzone, also from Pollit and Arnold, threw themselves into the defense of our union with unrestrained zeal. The union, as they found it, clung tenuously to life. It had yet to receive official status before the Ontario Labour Relations Board. There was no dues check-off, no bank account, and no immediate source of funding.

Prior to the formal decision to form a union, the members of the Portuguese fishing community had gathered $10,000 in donations from those interested in organizing. This incredible feat was destroyed when one of the prospective members absconded with the funds and left the country. Amazingly, the community rallied, began again. Dances, cultural events, and festivals were held. All gatherings became fundraisers. This activity raised an additional $30,000 which allowed the rental of a small office and — luxury of luxuries — a phone of our own. Communication was now possible on a consistent basis. Meeting halls could be rented, delegations could be dispatched; news releases written. We had enough money to tell our story to others and to stay together, but we couldn't pay huge legal bills.

Hard Times; Hard Choices

The Leamington campaign drew cultures and classes into a proximity which previously had not existed. A tightly organized group of working people, most born outside of Canada, were challenging the townspeople to change the way they did business. The underlying tensions between competing blocs of interests found in the town's structure flared with the rise of the union. Few people in the area were neutral, all rightly felt that something profound was at stake — to be won, or lost — because familiar parameters were threatened.

Press reports stressed that many of the men in the union were veterans of Portugal's colonial wars. Ironically, the families had come to Canada for peace — and found none. The reaction of non-union fishers and processing workers to the pro-union faction was a serious source of concern. Provocation from non-union Portuguese fish workers was common. At times, for union members, simply going to the store or the Post Office was a test of determination. There were heated arguments, fights, and flaring anger on all sides. Municipal politicians would call the union office and plead for calm. Meetings with the town police chief were common.

The development of the union became a two-front war which raged in the town and at the Labour Board. Union members were besieged culturally and legally. It forced them to co-operate with each other in a manner I have not ever seen in my capacity as a union organizer. With each attack, the group became stronger, more closely knit, more proud of their heritage and contribution to the world's work. The sleepy town of Leamington was waking up to the sound of Soca music, Fado laments, Carnival, soccer, and even to May Day marches. Those in power for generations were being forced to confront their prejudices. The Great Lakes Fishermen and Allied Workers were a force far beyond their numbers.

It was the law that rendered them helpless.

2B or Not to Be

The old rules of the Labour Board complicated an already confused legal picture. When lawyer Laurence Arnold first faced the company's representative, it was to argue what we called the 2B argument. This section of the labour relations act excluded farmers, trappers, salesmen, etc. from establishing collective bargaining units. If a unit fails the test of 2B, then all claims are denied, and the union has no legal standing to act on behalf of the workers.

In our case, companies desperate to deny us bargaining rights tried every legal manoeuvre possible, at times bordering on the absurd. Here's a true story of one argument.

On behalf of the nine companies opposing the union, lawyer Rod Goddard advanced a spirited, creative assault on the term "fisherman". For a day and a half, he presented evidence on how fish were caught in a gill net. His summation was that as fish were caught in nets by their gills and head, they were actually *trapped*. His argument held that the fishermen could call themselves what they will, but the facts were plain, they were actually fish *trappers* and consequently should be denied status before the board. This scintillating speculation by Goddard — which took our tax dollars and precious OLRB time — was energetically opposed by Arnold.

For my part, I had been acting as co-counsel with Arnold and had listened intently to Goddard's thesis. At the close of the union's summation, I remarked to the Chair of the Panel that I had nothing to say to Goddard's position other than to object his revision of the King James Bible. When the Chair asked for clarification, I pointed out, "The good counsel's argument suggests that Jesus of Nazareth had the Last Supper with twelve trappers, and the union rejects that argument."

With Our Freedom, We Are to Speak

While the OLRB was entertaining various arguments on jurisdiction, we had been given leave to proceed with actions against employers for violations of the act, specifically those firms who had taken action against union members. These were numerous and were divided between Arnold, Falzone, and myself. Many of these involved substantial sums of money in the form of back wages lost to individual members who, in the union's view, had been fired solely on the basis of union affiliation. A number of these cases continued for two years or more. The union won most cases. Over $400,000 in back wages were ordered paid to employees. These decisions were immediately challenged by the companies, again on the basis that the Board had no jurisdiction to preside over the issues. This required appeals to the Appeals Court of Ontario, the Supreme Court of Ontario, and finally, the Supreme Court of Canada.

The service rendered to the union during these proceedings by Arnold and Falzone was heroic. Such zeal would have been more readily understandable if the union had been able to pay for such service. No demands for payment were ever made. There was only a verbal agreement that should our actions against the employers result in monetary awards, then billing would be possible. This incredible gamble by the firm was inevitably rewarded when the rulings began to issue forth. The union won on almost all counts. Employees were ordered reinstated. Back wages of tens of thousands were awarded to desperate union members.

One such individual was Armindo Ferreira. He and his family were representative of most fired members, but his story is special because of his unwavering courage and the humour and wisdom he displayed through the ordeal.

Upon hearing talk of the desire to form a union, Ferreira's employer called together his thirty or so fishermen. At this captive meeting, the employer asked, "What do you have against my company?"

Only Ferreira stood up to say, "It is true. I have signed for the union. I am not against you, but in support of others, who work for companies where conditions are worse than ours."

Irrespective of Ferreira's unblemished seven year record with the firm, he and six others were fired without cause. The hearings on this matter took two years, and a total of twenty-six days in court. It was my task to prove that the company had full knowledge that the seven men were union supporters. Moreover, we had to prove the firings weren't based on "business conditions" but strictly "anti-union animus."

Ferreira was a man of high integrity. He was honest, and he was principled. His actions in support of his brothers and sisters caused him to lose a good job. No company would hire an individual who had taken recourse against his employer. Inevitably, Ferreira lost his recently purchased home. Unlike many of the members, Ferreira was highly educated. His three years in the Portuguese Marine Corps as a communications specialist had given him an advanced education. He loved opera. Luciano Pavarotti and Placido Domingo regularly poured out of his stereo. During his two year ordeal before the Board, Armindo never wavered or complained. He told and retold his story with consistency and candour.

Near the end of the formal hearings, Ferreira's employer's lawyer took advantage of the fact that I had put Armindo on the stand as my last witness. I felt that his clarity on the issues would be an excellent end to the union's case. In a somewhat bizarre tack, the opposing lawyer, Gary McLister, began to cross-examine Armindo on his knowlege of his former employer's adherence to Christianity.

"So, Mr. Ferreira, would you agree with me that my client (the employer), is a Christian?"

Ferreira required no time to consider the matter. "Mr. McLister, the most serious Christian in the world is the Devil. Who believes in Christ more than the Devil? But I wouldn't want him on my boat!"

The purity of this answer galvanized the room.

Regardless of the outcome of the gruelling proceedings, Ferreira had already lost his home, and was forced out of the industry. He moved to Toronto, where he found work as a construction labourer. Shortly thereafter, he slipped from a scaffold and broke his back. Armindo's recovery took years and he suffered terribly. The dislocation to his family was profound, yet he remained certain he had chosen well. Armindo's stoicism was representative of most people. He believed sincerely that struggle was hopeful and that acquiescence was "robbery of one's face."

Armindo Ferriera taught me much.

Bread and Peace

The primary legal question of jurisdiction, which began in 1986, was not resolved until 1991. Five long years of legal limbo, social and political pressure, fundraising, late-night visits from the police, lost homes, and daily conflict ended when the Supreme Court of Canada refused to grant the employers leave to appeal the Ontario Labour Relations Board's contention of Provincial jurisdiction for the Lake Erie fishers and allied workers. This cleared the way for the collection of the several hundred thousand dollars in awards.

During the five-year period, Arnold and Falzone had taken to calling the union their "hobby." The lawyers had opened their homes to the unionists. We stayed with their families, often four or five of us, and we were given transportation, meals, and unconditional support. Both Falzone and Arnold constantly reminded weary unionists that this struggle was worth it. They, too, were organizers, partisans, friends.

With the successful resolution to the legal mayhem, the union was now able to begin to bargain collective agreements. All were tired, but as companies reluctantly signed contracts, members began to come down from the five-year state of alert to acquire a more civilian approach to their workplace. Still, we knew we could not survive as either a lonely outpost of the UFAWU, or a wholly independent body.

In 1991, we merged the union into Canadian Auto Workers Local 444. We are now known as the Marine Division of that local. This merger seemed strange to many, but it has been a wise choice. The late Ken Gerard, CAW Local 444's President at the time of the merger was questioned as to why CAW 444 signed up the fishers and their families in the allied trades. "We're looking for good trade unionists," he said.

So were the fishers. We are very proud to be a part of the CAW and Local 444.

We Will Not Return to the Old Ways Again

There were a thousand times during that five-year period when I would consider the possibility that the Supreme Court might choose to rule in favour of the fish companies. We had been warned by Arnold that the possibility existed. It was too bitter to contemplate, so I kept a positive attitude externally, while privately I was in a high state of anxiety. Of particular worry were those many members whose cases hung in the balance. When notification was sent to the union that jurisdiction had been irrevocably granted, the mood was sombre. We shook hands, and quietly spoke to one another. There was no elation or spontaneous outburst. We were all tired. More to the point, there was a universal feeling that we were at last receiving what was our due. Each member, irrespective of the degree of participation, would be forced to rationalize the experience through the prism of their own lives. It was never a story of "Portuguese workers" to us. It was always a struggle for democracy against arbitrary measures, and for equity.

Were lessons learned? Of course. Individual acts of courage were many. Alternatively, there were those individuals who let us down, disappointed us. But in the end, the ruling that covered the Leamington fish workers covered all fish workers in Canada. Immediate access to codified bargaining rights, provincial health and safety regulations, etc., are now the status quo for all fishers and shore workers. The hard struggle of the few has established the legal framework for the many. Local action brought national results.

What was the dynamic that drew together the players on a national basis? What made the UFAWU spend $80,000 on a struggle they would not even benefit from through increased membership? What of Arnold, Falzone — what could have been their motive? Why would the UE and Dick Barry, the CAW and other unions involve themselves in a messy dispute involving a mere three hundred or so people in an obscure section of Ontario?

When the violent nature of the campaign threatened to isolate the fish workers from the mainstream, why did MP Steven Langdon visit us, help us, and ultimately call on over three hundred New Democrats gathered to honour Ed Broadbent in Windsor, Ontario, to give unequivocal support to this struggling group of workers? That night, Broadbent himself met and shook hands with us. It confirmed to us our campaign had high sanction, and cleared away the doubts of some others in the room. We were partners in the struggle.

If there are lessons to be drawn, then surely we must look at the alternatives to the actions taken by the workers. What were they? Continued acceptance of their situation? Stoic suffering? Grateful acquiescence to their lot in a new land? These are hardly acceptable alternatives for humans about to enter a new century.

Struggle distils the essence of human character. It defines us. While it is indeed understandable that we sometimes turn away from confrontation, we must inevitably agitate for the right to define ourselves. To have no agenda is to be captive to someone else's agenda. For my own part, I had seen workers fight for recognition prior to coming to Ontario, but nothing prepared me for a contest of the intensity or duration which culminated in union recognition for this group of workers. What could have been for me a few weeks' visit turned into an oddessy, five years of which were caught up in an adrenaline-pumping, day-to-day fight for survival.

Has unionization solved all the problems of the industry? Obviously not. What has been handed to the fish workers are the tools to defend themselves. Have the attitudes of the employers changed? Immensely. The employers have no love for the union, but obviously are no longer prepared to do daily battle with its right to exist. It has become an accepted entity, attitudes have changed. Have the towns-people accepted this group of people as part of the community? More have — certainly not all, though the former Mayor and others now often join us for celebrations.

I have taken the opportunity in this offering to point out individuals who I felt were key in this story. It is not possible to mention all who played an important role, but they are thought of often. I would not turn back the clock, nor would I willingly choose to revisit the period dealt with in this article. But it is sufficient to say that we do not change our circumstances without conviction. This must be accompanied by collective action, and finally, by a heightened awareness. To fail to actively challenge inequity and arbitrary power means that we — not the powerful or wealthy — rob our lives of meaning.

Michael Darnell is an Executive Board Member of CAW Local 444. He continues to represent the fishers and allied workers as Local 444's Marine Division director. During his working life, Darnell has worked as an organizer, horse trainer, and fisherman. Darnell has served as a member of the town council in Prince Rupert, B.C., and was the New Democrat candidate for the 1993 federal election in the riding of Essex Kent.

ENDNOTES

1. John Rodrigues is not his real name. Throughout this, I have used pseudonyms for some people. There are still some outstanding legal issues, and possible personal repercussions for the individuals involved if "old" stories are dredged up. So I've changed a few names.

Gaivota

Uma gaivota voava, voava.
Asas de vento, coração de mar.
Como ela, somos livres.
Somos livres, de voar.

Uma papoila crescia, crescia.
Milho vermelho num campo qualquer.
Como ela, somos livres.
Somos livres, de crescer.

Uma criança dizia, dizia.
"Quando for grande não vou combater."
Como ela, somos livres.
Somos livres, de dizer.

Somos un povo que segue em fileiras.
Parte em conquista do pão e da paz.
Somos livres, somos livres.
Não voltaremos atrás.

Jose Afonso

The Seagull

The seagull flew, flew
Her wings of the wind, her heart of the sea.
Like the seagull, we are free.
With our freedom, we are to fly.

A red poppy grew, grew,
It grows like corn, it grows in fields somewhere.
Like the poppy, we are free.
With our freedom, we are to grow.

A child said, said,
"When I grow up, I will not go to war."
Like the child, we are free.
With our freedom, we are to speak.

We are a people who follow others' rules.
Go forward now for freedom, in conquest for bread and
peace.
With our freedom, our freedom,
We will not return to the old ways again.

The editors gratefully acknowledge translation assistance from Ina A. Fernandes, Joseph Salema, John Couto and Len Wallace.

The Political Economy
of Change

. . . .

Above all, step by step, Canadian communities are beginning to see that they can shape their own future.   That's what the progressive politics of this next decade will be about, more power for people in their communities.

Steven Langdon
Debts, Deficits and Human Communities:
A New Approach

Charting the Course For New Jerusalem

by Howard Pawley

With the New Democratic Party embarking upon its renewal process following its catastrophic federal election results, the press has written about divisions between the so-called "traditionalists" and "pragmatists." This is a subtle substitution for the usual reference to the party's right and left wings. However, terms such as traditionalist or pragmatist do not appropriately describe the debate in our party. The discussions focus on meaningful alternatives that appeal to our natural constituency without causing us to indulge excessively in ideological or utopian debate. A more worrisome outcome is the prospect that we may back-peddle on some basic policies and consequently, become indistinguishable from other existing parties, those which support the capitalist structure.

With this in mind, I will attempt to outline some suggestions for the New Democratic Party as it enters into this critical period of its history. It must examine the present scene, determine its *raison d'etre* in terms of greater equality and enhanced democratization. It must then review the process by which we function as a political party and finally, be prepared to answer some very difficult questions.

In the past decade, in Canada and throughout the world, democratic-socialism has been shoved onto the defensive, despite a surge in poverty and unemployment, by powerful neo-conservative forces.

Persistent studies show income and wealth disparities intensifying not only in Canada but throughout the world. Rising levels of economic and human wreckage litter every corner of our nation. The social safety net is steadily eroded while the tax system becomes more regressive. Today, nine out of 10 companies in Canada employ fewer people than they did 10 years ago. Corporate downsizing continues to claim jobs daily. Canadian governments fail to recognize the uselessness of job creation by corporate coddling. The results are that a new generation of Canadians, unlike any previous one, no longer expects to do as well as its parents, and worst of all, a spirit of hopelessness pervades all levels of modern society.

Although the promotion of the competitive agenda has resulted in enormous economic and social damage, governments today are seen as incapable of bettering the human condition. Even with the defeat of neo-conservative governments, including that of Bush-Reagan by Bill Clinton in 1992, and the near wipe out of the Mulroney-Campbell Conservatives, these fallacious assumptions about governments persist. Despite changes in administrations, the newly elected neo-Liberal governments have continued the neo-conservative policies of their predecessors, including the backing of the North American Free Trade Agreement (NAFTA), encouragement of privatization and the slashing of social programs. Sadly, throughout the world the parties of the Left, whether in or not in power, are no longer seen as alternatives to the inequitable capitalist system. In the past, social democratic or democratic-socialist parties have based their popular appeal on their ability to stimulate economic growth to adequately fund the welfare system and to maintain full employment. However, socialist parties are now confronted by the dilemma of how to contend with the functioning of modern transnational corporations that are successfully weakening the capacity of national state governments to pursue Keynesian/welfare state programs. Moreover, surpluses in government revenues no longer exist. They have been replaced by mounting deficits.

Many of us can recall how vivid the political choices once were. The vision of the "New Jerusalem" was clear. We did not shy from identifying the evils of an inequitable economic system. We described how it disempowered and exploited working people. A lifetime commitment to the cause of democratic-socialism was undertaken, neither for career aspiration nor personal enhancement, but to do our bit to construct a more egalitarian society.

Regrettably, somewhere along the way, our vision has became less recognizable while those on the right of the political spectrum have gained momentum. Often, we appeared ambiguous in our articulation of an alternative agenda to that espoused by the Thatchers, Reagans and Mulroneys of the world. Ironically, the collapse of communism has been interpreted not as an indictment of totalitarianism, but of socialism. The impression grew that we have become lost without a compass to guide us. Sadly, our actions frequently implied that we lacked a viable alternative, though one had never been more essential than since the 1930s depression.

The Party's Ethos

Fortunately the party's renewal process at long last, provides us with the opportunity to think about a revitalized ethos or *raison d'etre* for our party.

The New Democratic Party has best functioned as a party unlike the others. Whenever it steered too closely toward the political centre it has usually failed to inspire either political or moral support. To some, it appeared to forget its roots in the pursuit of power. It alienated or caused indifference among its traditional base while simultaneously failing to attract any new constituency. The party's vitality depends upon the inspiration it can generate among those less powerful in our society, its advocacy of the public interest against those enjoying excessive power and wealth. The party must cause people to think differently about politics. It must show a preparedness to do things differently, including changing the system itself, so that "people before profits" may prevail.

The rejection by the Canadian public of the Charlottetown Accord, harmed the NDP more than any other party because we were seen as part of the elite of political, business, media and labour leaders. Today, ironically, many perceive the Reform Party and the Bloc Québecois and not the NDP as the outsiders. The NDP is seen as too anxious to accommodate itself to the elite, and worse still, not offering anything different, we are no longer seen as an anti-establishment party.

Traditionally, it has been our party that has spoken on behalf of the unrepresented, and we should continue to be seen as the voice for those disempowered by the system. A firm resolve to achieve a fairer distribution of wealth and power must be the principal characteristic, and the principle that provides the NDP with its distinctiveness from other parties. Our overriding concern must be greater equality rather than less. All policies should be judged accordingly.

It is true that we now must contend with scarcity rather than abundance, as governments enjoy fewer resources than previously. Curiously, while those living below the poverty line are under great pressure from mainstream business, academic and media analysts, those reaping the advantages from the subsidies in our tax system are immune from pressure. We must be prepared to tackle this contradiction head on.

The swing to conservatism in recent years has seen the abolition of estate taxes, the introduction of more consumer taxes and a reduction of taxation for high earners and corporations. A recent report by Statistics Canada on wealthy Ontarians shows that the rich have made more use of deductions and credits to avoid paying taxes than other taxpayers. The analysis indicates that almost one in 10 of the top one per cent of the taxpayers with an annual average income of $286,000 a year, succeeded in paying an effective tax rate of less than 10 per cent in 1990. It also disclosed that the top five per cent made the greatest use of loopholes. For instance, 60 per cent of this group made use of Registered Retirement Savings Plans compared to just under 22 per cent in middle or lower income groups.[1]

I remember fondly the experience in Manitoba in 1969 when the Schreyer government, as its first official act, replaced the regressive health poll tax with higher income taxes. Later, a cost of living allowance was instituted for low income categories. In 1987, my government, rather than undertake draconian cuts to social spending, enacted limited though progressive changes on those most able to pay. We were bombarded by criticism, however, as a less well-off province compelled to work within the framework of the existing unfair taxation system, we succeeded in making more equal the distribution of income. To do so, we stuck to our guns. We did make the distribution of income a little fairer.

Today, with no surplus to equitably distribute, we must devise more of such alternatives to ensure the most vulnerable are not casualties in the name of protracted restraint. Unlike the other parties, we accept the interdependence of both the social and economic thrusts and while endorsing a solid and expanding economic base as a requisite for the enrichment and enhancement of our lives, we also know that public services in the social sector contribute to economic growth. The European experience verifies this. The two must go together. Contrary to popular belief, the current system has not done well on either front.

I am not suggesting the NDP bite off more than it can chew but rather for the party to focus on its own priorities, relating to the interests of its constituency base. It must avoid being deflected from priority issues, for peripheral ones will only distract the public from interpreting properly the party's achievements as well as its objectives.

For instance, in Manitoba in 1983, my government's seeming preoccupation, albeit compelled by circumstance, on the French language issue hindered it from projecting the emphasis that we wished to portray, namely the assault on unemployment during the recession of the early 1980s. It was only when we were able to extract ourselves from this contentious though admirable issue and concentrate on our principal objectives in the latter half of our mandate that we were able to achieve re-election.

Democratization

The extension of democracy is essential to improving participation and accountability at all levels of human endeavour. Surely democracy must include not just political but also the economic and social participation as argued by David Lewis and Frank Scott in *Make This Your Canada*. Do adequate measures exist to ensure accountability to citizens? Is there a need to strengthen participation at the community, municipal and provincial levels? Increased democratization at the community level can be promoted in a wide array of instances such as health, justice and local economic development. In both the free trade debate and on the question of monetary policy, the role of citizens, the role of public opinion was lessened in relation to that of government. How do we reverse the trend to lessened citizen influence? What we must seek is clearly more empowerment by individuals and the loosening of the social and economic grip by the elite on the determination of public policy.

Process and Operations

A further challenge is the preoccupation by supporters in progressive interest groups. Instead of channeling their efforts to the party, these activists sometimes find greater satisfaction freed from the need to compromise demanded by the political process. Some party members complain, understandably, that we have become overly reliant upon such groups that measure progress strictly through the lens of a particular issue rather than through a total package of policy.

To be successful, coalition politics needs articulation of a respective party — interest group role. While the interest group represents a narrower range of concern, the party must reflect an all-encompassing vision. However, one can't fault friendly interest groups for our current predicament as a philosophic framework is lacking. David Mackenzie is certainly not helpful in his submission to the Renewal Conference when he denigrates interest groups who, after all, are but fulfilling their own missions, all without the hefty resources available to the corporate community, when he describes them as "coalitions of veteran fringe leftists of anti-NDP persuasion" the "old Marxists of the hard Left."[2] Although I often resented as well what I occasionally perceived as the unfairness by such groups to my government, I hope I never permitted this frustration to cloud my recognition of their legitimate role. A social democratic government can wisely benefit from these groups effectively countering the well-organized and financed campaigns by the Right. To do this, however, trust must be maintained so that paranoia does not poison what should be a healthy relationship. We need an affinity that will successfully persuade a coalition of sympathetic coteries to strengthen the party organizationally.

There have, at times, while especially in power, been strains between the party and the labour movement. In Ontario, during the confrontation between the government and labour over the so-called "social contract," neither side was adequately understanding of the other's role. If they had, I believe there would have been greater trust contributing to a successful conclusion. I speak not theoretically but rather from my experiencing the co-operation that was achieved between our government and its employees' union in similar circumstances occurring in Manitoba in 1983. At that time, rather than deficit-fighting, the major emphasis was on the need for job creation in direct ministerial-union leadership, low-profile discussions where it was made worthwhile for labour's co-operation not by financial incentives but by their participating in the creation of a Jobs Fund to reduce unemployment.

One can only marvel at the organizational success of the Parti Québecois and the Bloc Québecois, pooling supporters from a diverse ideological spectrum and competing interests with a predominant belief, namely: sovereignty for Québec. There must be a common vision behind our package of policies so that it doesn't only cater to a cacophony of demands.

In contemporary politics, the advent of professional market testing provides greater feedback than ever to the political leadership exceeding traditional debate among traditional party activists. This unfortunate trend was accelerated with adverse consequences in the 1988 and 1993 federal election campaigns. Opinion polling, focus groups and other modern technological developments obviously contribute a major way to electoral strategy but they should not determine which policies we pursue. It is widely acknowledged that the American pollsters and their marketing advice in the 1988 campaign "to play down the free trade issue" permitted Liberal leader John Turner to seize the initiative from us.

If, in Saskatchewan during the 70s, the Blakeney government had followed the advice of its pollsters, they wouldn't have transferred much of the potash industry from private to public hands. Polling was not used when Tommy Douglas implemented a comprehensive health insurance package in Saskatchewan, nor when the Ed Schreyer government enacted public auto insurance in Manitoba.

These modern techniques, including polling and focus groups, have distracted us from the traditional emphasis on party organization and party education. A shrinking membership base is invited to only participate in party functions at election time. To the Liberal and Conservative parties, which are cadre rather than mass membership parties, the consequences have been less debilitating than with the NDP. The Liberal and Conservative Parties enjoy the luxury of support from Canada's governing elite. Corporate interests and a friendly media ensure them support but the NDP can only offset such disadvantages by an active membership and organization. Clever media techniques and public relations expertise, though helpful, fall far short of what is required. A large and energized membership can only be derived from democratic forms existing in the party for membership to control policy development.

Reversals in major election commitments should, at all costs, be avoided. To temporize or compromise is understandable and often desirable but the engagement in full scale abandonment of a key policy, one that has been dear to the party's membership and conveyed to the public in an election campaign, can result in massive demoralization for the membership with inevitable reduction in its credibility by the public. Indeed, to confidently press ahead, even in the face of momentary poor polling results, against a powerful opposition, can demonstrate a commitment and a confident sense of purpose. In the Manitoba election of 1973, one heard repeatedly favourable comments on the government's success against enormous odds when in its first term it legislated and implemented public auto insurance. It was a crucial factor in the Schreyer government's re-election.

It has always been my experience that charisma in leadership provides but short term political advantage. A party such as the NDP, dependent upon vitality and an energized organization, needs primarily an emphasis on a team approach — leader, caucus and party membership. To do otherwise, will generally result in a listless and declining organizational base, proving itself ineffective under any circumstances.

Finally, the party in this renewal process should be prepared to re-examine its system of affiliate membership. Is it an invigorating method of encouraging participation within the party? Does it suggest a two-tier membership system? Can the encouragement of a greater involvement by union membership in the NDP be enhanced by an emphasis on individual membership?

We must encourage a wide ranging party debate for today our party suffers from insufficient discussion about real policy alternatives. According to Joseph Wearing, the policy making process in the three political parties can be described as: " . . . an over simplification — though not so very far from the truth — to say that the Conservatives deal with this problem by not having policy conventions, the Liberals have policy conventions but forge the resolutions once the conventions are over, and the NDP leadership makes sure it gets the resolutions it wants."

This may be an exaggeration, but we do need a structure for mutual discussion, criticism and debate that brings together the membership without necessarily requiring agreement on policy. We certainly cannot justify any organization in which a membership base is used to principally support a staff or headquarters. Rather, we need an organization that is an inclusive forum, providing opportunities for systematic debating of ideas and reflection on local experience in a critical but supportive manner. It may be that the renewal process will provide a long overdue opportunity for just such a discussion to take place. Finally, let us prevent the process from solely descending into embracing the latest fashionable trends whether right or wrong.

Globalization

It is my intent to deal with three policy areas: trade, capital mobility and taxation. These major topics encompass the major transformations that are taking form in a manner that handicap the effectiveness of the nation state government as we edge toward the 21st Century. It will be incumbent on the NDP to address these fundamental questions.

The functioning of the modern multi-national corporations, beyond the control of party or national government, not just complicates but also globally hinders the achievement of democratic-socialism. The renewal process demands more sharp economic analysis than what has been evident in NDP pronouncements during the past decade.

Canada's entry into the U.S./Canada Free Trade Agreement and, then NAFTA, resulted in increased joblessness and plant closures. The values of Canada, contributing to our being a caring nation with collectivist aspirations, have been undermined. Canadian workers have been compelled to submit to continuing concessions for their survival from the competition with Mexico and the southern United States. Corporations are transferring elsewhere their corporate activities to gain benefits from various right-to-work laws, a weak trade union movement and substandard environmental provisions. The elites of some foreign nations prosper by denying their workers fundamental democratic, human and labour rights. Unbelievably, the NDP is now being told by some within its own ranks that it should endorse such trade arrangements. Although the NDP was dealt a severe political blow electorally; it was not due to its opposition to the trade deals. Other factors dominated the campaign. Indeed, a unique opportunity currently exists for the NDP, with the Liberals' abandonment of any pretence on its part to re-negotiate either the FTA or NAFTA, to develop and strengthen trade policy unreservedly guaranteeing that Canadians workers are protected against social dumping by foreign firms. Countervailing levies should be imposed against all imports benefiting from practices that allow subsidization of foreign imports by violating basic human, democratic, labour and environmental standards.

In 1993, the NDP assumed a principled and correct position on trade. The party has been effectively sidelined in the creation of a comprehensive policy due to the impact of modern globe-trotting capital traders and the debate about whether there are any means available to contend with such pervasive power. Nation states have a lessened capacity to do the steering that Keynesian/welfare state programs demand. Today we must contend with capital flight and the consequent role of the international bond holders and commodity traders. These money-men, along with the banks and financial institutions operate without any accountability to elected governments and dominate the direction of monetary policy. Unless the NDP and other likeminded Parties strengthen globally their financial policies by recognizing the necessity of effective public control of the banking and financial sector, they will surely fail to accomplish their social or economic priorities. Future governments will be condemned to relegating their principal purposes for governing to representing the priorities of international capital.

Our system of taxation is rapidly becoming more regressive. Increasingly, schemes to build off-shore nest eggs are advocated in publications showing how to avoid taxation by systematically accumulating secret money offshore. They disclose in which Caribbean island you can live off either the interest earnings of your Swiss capital investments or the dividends from your own local factory — without paying any taxes. Thus, it is inexplicable to read in the submission by Hugh Mackenzie, who, as executive director of the Ontario Fair Tax Commission oversaw the $9 million, three-year study of taxation in Ontario, when he writes that: "Campaigns based on our traditional notions of tax fairness create unrealistic expectations of tax relief for middle income people."[3] Is it any wonder that so little has resulted from the Commission's efforts?

An area of policy making where international capital surely influenced the Canadian government occurred in the instance of the Goods and Services Tax, a regressive tax that reflects the trend to more taxation being paid by individuals and less by corporations. Worse, to the obvious detriment of the nation's taxpayers, it fails to even apply to that part of the economy representing the new forces of globalization.

It is up to the NDP to identify an alternative. A fair system of taxation ensures financial interests are not excused from the obligations levied on all other citizens. For example, in 1993, the real Canadian economy produced a GNP of approximately $700 billion,[4] the financial economy, trading on the Toronto Stock Exchange was valued at $147 billion, the value of trading on the Canadian bond market reached $1.4 trillion and the short term money markets turned over $1.9 trillion.[5] The real economy grew by three per cent in 1993 while trading on the financial markets rose 33 per cent. In today's economy, speculative profits dwarf those from producing real goods and services and moreover, they fail to really produce anything. As Kenneth Galbraith has recently stated, the value of the Canadian dollar is no longer established by what Canada produces but rather by the level of interest rates and the skills exercised by the international bond traders. Indeed, as the recent activity on the Toronto Stock Exchange has proven, the advent of positive economic news in Canada or U.S.A. has ironically had an adverse influence. So why should investments in goods and services attract the GST while those involving financial services, interest, bank charges, brokerage commissions be exempt? Why shouldn't the broader transactions of the financial community be taxed?

Instead of bowing out of this debate, the NDP should advocate the extension of the GST, if it is continued, to at least include financial services and purchases of financial instruments to reduce the overall rate, something not done by the Mulroney government probably due to former finance minister Michael Wilson's affinity to Bay Street. Above all, the NDP must realize that it cannot be mushy or bland about how it would deal with global finance. How it responds will mark the difference from the other parties and potentially restore the relevancy of the NDP again.

Conclusion

We must as a party in co-operation with other progressive groups and members of the Socialist International and labour, develop the cross border co-operation and activism as was so recently evident in the battle against NAFTA. As we edge toward the 21st Century, greater internationalization by the Left is required. Ironically, the decline of the threat of Communism may provide more impetus to increased cohesion to the world democratic and Left forces in the post Cold War era. The links may be encouraged as well by the necessity to protect and enhance social and economic advance from the assault by internationalization of trade and capital in the modern world community.

The NDP ethos depends on the difference rather than similarity to other parties. It must function within a democratic-socialist philosophic framework or lose its reason for existence. This must be reflected organizationally by a commitment to a mass party rather than a cadre party, where the membership will perform an important role in influencing policy direction.

The test of our success in the making of policy, whether directly or indirectly, depends not upon whether we have enhanced the wealthy and powerful but whether we have added more to those with little. This will be achieved by greater democratic control over political and economic decisions and structures and an expansion of human rights; so that every person will receive adequate housing, health care, genuine education and employment.

The political ship, the NDP, built by Woodsworth, Coldwell, Lewis and Douglas, though still sailing, is badly listing. Can it survive the turbulent waters of the 21st Century? Is there a future for the global Left as well? With proper leadership and crew and above all, a compass to provide directions, it can yet reach its destination, the distant port — the New Jerusaleum that Tommy Douglas once described, in his many speeches in community halls across this nation.

Howard Pawley has been an active New Democrat for all his adult life. A lawyer by trade, Pawley served in the Schreyer government, establishing Public Auto Insurance. Pawley led the Manitoba New Democrats to two victories at the polls. Since 1990, Pawley has been teaching at the University of Windsor and working closely with Windsor-area community groups and activists.

ENDNOTES

1. The *Globe and Mail*, "Wealthy Ontarians Find More Ways to Avoid Paying Taxes," June 24, 1994, p. B5.
2. Brief to NDP Renewal Conference, Ottawa, Ontario, August 27, 1994.
3. Brief to NDP Renewal Conference, Ottawa, Ontario, August 27, 1994.
4. Statistics Canada, Canadian Economic Observer, Catalogue 11-210.
5. Bank of Canada Review, Summer 1994, tables H1, H3, and H4.

Youth, Social Responsibility and Social Change

by Brian Mayes and Simon Blackstone

I n writing this "youth policy" paper, we open with the traditional disclaimer, as voiced by everyone from F. Scott Fitzgerald to Douglas Coupland, that we do not claim to speak for a generation. We do not claim to speak for anyone but ourselves, two middle-class white men born in 1962 and 1971. We do, however, want to speak out about our impressions about progressive policies for youth, the New Democratic Party's failure to address these policies, and the opportunities that exist for progressive youth policy in 1990s.

In Canada, the first half of the 1990s have been marked by a prolonged recession with consequent increase in unemployment, a substantial increase in post-secondary tuition fees and on the federal scene, a collapse of electoral support for the only political party that is avowedly social democratic. Meanwhile, there has been a steady increase in the debt load carried by most provincial governments as well as by the federal government.

The economic problems facing this country make it appealing for young people to blame the economic situation on some "other" (i.e., immigrants, unions, feminists) and to vote for a right wing alternative (i.e., Reform) that will "eliminate" that problem, and bring back a return to prosperity.

Within this context, what steps can be taken to assist young people in pursuing employment and post-secondary education, and in viewing society in a social democratic manner? We do not claim to have all the answers to these questions, but there are some areas that deserve a fuller debate in regards to their potential benefit for young people in today's society. This means social democrats have to take a serious look at existing policy on such issues as pensions, youth services programs and training/education, and perhaps most fundamentally to join the debate over rights and responsibilities.

Rights and Responsibilities

The Communitarian school of thought is rapidly gaining attention in the United States. The discussion focuses around "the responsive community" that has both rights and responsibilities. Pollster Daniel Yankelovich in a 1992 study stated,

> When it comes to social policy, as represented by government mandated benefits, the concept of need-based entitlements, where nothing is expected in return, leads the country into all manner of contradictions and conflicts... It is clear from this study that most Americans would embrace the idea of government programs grounded in reciprocity...[1]

Aside from "make the corporations and the wealthy pay their fair share of taxes" (a commendable thing), there has been little debate on communitarianism in Canadian social democratic circles. A debate over rights and responsibilities does not mean an endorsement of the existing distribution of wealth and the existing distribution of power. Such a debate should demonstrate a sense of interdependence and co-operation, while acknowledging that the government is not simply a vehicle for entitlement programs.

The focus for social democrats should be the development of a policy that will provide some sense of local community, as well as national identity. Fundamentally, such a policy will provide young people with hope in the future, and provide a vision that progressive forces have a realistic "co-operativeness agenda" that offers a better future than the right-wing "competitiveness agenda."

What are the responsibilities a Canadian society and state ask of people, particularly young people? A policy of generational equity should be key for social democrats in Canada. This policy would have to take many forms, and we wish to discuss only a few of them, specifically the approach to national service, the approach to "social security" (i.e., state provided pensions and unemployment insurance), and the concept of full employment.

National Service

A fundamental part of the generational equity policy should be the establishment of a national service requirement for young people. This service requirement could perhaps be eight months service, in four-month semesters during the age span of 18-25. Whether this service requirement would be mandatory and universal, as in most western European countries, or simply voluntary is obviously a controversial subject for debate. It is worth noting that Canada, the U.S., Japan and Britain are the only major industrial countries without some form of mandatory service.

The Canadian social democratic perspective on this issue is unclear. The New Democratic Party completely ceded this turf to the Liberals in the 1993 Canadian federal election campaign, to the extent that the "Community Youth Service" plan promised in the NDP's "Strategy for a Full-Employment Economy" was never even produced.

The German military draft offers an option that allows draftees to opt for national service over military service. The *Zivildienstleistende,* or *Zivis,* serve for 15 months (versus 12 months military service) between ages 18 and 28 in a variety of public service jobs. The program covers 135,000 participants at a cost of just over $3 billion per year. Similar programs are in place in Denmark, France and Portugal.[2]

The argument for a universal national service in the United States has been put forward by Michael Lerner of *Tikkun* magazine, in "Memo to Clinton," where he states:

> Don't expect people to make sacrifices for their country if they think that lots of others are getting away with something. National service will generate little idealism if it is only for those who can't afford to pay back college loans... Your administration must generate a new paradigm of communal responsibility, and embody that paradigm by appearing to insist on equal responsibility and equal sacrifice from all sectors of the population.[3]

A National Service corps could start to deal with some of Canada's urban problems (i.e., nothing for drop-outs to do, lack of structure for young people with no job or no education). This program should be a "public works" type of project — but with some options for training in certain areas. By avoiding the more idiotic limits on freedoms (i.e., no haircuts required) this corps could offer some opportunity to a lot of young people.

This program should be part of a generational equity trade-off. In return for service to your country there is some form of employment guarantee, or there is some guarantee of college/university tuition credit. In this way there is neither an expectation of full funding from the state, nor is there is a rejection of state initiatives. The government of the day could assess its priorities and weight national service credits differently (i.e., to encourage training in skilled trades, allowing two years of tuition for every year completed, versus one year of university credit).

It would be overly idealistic to think such a program would avoid the pitfalls of bureaucracy and "make work" projects. Nevertheless, if a community focus is retained there is hope that the program would be more than a kind of national boot-camp. National service could also be part of an effort to build national unity, to promote regional economic development and to show all Canadians a "government that works."

There are obvious labour relations implications for such a program. It serves as an opportunity for the Canadian labour movement to convince a generation of young Canadians that organized labour is an equal economic stakeholder along with business and government. Thus, while labour should insist that no worker lose his/her job to one of the youth corps members, it should join in the design of a new youth program. This includes remaining open to the types of public sector work that are to be done, and recognizing the model of Germany and other countries in terms of remuneration for corps members. This participation could be encouraged by placing youth corps members in a bargaining unit represented by a public sector union.

Some observers have criticized existing voluntary youth service programs, as exemplified by City Year in Boston, or Serve Canada in Toronto, for "neglecting analysis of the economic and social forces that create inequality, powerlessness and other community problems."[4] However, it is also true that at their best, such programs bring together young people from different backgrounds to co-operatively address real-world problems. Such a program will not build a revolution, but it will try to build a sense of community. Writing about the murder of a City Year participant in Boston, Suzanne Goldsmith said:

> ... And now, when we read in the paper about another black male getting shot, we don't just turn the page quickly, relieved that we are not part of that world. We know that we are. That is what national service can deliver. And that is enough. [5]

Social Security

Some romantics on the left argue that in a few years young people in Canada will adopt the attitude that Canada should repudiate its debt obligations. These debts obviously limit the flexibility of governments and the opportunities open to young people. It is vaguely felt that youth will somehow rise up under the slogan "Hell no, we won't pay" and force government to consider repudiating on its debt commitments. Through some sort of inchoate social democratic dream, the bad guys (i.e., the banks, bondholders) will be left holding the bag for the government deficits of the last 30 years, while the radicalized youth lead the way to a new social democratic paradise.

The more responsible among those who prophesize this movement

among young people recognize the economic risks, if not impossibili-
ty, of this sort of action. What is not said, is the likelihood that such a
call to economic arms for young people is just as likely to have a right
wing focus (i.e., cut the benefits of the injured, the unemployed, the
elderly) as to be the root of a new progressive movement.

A more responsible alternative is to come up with a plan that admits
that uncontrolled growth in the debt is a problem, a problem that may
take a generation to reduce. Part of this is present a plan that shows
the continued economic viability of state-run pension funds, and the
value of unemployment insurance.

For example, the Canadian Institute of Actuaries in its 1993 report
on the Canadian Pension Plan called on the federal government to
"open a public debate on CPP's future long before young workers and
voters rebel against high contribution rates in the next century." The
chair of the committee stated, that "there is widespread public fear
that CPP will go broke or disappear because young workers refuse to
pay high contribution rates, or that benefits will be clawed back."[6]
Similarly, a recent poll in the United States indicates that a higher percentage of American "Generation Xers" believe in UFOs than believe
that the social system will pay them retirement benefits (46 per cent to
9 per cent).[7] This loss of faith in the existing system plays into the right
wing agenda for dismantling the social safety net, and destroys the
belief that we are all part of a community, contributing to each other.

Are there progressive alternatives that social democrats can put forward? How can progressives show that this sort of program is vital to
a sense of Canadian community, and is not simply a cumbersome
bureaucratic subsidy for baby boomers? Social democrats need to
make clear long-term policy and budgetary commitments to those fundamental programs like CPP which affect a broad spectrum of society,
and which grew out of a broad-based majority support. One possibility is an increase in contribution rates based on age (i.e., increase at age
40) to encourage younger people that they are not simply subsidizing
an older generation.

It is this sort of policy development that will show young people
that there is a realistic plan for the future, and not simply a plan to
"spend our way out of this mess." If social democrats are to make a
clear case for a full-employment strategy it will require more than
dime-store Keynesianism.

There is no guarantee of what will happen in 20 years, but if young
people are shown that social democrats have a realistic plan to keep
the pension system viable, the risk of a revolt against the plan, and
other government measures, will be much reduced.

Full Employment

As of June 1993, youth unemployment stood at 18.6 per cent. Statistics Canada figures show that in 1990, families headed by those under age 25 earned 20 per cent less than families in that age group did in 1980.[8] Clearly, these numbers indicate the seeds of a longer-term problem, both in regard to on-the-job training and economic security.

A 1993 study by Canadian economist Judith Maxwell called "Globalization and Family Security" contained several recommendations for youth policy, including:

- Create a Job Corps for both youth and older workers who are unemployed or retired, which will channel their unused energy into community services like Head-Start, child care, care of the elderly, remedial teaching systems for children with problems at school and so on . . .

- Commit to a policy of full employment for young people. No Canadian under the age of 25 should be eligible for unemployment insurance. If they are not working, they should sign up for the Job Corps or enrol in a formal education or training program. As long as they are committed in this way, they should be eligible for income support . . .

Leaving aside the inequitable Unemployment Insurance issue, do these proposals really equate to a full employment program? Theoretically yes, but there it leaves the question of how to promote "full employment" that includes jobs outside the public sector. In an era of the information highway, our society's main assets are our infrastructure, our training and our education. Even if we devise schemes that promote life-long learning and skills training, how can we be sure that we are training for jobs that exist?

Maxwell offers some suggestions on this front:

- offer a full range of apprenticeship, vocational and technical training focused on skills that are needed by local employers.

- reduce payroll taxes paid by employers and employees in return for on-the-job training and skills upgrading programs.

These are commendable sentiments, though they leave aside the funding issue. What are the options for social democrats?

For "full employment" to seem like more than a utopian dream in the 1990s social democrats must vigorously pursue a course of economic imagination that will produce ideas about community controlled capital, and resultant job creation. Part of the answer lies in a more corporatist, community-focused approach to policy development, if this is possible in Canada. Government-run training will undoubtedly be more successful if it is clear what kinds of jobs are available in the short run, or what sort of retraining needs to be done. Encouraging workers and employers to address this issue, both through tax measures and through legislation, is one step towards answering the issue of "training for what?"

A full employment strategy exclusively for young people is not an equitable policy, unless there is a general commitment to full employment. A major part of this commitment will need to be a serious study of work sharing and its ramifications for business, workers and young people. Again, social democrats have to return to the consideration of a "co-operativeness agenda" that will promote sharing of resources, rather than simply training to defeat some unseen foreign competitor.

Conclusion

The concepts of "generational equity" and "rights and responsibilities" are not broad ideological platforms. Rather, they are part of the larger process of developing an ideology for the new "New Left." It will be up to social democrats to consider these ideas, and to determine if they offer a useful basis for future policy making. By focusing on a community of interest among the generations, and among all Canadians we may be able to build a sustainable platform for the future. Instead of simply proclaiming that the "corporate agenda" must be rejected, we need a realistic, achievable agenda of our own. If we don't provide a real alternative, the march to progress will remain only a book title rather than reality.

Brian Mayes and Simon Blackstone are co-founders of the zoodemocrats, a discussion group for those who cruise the information highway. Mayes works as a negotiator for the Ontario Public Service Employees Union, and serves on the Board for Serve Canada. Blackstone is a Political Science student at McMaster University.

Endnotes

1. Daniel Yankelovich quoted in: Marshall, Will. "The Politics of Reciprocity". Democratic Leadership Council, *The New Democrat*. (Volume 4, No. 3) July 1992, p.6

2. Figures from Clark, Nicola. "The German Draft: A Model for America?" *The Responsive Community; Rights and Responsibilities*. (Volume 3, No. 4) Fall 1993, pp. 38-41.

3. Lerner, Michael. "Memo to Clinton"; *Tikkun*. (Volume 8, No. 1) January/February 1993, p.10.

4. Derber, Charles. "National Service: The Sixties Meet the Nineties." *Tikkun*. (Volume 8, No. 3) May/June 1993, pp. 19-21.

5. Goldsmith, Suzanne. "Crossing the Tracks: A Lesson in Public Service." *The Responsive Community: Rights and Responsibilities*. (Volume 2, No. 4) Fall, 1992, pp. 53-60.

6. C.S. Moore (chair), and previous quote, quoted in Daw, James. "Future Pensions Safe If Payout Delayed to age 70, Actuaries Say." *Toronto Star*, November 13, 1993, p.E1.

7. "Younger Generation puts faith in UFOs." *Vancouver Sun*, September 27, 1994, p.A13.

8. Figures and quotes from Maxwell, Judith. "Globalization and Family Security," pp. 19-55, and Forum Directors Group Keynote Paper, pp. 1-18, both in: *Family Security in Insecure Times; National Forum on Family Security*. (Ottawa: Canadian Council on Social Development, 1993).

Towards Citizen Welfare and Democratic Citizenship:
Democratic Socialist Perspectives on Social Policy

by Judy Wasylycia-Leis

T he critical situation facing the New Democratic Party and the lack of a common vision on the democratic-socialist left in Canada require wide-open debate and dialogue on all fronts. The social policy field is no exception. It goes hand in hand with economic policy and is a key element in the development of democratic socialist theory and practice.

Social policy flows from a clearly-defined vision and complements economic direction and activity. To the extent that the debate about vision and an alternative economic agenda for the NDP and the left generally is only just beginning, any attempt to delineate new social policy directions has to be considered preliminary and partial at best. As well, it would be premature and counterproductive at this point to propose a specific social program or plan for government. A major rethinking process is required first. Social policy is an integral part of rebuilding on the left in Canada and can only be developed after much debate and within the context of a new framework for democratic socialism.

There is very little in the literature on the left about new directions for social policy. New models for social policy in democratic socialism are virtually non-existent. In this absence, two approaches have occupied the field. One expresses the view that when it comes to social policy, this area is the least of our worries since the policies of the NDP and the record of social democracy are significant. Past achievements such as medicare and public pensions are held up as good social policy that may require strategic but not substantive review. The other approach is that the era of relative growth in social spending has simply come to an end and that the changing world economy demands a reconsideration of such ideas as the welfare state and public sector administration.

Both arguments are problematic and detract from the necessary task of working towards the development of a new or renewed political program on the left. Neither approach constitutes an effective force against the right wing assault on social services nor envisages the use of social policy as one tool in the transformation of society. This is not to deny the significance of social democratic reforms and the major contribution of the CCF/NDP in the establishment of Canada's social safety net. As a result of such efforts, access to health care and education became recognized as a fundamental right and freedom. The belief that people should be sheltered from the risks of economic life resulted in programs like Unemployment Insurance, Family Allowance, Canada Assistance, Old Age Security and the Canada Pension Plan. The idea of an active state led to inroads in labour standards, workplace health and safety regulations, and environmental protections. A commitment to co-operative action and collective responsibility helped shape Canada as a caring, sharing nation.

The Assault on Social Programs

All of these achievements are under attack now. Many have already been eliminated or fundamentally altered and what remains is being dismantled under the guise of review and reform. Federal funding to provinces for health care and post-secondary education is being phased out. Caps on equalization and Canada Assistance payments, the elimination of Family Allowance, clawbacks of Old Age Security and cutbacks to Unemployment Insurance have taken place. And dozens of programs and organizations have had their funding reduced or eliminated. All of this and more is happening in the move to restrain and cutback our social welfare system and to reduce the role of government in public services.

The free trade agreements advance this agenda by designating areas traditionally reserved for non-profit administration as appropriate for commercial enterprise and private sector management, opening the floodgates for massive marketization and privatization of social programs. The withdrawal of government from much of the social policy field makes this one of the most lucrative markets for new or expanded private sector enterprise. Once considered "sacred trusts," health care and education are now up for sale and takeover. In March 1994, headlines out of Alberta said, "hospital for profit weighed." In Manitoba, numerous private home care firms opened up for business.

And then in June of this year reports from Nova Scotia said, "private firms to own schools."

Under the new federal Liberal administration, free trade remains unchallenged and, in fact, provides the rationale for the downsizing of state responsibility for economic and social equity. The assault on the welfare state generally has been continued under this government with additional clawbacks, funding cuts and program reductions. The February 1994 budget announced that the freeze on transfer payments for health care and post-secondary education would continue for 1994/95, and that the Mulroney formula cutting transfers by three per cent per year would also continue at least until 1996/97. This same budget reduced Unemployment Insurance benefits and indicated that transfers under the Canada Assistance Plan, which had been capped in Ontario, Alberta and British Columbia, would now be capped in all provinces and not exceed 1994/95 levels for at least two years. The net result is further privatization of health care, lack of access to post-secondary education and impoverishment of the already poor.

The current assault on the state and the scope of the agenda being pursued by transnational business and its allies are unprecedented and all-pervasive. This is best summarized by Daniel Drache and Meric S. Gertler:

> No area of government policy has been spared. Across a broad front that includes not only trade but regional development, tax and fiscal policies, old age pensions, family allowance, labour market policy, social income programs, and collective bargain-ing, the government has moved persistently and systematically to reshape the institutional and legislative character of Canada. Its strategy is to water down Canadian redistributional programs so as to make them equivalent to the (American) lowest common denominator, and to cut the direct and indirect labour costs to business.[1]

Rethinking Social Policy

Effective opposition and alternative policies to this agenda require major rethinking and rebuilding on the left in Canada. It means chart-ing new directions and not drifting towards neo-liberalism which accepts the "limits to growth" argument and suggests expectations are out of line with reality. For neo-liberals, eliminating universality in favour of selectivity, moving unemployment programs from insurance to short-term assistance, and requiring those on welfare to work are sold as necessary to keep Canada competitive in the new economic order that emphasizes knowledge, human capital, economic integration, efficiency, flexibility and mobility. This approach is essentially the so-called "neo-socialism" being advocated by a segment within the NDP. It focuses on fiscal pressures facing the state, accepts that "an economic policy of human capital-efficiency-mobility is a reasoned response to a global reality"[2], and argues that the role of social policy is to ensure that this change is accomplished as humanely and effectively as possible. Such an approach does not address the growing incidence of poverty, increasing social dislocation, increasing unemployment and new forms of powerlessness. As Gregory Albo reminds us:

> Indeed the drift of social democratic politics towards neo-liberal policies compounds the difficulties by ceding further ground to marketization and adding to the public's disillusionment with political life.[3]

Meaningful social policy will not emerge from this approach. Nor will the answer be found in a return to the "good old days" of the Regina Manifesto. It is not realistic to argue that the task is simply one of finding the right economic strategy so we can put people back to work at good-paying jobs thereby ensuring the state the necessary resources for reinstating the social safety net. For one thing, this argument neglects to consider that only by pursuing economic and social policies in tandem will meaningful policy be developed. New definitions of productive work, new models for economic development, and new values attached to social, cultural and recreational life all have to be included in a new societal paradigm. Secondly, it cannot be said that social equality will automatically follow economic equality unless it is included and integrated in all aspects of the planning and development of specific programs or the project as a whole.

Finally, the scope of the attack on our social system and the powerful nature of the hegemonic project on the right require policies that move beyond social democracy. However beneficial social democratic reforms have been, they have by and large not been able to withstand the assault on social programs nor leave a legacy of lasting social change. Reforms under social democracy were generally pursued as ends in themselves and not as goals toward the transformation of society. In fact some have argued that these reforms enhanced market conditions by ensuring the necessary infrastructure required by capital and by reducing social unrest caused by the hardships of the market economy.

The experience of social democracy offers valuable lessons for pursuing new directions in social policy and the reforms achieved should never be discarded without an all-out effort on the left to stop the cutbacks. However, the longer-term agenda requires policies to over-come the limitations and shortcomings of social democracy.

Searching for New Social Policy Directions

The first task is recognizing the relevance of social policy for build-ing the kind of society envisaged for the future. Too often social poli-cy is relegated to the sidelines as something to be discussed once the "bigger" economic issues have been resolved. Very few new social policy ideas have been advanced in the past decade. Concern about public reaction to new initiatives requiring public funds or lack of will to challenge market-driven delivery systems as in health care have cre-ated a social policy vacuum. Or to use the words of John Myles, "we have an exhausted social policy paradigm."[4] New priority must be given to social policy in order to encourage the research, resolutions, debate and consultation so necessary for the development of new directions.

Along with a renewed emphasis on social policy, a comprehensive review of all existing social programs needs to be undertaken. It is being done by the new right and neo-liberals for purposes of downsiz-ing and off-loading. It should be done by the left for identifying gaps in social programs, pursuing new and more democratic models of administration, and altering out-dated and unresponsive policy struc-tures. It needs to be reviewed in the context of democratic-socialist principles with the goal of developing a comprehensive and a planned approach to the social service delivery system. The present social safe-ty net is the result of an incremental approach that involved consider-able political compromise and expediency. As Doug Smith states:

> Each one of the ropes which make up the social safety net was woven in such a way to buy as much social peace at as low a price as possible. As a result the safety net was never conceived of as an integrated series of benefits that would provide Canadians with a decent level of income. It has succeeded in meeting its goals — today we have horrendous levels of child poverty and no rioting in the streets.[5]

Social policy is defined as the state response to particular economic and political conditions in our society. For the new right it means a system of cost-cutting in order to enhance the competitive advantage of the private sector. For neo-liberals it is essentially the same but dis-guised with expressions of do-gooder sentiment. For democratic socialists it is the tool for redressing material and political inequalities.

This dual aspect of inequality is described by Leo Panitch and Donald Swartz:

> These inequalities pertain to marked differences in income, wealth, and life chances, but also to who decides what is to be done and how, to who works and produces, and to who is responsible for the work of reproduction while others decide and give orders.[6]

Rethinking social policy and reviewing the existing system are, therefore, necessary not only for developing new and better social programs that will help eradicate poverty and economic insecurity but also for democratizing the state and giving people more say over decisions that affect their lives. The twin goals are citizen welfare and democratic citizenship with both being recognized as norms in a civilized society.

Democratization vs. Privatization

Although little has been written about a social policy paradigm for democratic socialism, the issue of democratizing the welfare state has received considerable focus recently. This approach gives clear direction for the development of social policy on the left. It calls for a fundamental shift in the organization of the state and the public sector. Specifically, it points to central control, top-down decision-making, and lack of accountability between the state and its citizens as contrary to the very essence of democratic-socialism which is empowerment, participation and co-operation. This approach may be a topic of some attention today but it is not new. It has been a consistent theme of the women's movement and in fact is a defining characteristic of feminism. Women's organizations have long advocated a process of individual empowerment and collective development through participation, shared responsibility and consensual decision-making. For both feminism and socialism, democratization represents recognition of human potential and collective capacity for creating a society governed by justice, equality and community.

Discontent with big government and distrust of politicians have certainly been a dominant concern in the population as a whole over the past decade or more. Increasingly, issues of out-of-touch decisions, patronage appointments, bureaucratic red tape and program inflexibility have dominated the public agenda. Clearly, such feelings arise from the dominance of right wing forces which depend on a passive citizenry and minimal impediments to corporate concentration of power. However, it is the right which has been able to play upon this prevailing discontent by presenting privatization as the only way out of this "mess." According to Gregory Albo, the new right argues that "markets constitute the only alternative to the inefficiencies of bureaucratic administration; consumers of public services should have choices, rather than suffer through a centrally-controlled allocation of goods."[7] Albo and others argue that the challenge for the left is to present democratization, not privatization or marketization, of the public sector as the solution to current frustrations with the state and the growing sense of alienation, isolation and powerlessness.

Democracy and the State Apparatus

The difficulties to date in mounting massive public opposition to privatization are related to feelings of ambivalence about the alternative. Democratic shortcomings in the state apparatus and serious flaws in the public provision of services have undermined support for an active role by the state in both the provision and delivery of social programs. Social democratic governments have not been able to fundamentally alter existing state administrations and services and hence to serve as a catalyst for public opposition to government off-loading and cutbacks.

In many ways, the critical situation facing the NDP today is related to the popular perception that big government and central control are synonymous with the NDP. The practice of NDP governments to pursue as a general rule conventional models of politics and administration has contributed to this belief. It should also be noted that many social programs are being dismantled today without much public outcry because of a failure to create a sense of citizen ownership over those programs, something which has more chance of happening when knowledge and power are shared.

The potential for democratizing the state is greatest in provincial and municipal jurisdictions. The closer government is to the people it is serving and the more it is involved in the daily life of families and communities, the greater the possibilities for achieving accountability and for entrenching the right of citizenship to plan and control the delivery of services. This potential has not been realized even among NDP governments with the best of intentions. A significant barrier is created by federal off-loading and the increasing loss of regulative capacity at the national level. The dramatic drop in federal government financial support for social programs and the commensurate loss in ability to uphold and enforce national standards have virtually tied the hands of provincial governments committed to administrative reform.

Revamping the health care system becomes almost impossible with significantly-reduced finances. Restructuring the taxation system to shift the tax burden onto the wealthy and to raise revenue for needed services requires federal leadership and initiative. Equality of access to child care, education and other services remains a distant goal without national funding, policies and standards.

While federal off-loading creates major obstacles to democratic reforms, it is also the case that democratization has received no or very low priority in the NDP. This has not been by deliberate choice but by the failure to understand that control over decisions affecting one's life is just as intrinsic to democratic-socialism as economic equality and wealth redistribution. NDP governments have developed strategies and campaigned on promises to expand services but rarely has citizen participation in the delivery of those services been on the agenda. Without a major commitment to democratic reforms and a clear and realistic agenda for accomplishing this objective, it is impossible to make democratization a priority once in government. In Manitoba, democratic reforms in health care were recommended in the early 70s but were not taken seriously until the mid-80s when fiscal pressures finally forced the matter. Between 1981 and 1988 in Manitoba, demands from the popular sector for more control over decision-making were addressed on an ad hoc basis and met with varying degrees of success depending on the nature of the group or the forcefulness of individual ministers. Priority was given to consultation but there was no overall plan for systematic involvement of people in decision-making.

This is not to say that the NDP has been unconcerned about altering the relationship between government and the governed. A number of innovative measures can be attributed to NDP governments. They include decentralized child and family services and parent-run child daycare centres in Manitoba; community health clinics in Saskatchewan; Community Resource Boards in British Columbia; and a Community Economic Development program in Ontario. These initiatives offer helpful lessons for the objective of pursuing socialist planning through decentralized and democratic means. Based on the specific example of the Winnipeg Child and Family Services system, some of those lessons include: ample time for planning and consultation at the policy development stage; adequate funding based on accurate projections of demand; greater delegation of decision-making and empowerment of staff and board members; alternatives to government appointments for ensuring board make-up reflects the diversity of the community it is serving; and adequate education and information to encourage active community participation as well as public understanding.

An agenda for change in the administration of the state is a major undertaking and requires measures to both increase accountability and citizen participation. At the time of serving as a minister in Manitoba between 1986 and 1988, it seemed as if great progress was being made in both areas. A central policy and planning group separate from the bureaucracy, ministerial advisory committees, pre-budgetary consultations, affirmative action appointments to boards and commissions, agenda planning with key groups like organized labour, and an open door policy for public input — all these measures and more seemed to be sufficient to meet the goals of open government and participatory democracy. With the benefit of hindsight, it is clear that these measures, however significant, did not fundamentally shift power within the state or significantly increase citizen participation in the workings of government. The central planning group became preoccupied with crisis management. The consultations became vehicles for seeking approval not alternative viewpoints. Risk-taking that met with failure or public criticism led to retreat. Concern about "catering to special interest groups" inhibited support for citizen coalitions and popular movements. Service to constituents and community groups was undertaken more in the spirit of benevolent paternalism than out of commitment to the concept of self-help. Innovative plans were often hijacked, held up, or significantly altered as a result of bureaucratic control and influence.

It has become increasingly clear that selective measures and isolated reforms, while steps towards democratization, are not sufficient to turn back the tide of privatization. There has to be a comprehensive, far-reaching approach as suggested by Leo Panitch:

1. The first requirement for democratic reform is frank and full recognition that our political institutions still operate in the context of the inegalitarian dimensions of class, gender and race.

2. We need to shake the bureaucratic model to its foundations.

3. The task of democratic leaders and administrators, the skill they have to learn, is to encourage and facilitate the organization of communities of identity and interest.[8]

Democratization on its own will not transform society. But as more and more communities seek local-based decision-making and as popular movements oppose both the squeeze on services and the way existing services are run the more likely an effective challenge to the new right becomes. Similar struggles for democratization by labour, the women's movement, citizen coalitions, environmental groups and the Aboriginal community point to the potential for rebuilding on the left. As well the integration of social policy focused on equality and democratization with economic policy based on a redefinition of productive activity and on community-centred development could be the makings of a significant force on the left.

Work, Reproduction and Family

The struggles of popular movements offer more than the possibilities of organizing an effective alliance on the left. They offer invaluable insights into the development of a social policy paradigm for democratic-socialism and provide direction for the way ahead. The popular sector, particularly the women's movement, takes our thinking beyond traditional notions of work, narrow definitions of economic activity, and identities based primarily on the marketplace. As Meg Luxton and Heather Jon Maroney state, "It offers a place to begin thinking strategically: from the social location of women and men whose lives are lived at the intersection of production of goods in the workplace, of life in the household and community."[1] It draws our attention to such issues as the content of work, value of reproduction, care of children, role of the family, attachment to community, and emotional and spiritual needs.

A critique of work, reproduction and family is critical for the development of new directions on the left. Yet it represents one of the most underdeveloped areas in social policy development. One of the greatest failings of the NDP has been to dismiss the demands of the popular movements as self-interest on the part of single-interest groups. The left generally has underestimated the significance of possibilities inherent in the popular sector and in socialist-feminist theory. Only rarely has the left addressed economic and social policies that are not in direct response to productive work even though, as Jane Jenson states, "production-based politics and production-based identities no longer mobilize as much, as easily, or as convincingly as they once did."[10]

Broadening this understanding in terms of identities based on class, race and gender and of political spaces that evolve from family and community as well as the marketplace is essential for understanding the full nature of the right wing agenda and for developing a meaningful alternative on the left.

ault on the state by market forces and the political right
beyond the privatization and marketization of public services
to other areas: (1) creating a large reserve of cheap labour and
assigning low value to significant areas of work; and (2) shifting the
burden for the provision of services from both the public and private
spheres to unpaid volunteer and household workers. The different
impact of this agenda on women compared to men is significant for
social policy development. This is best understood by considering the
spaces defined for women by the market, the state and the family
under patriarchy and capitalism.

Market forces have consistently viewed women as a cheap source of
labour to be moved in and out of the labour force as economic conditions require. This is more apparent than ever under current economic conditions. Globalization has required a much larger low-wage, low-
skill economy with even greater reliance on the undervaluation of
women's work. Women remain concentrated in poorly-paid sales and
service occupations, employed more often than not on a short-term,
temporary-help basis, with no entitlement to benefits, and receiving on
average 50 per cent less than male counterparts. In the interest of
minimizing labour costs and maintaining a dependent workforce,
employers have come to rely on the gender gap and job ghettos as permanent features of the economy.

The role of the capitalist state is to compliment and support the
needs of market forces. It does so by allowing the minimum wage to
decline in real terms which means even lower pay for women and
other vulnerable workers. It also does so by maintaining job ghettos
and gender bias within the public sector workforce and by doing very
little to redress the undervaluation of women's work. The state
accomplishes this not only through the erosion of the minimum wage
and the absence of tough pay equity provisions, but also by restructuring or downsizing the service sector and replacing high-skilled, well-
paid jobs with low-wage, deskilled personal services. Thus in the few
areas where women are remunerated according to their training and
qualifications, the state has chosen to intrude and to downgrade the
quality of those jobs. As one example, in Manitoba, the Conservative
government has decided to change the mix of services in the health
care sector by laying-off a significant number of registered nurses,
eliminating the licensed practical nursing profession, and hiring low-
wage, low-skilled health care aids. Similarly in the daycare sector,
efforts to raise education requirements and enhance salaries have been
abandoned ensuring child care workers, most of whom are women,
are relegated to the bottom of the wage scale. Instead of giving value

to the work of child care, the state has chosen to treat it as an unskilled, babysitting service.

The goal of a reduced welfare state in line with corporate wishes clearly has a disproportionate impact on women. Privatization, cutbacks and downsizing not only affect employment opportunities for women but also restrict access to services for women and others at the bottom of the wage economy. The resulting insecurity and uncertainty only serve to entrench relationships of dependency between women and employers and women and service providers. What remains of the social safety net is being delivered on a much narrower, selective basis with a host of new rules to follow and new hoops to go through in order to prove eligibility. Users increasingly feel subordinate and personally to blame for their situation. The paternalism inherent in this approach contributes further to the loss of dignity and self-worth already felt by women in a system that undervalues their work and contribution generally.

The subordination of women by the market-driven state is most apparent in its attempts to shift the burden for the provision of services from government to unpaid volunteers and household workers. This essentially has meant increasing the responsibility already born by women for unpaid work in the family and the community. It is an essential feature of the patriarchal capitalist political culture that needs to be acknowledged and challenged. As Carole Pateman states:

> The "work" of a housewife can include the care of invalid husbands and elderly, perhaps infirm, relatives. Welfare-state policies have ensured in various ways that wives/women provide welfare services gratis, disguised as part of their responsibility for the private sphere. A good deal has been written about the fiscal crisis of the welfare state, but it would have been more acute if certain areas of welfare had not been seen as a private, women's matter.[11]

The right wing agenda to off-load responsibility for welfare services onto the shoulders of women has required a renewed focus on the family as the source of social stability and the centre for loving care. It is no coincidence that current media campaigns expounding the virtues of volunteerism and the family are taking place in the midst of an assault on the welfare state. Implicit in this message is the view of family as a heterosexual nuclear unit where men are primarily income providers and women by nature are nurturers. It sees care of family members primarily in terms of personal obligations. It relates youth crime to problems of working women and daycares. It treats stress caused by juggling paid employment and family responsibilities as a character flaw. And it considers violence against women as an individual problem as opposed to a systemic or structural feature of capitalism and patriarchy.

From this analysis of the state and family under capitalism and patriarchy, several new policy directions begin to take shape. First, it makes sense to consider a redefinition of work based on the welfare activity provided largely by women either in the wage-labour sector on an undervalued basis or in the voluntary sector where it receives no value. This has been a long-standing, largely unheeded recommendation by socialist-feminists. Given the current unprecedented assault on the state, it is more urgent than ever for the left to take up the challenge of shaping the economy to meet the needs of society. It means recognizing that the nurturing of children and caring for the sick and elderly are no less productive than jobs in the competitive wage-labour sector. The development of high-skilled, well-paid caregiver services within the public sector makes economic sense and serves to help eliminate gender bias so prevalent in society today.

New directions in social policy also require much greater focus on the value of reproduction, both by recognizing it as meaningful activity that should be socially supported and by ensuring the right of individual women to decide whether or not to have children. It means ensuring access for all women, regardless of sexual orientation, class, race or disabilities to health and social services which support childbearing and raising. It means challenging patriarchy and homophobia and recognizing the family as an institution based on the values of love, caring, co-operation and equality. It means extended maternity and paternity benefits and other supports which recognize the social importance of childrearing. And it means supporting demands for safe birth control, abortion access and a moratorium on the development of new reproductive technologies.

Finally, new directions in social policy must consider what people need to live humanely at the intersection of work, family and leisure. Issues that arise around part-time work, job sharing, new work practices and home-based employment provide direction for more effective integration of these aspects of life. Some of these ideas have become fashionable in right wing circles but they have been implemented solely as cost-saving measures and for softening the impact of lay-offs and downsizing. In the context of progressive policies around income security, pro-rated benefits and adequate support services, a rethinking of the work week is a key aspect of policy development on the left. Options that need to be pursued under this approach include the four-day work week, employment rights and benefits for part-time workers, paid education leave, paid family responsibility leave and impediments to unpaid overtime. Sharing the work and creating flexible work-leisure choices can make for healthier workplaces, richer family life, stronger community ties, and space for emotional and spiritual needs. As Bruce O'Hara states, it also offers us the opportunity to create full employment without the environmental damage inherent in rapid economic growth.[12]

National Standards and Transfer Payments

Discussion, debate and consensus around a framework for social policy must precede the setting of specific priorities and issues. Otherwise the debate is deflected over fiscal and constitutional matters and the sense of purpose is lost. At the federal level of government the debate about an effective social policy has been buried under questions about jurisdiction and method of payment. As Richard Simeon notes:

> Social policy debate is obscured by the veil of fiscal federalism; it is hard for citizens to understand that a debate about CAP, EPF and Canadian Health Act is really a debate about social policy. So the objectives of social policy are lost in the intricacies of funding arrangements; and social programs are shaped by the design of fiscal transfers in ways which few of us can comprehend.[13]

A focus on fiscalism and constitutional matters has also obscured the significance of the changes being advanced by the new right. The key target or central playing field of right wing forces has been the federal government. By undermining the role of the nation-state and weakening the federal government, the whole system begins to unravel. Using the tools of monetary policy, constitutional debate and free trade agreements, the agenda is advanced but also clouded. The roots of the problem are lost in jurisdictional wrangles and legal battles. Public discontent is misdirected as blame is passed back and forth between three levels of government or put to rest on international forces said to be beyond anyone's control. Some activists and academics concede that the nation-state has lost regulative capacity and recommend activity be shifted to the local level.

The call to "act locally and act globally"[14] is important but not to the detriment of national priorities and federally-focused activity. A social policy focus on democratization should in no way be seen as a recommendation for moving to local-based politics and forsaking the national scene. Rather it is the pursuit of more decentralized and democratic decision-making in the context of a strong central government that enforces national standards and advances national priorities. The social policy goal of citizen welfare is the pursuit of equality for all people regardless of sex, race or region. The absence of a strong nation-state would make it impossible to achieve this goal.

Transfer payments constitute a critical social policy tool within the nation-state for achieving the objective of redistributing wealth and power. As presently designed they are a complex set of arrangements by which money and taxing power are allocated between the central government and the provinces. Whether talking about Equalization, Established Program Financing (EPF) or the Canada Assistance Plan (CAP), fiscal transfers are intended to be regionally redistributive programs responding to revenue imbalances and wealth disparities between provinces. Some would argue fiscal transfers are the glue that holds this country together. That may be but more importantly for this debate is the extent to which goals of mutuality and citizen welfare are seen as the underpinnings of fiscal transfers.

When it comes to transfer payments, the major current issue is that they are being squeezed out of existence. Payments under EPF for health care and post-secondary education are scheduled to end in the near future. As well equalization and CAP payments have been capped. The Liberal review of social services is likely to lead to further cutbacks and off-loading under the guise of new or redesigned programs. For example, there are reports that a Guaranteed Annual Income (GAI) is being seriously considered but that it will mean the collapse of several income security programs under the rubric of a GAI with less funding than is available currently for those programs. As John Myles predicted in 1988:

> There are any number of variants of the liberal GAI, and some are more "liberal" than others. The less liberal versions emphasize the need to shift resources from existing income security programs (especially Unemployment Insurance and Family Allowances) to finance a GAI. The result is a tendency to reduce wage replacement in order to finance wage subsidies.[15]

A GAI could be a positive and progressive approach to redressing inequality but it needs to be funded adequately, go beyond the subsistence approach and not eliminate labour market incentives.

Equally disconcerting are the Liberal proposals for workfare, a program requiring recipients to work in return for welfare. It takes no account of the fact that jobs paying adequate wages are just not available or that many welfare recipients, like single parent women, would like to work but simply cannot afford to do so. The problems with workfare are summarized best by Allan Moscovitch:

> *Workfare is an approach to minimum income provision inspired more by the past than the present or future — by a desire to punish people who are poor for their poverty rather than by a desire to provide them with the skills, education, support, financial assistance and paid employment necessary to leave poverty behind.[16]*

Moscovitch suggests a more sensible approach to help welfare recipients, who are able to work, find employment. This would involve revisions to CAP making it possible for welfare recipients to pursue education and training, including voluntary participation in workplace and community service training programs. Other alternatives include increasing the minimum wage, pay equity, subsidized child care and assistance to people with disabilities to cover the additional costs involved in getting a job.

The erosion of fiscal transfers creates serious problems at the provincial level and puts programs like medicare in jeopardy. It also means the abdication of federal responsibility for the welfare state and lost potential for influencing the direction of social programs consistent with the goal of democratization.

While the matter of preserving a system of transfer payments is an urgent priority, it is also clear that the complex and confusing method of payment has to be revamped in the longer term. Numerous proposals have been made including the splitting of the current EPF system into separate blocks for health and higher education, using the actual current provincial spending as the basis for the split. A different strategy has been proposed by Michael Mendelson and is summarized as follows: (1) the "write down" of provincial debt to provide a basis for restructuring on a healthy fiscal foundation; (2) a Constitutional amendment requiring provinces to "balance their budgets" in exchange for massive relief from their debt; and (3) a further Constitutional amendment which would protect federal-provincial arrangements, making them truly "federal-provincial" programs, not subject to unilateral federal decisions.[17] An analysis of these or any other proposals is beyond the scope of this paper. However, it needs to be said that any discussion of redesign in transfer payments and fiscal federalism must take place beyond closed federal-provincial conferences, involve an open, consultative process, and ensure adequate time and resources for citizen intervention.

Priorities: The Basis for Agreement

It would be premature to outline a specific social policy plan or a program for government action. However, using the goals of citizen welfare and democratic citizenship, it is possible to delineate the basis for agreement to determine those priorities.

- *National standards and assured, stable funding*

Although much of the focus of this paper has been on democratization, the first requirement in the social policy field is adequate funding and benefit levels. Meaningful change will mean a significant increase in public spending. It does not mean doing more with less nor is it about decentralized cash transfers. A strong federal role in program development, national standards and targeted cash payments is essential for ensuring equality of access. Clear and straightforward regulations help ensure the provision of services as a matter of entitlement and allow citizens to claim those rights without having to face user fees or to move to another district or province in order to access necessary services. The combination of national standards and cash transfers gives the federal government the leverage for far-reaching changes at all levels of the welfare state.

- *Democratic decision-making and control centred on community — not corporate — needs.*

Any new programs or changes to existing programs need to be developed and delivered on a community-based, democratically-run model. In some areas like health care, the challenge will be to transform what is basically a privately-run, market-driven system to one that is consumer-driven and community-centred. Elected hospital and clinic boards, patient advocates, access to health care records, funding of user groups and watchdog organizations to provide independent advice and external pressure, and self-management projects are some of the ways this can be done. Similarly in education, the corporate invasion of the classroom has to be challenged, the notion of vouchers for parents or students has to be vehemently opposed, and models for school-based decision-making as well as parent advisory bodies have to be supported and expanded. Whatever the service area, the goal of democratic and community-centred decision-making requires an organized, informed and demanding public. And it is in this development of democratic capacities that a political support base sufficient to resist the dismantling of innovative programs is built.

• *A collective, participatory approach in the workplace reflecting a holistic approach to the work at hand.*

Active consumer and community involvement in decision-making cannot be accomplished if the agencies or departments they are working with maintain hierarchical, top-down management practices. Changing the internal operations of public bodies based on collective, co-operative models is critical for achieving the goal of democratization. Some of the suggestions for doing this include de-layering of the bureaucracy, reducing the wage differentials between staff, establishing multi-disciplinary planning teams, devolving decision-making to lower levels within the organization, and multiplying points of citizen access. Just as innovative ideas and constructive criticism must be encouraged from users and community activists, so to must risk-taking and networking among the providers be rewarded. Key to successful social policy is the ability to cross departmental lines, avoid inflexibility and secrecy, and develop holistic approaches to the work at hand.

Conclusion

The issues discussed in this paper barely scrape the surface of the social policy field. The main purpose has been to spark the debate, stress the significance of social policy in building a democratic socialist movement, and propose a framework for future policy development. Central to the approach proposed are the goals of citizen welfare and democratic citizenship. The application of these goals must go beyond the paid labour force and extend to the unpaid voluntary sector. Meaningful social policy can only be developed by rethinking the notion of work itself and by defining the undervalued and unpaid work of women and others in the popular sector as productive activity and of economic value. It is in this integration of social and economic policy that new policy directions take form. The potential for building a viable political alternative on the democratic socialist left is enormous. But it requires a major rethinking on all policy fronts, far-reaching and frank debate, genuine openness to the ideas in the popular sector and serious coalition-building work. It means the goals of equality and democratization apply as much to the process of building the movement and the political alternative as they do to the developing of policies and the creation of a democratic socialist state.

Judy Wasylycia-Leis is a 20-year member of the New Democratic Party, serving in a variety of capacities on local, provincial and fed-

eral executives. She served as the NDP MLA for St. Johns in the Manitoba Legislature between 1986 and 1993, when she resigned her seat to run federally in Winnipeg North. Between 1986 and 1988 she held several Cabinet Portfolios in the Pawley NDP government. She has also worked as the federal NDP women's organizer, Executive Assistant to Ed Broadbent and a co-ordinator of the Manitoba Government's Women's Directorate.

ENDNOTES

1. Daniel Drache and Meric S. Gertler, "The World Economy and the Nation-State: The New International Order", in Daniel Drache and Meric S. Gertler, eds, *The New Era of Global Competition:* State Policy and Market Power (Montreal: McGill-Queen's University Press, 1991), 17.

2. George Fallis, "Thinking Again About Equalization", in Sherri Torjman, ed., *Fiscal Federalism for the 21st Century* (Ottawa: The Caledon Institute of Social Policy, 1993), 52.

3. Gregory Albo, "Democratic Citizenship And The Future of Public Management", in Gregory Albo, David Langille and Leo Panitch, eds, *A Different Kind of State? Popular Power and Democratic Administration* (Toronto: Oxford University Press, 1993), 32.

4. John Myles, "Decline or Impasse? The Current State of the Welfare State", Studies in Political Economy 26 (Summer 1988), 83.

5. Doug Smith, "Modernizing the safety net", Inner City Voice, (Winnipeg: January 1994), 4.

6. Leo Panitch and Donald Swartz, "The Case for Socialist Democracy", in Simon Rosenblum and Peter Findlay, eds, *Debating Canada's Future: Views From The Left* (Toronto: James Lorimer & Company, Publishers, 1991) 32.

7. Albo, "Democratic Citizenship", 23.

8. Leo Panitch, "A Different Kind of State?", in Albo et. al. eds, *A Different Kind of State? Popular Power and Democratic Representation,* 10-11.

9. Meg Luxton and Heather Jon Maroney, "Begetting Babies, Raising Children: The Politics of Parenting", in Jos. Roberts and Jesse Vorst, eds, *Socialism in Crisis? Canadian Perspectives* (Winnipeg: Society for Socialist Studies, 1992), 185.

10. Jane Jenson, "All the World's a Stage: Ideas, Spaces and Times in Canadian Political Economy", Studies in Political Economy, 36 (Autumn, 1991), 49.

11. Carole Pateman, "The Patriarchal Welfare State", in Amy Gutman, ed., *Democracy and the Welfare State* (Princeton: Princeton University Press, 1988), 247.

12. Bruce O'Hara, "Job sharing works for all", Winnipeg Free Press, March 16, 1994, A7.

13. Richard Simeon, "Concluding Comments: Can We Do Federalism in Hard Times?", in Sherri Torjman, ed., *Fiscal Federalism,* 79.

14. Harriet Friedmann, "New Wines, New Bottles: The Regulation of Capital on a World Scale", Studies in Political Economy 36 (Autumn 1991), 38.

15. Myles, Decline or Impasse, 95.

16. Allan Moscovitch, "The Canada Assistance Plan", in Sherri Torjman, ed., *Fiscal Federalism,* 62.

17. Michael Mendelson, "Fundamental Reform of Fiscal Federalism", in Sherri Torjman, ed., *Fiscal Federalism,* 15-17.

Debts, Deficits and Human Communities:
A New Approach

Steven Langdon

> *The enemy of the conventional wisdom is not ideas but the march of events.*

John Kenneth Galbraith, *The Affluent Society*

The conventional wisdom in Canada in 1994-95 says that public debt and budget deficits are disastrous. "We are about to hit the wall," the alarmists shout; "the IMF will take us over!" cry financial analysts who have never seen an IMF agreement; "the world will stop lending us money," claim other Cassandras.

And so the conventional wisdom clamours for massive cuts in social support for the jobless, for more closures and layoffs in hospitals, and for attacks on old age pension benefits.

But all this conventional wisdom, repeated over and over again, cannot hide the hard truths that represent the real march of events in Canada.

This essay examines three of these hard truths, and draws policy conclusions from the analysis. The article also suggests a new approach to the budget deficit question. First, the essay shows that the *private sector* has also dramatically increased its debt — but the mechanisms of private debt expansion significantly disguise this fact.

Second, the essay stresses that the present system of economic measurement, and the differential way in which market and non-market output is treated in conventional economic analysis, lead to strong biases against public sector activity and debt expansion in Canada. Third, the study suggests how this bias against the public sector is severely damaging future Canadian development. Finally, the conclusion of the essay points to policy moves that should be taken to compensate for and help overcome this built-in bias in a market-based economy.

Debt and the Private Sector

The marked increase in public sector debt in Canada has not been an isolated event. It has been matched, as a percentage of National Income, by fiscal performance in the U.S., and even exceeded in a number of European countries.[1]

More significantly, increasing public fiscal deficits have been only a part of a general and massive increase in capital availability and subsequent debt generated throughout the world after the first large oil price increases by OPEC in 1973. Official U.S. dollar reserves held by all countries outside the U.S. more than tripled over the 1970s to well over US$200 billion. And the recycling of petrodollars back into the world banking system pumped hundreds of billions in new funds into world capital markets — so that even developing countries saw their combined debts rise from US$70 billion to $300 billion over 1970-1979.[2]

Beyond this recycling of petrodollars, the private sector also developed new mechanisms to tap sources of capital. The leveraged buyout became common-place, often using so-called "junk bonds" (high interest, high risk company bond issues) as the means to carry through such takeovers. An "over-the-counter" stock transaction institution also became established — the "Nasdaq" in the U.S. permitting easier access for newer firms to equity capital (for which the return is variable dividends based on variable profits, not a pre-established interest rate locked into a bond or bank loan). As the federal Conservative government had to concede in the 1992 national budget, "corporate leverage and thus debt burdens are high in both Canada and the United States; the rise in corporate indebtedness has been especially pronounced in the United States."[3]

There *were* spectacular failures associated with the new paper empires that heavy borrowing helped build — Campeau in Canada, the Reichmanns, and the savings and loan company collapses in the U.S. But the main point to emphasize is the extremely widespread use of heavy debt financing by the private sector — in marked contrast to the common assumption that only governments borrowed money.

Both private and public sectors borrowed from capital markets. But a key point of difference was that the way the private sector in Canada obtained its expanded capital was more varied and complex, obscuring both the fact and the effect of this borrowing.

The case of Alcan Corporation demonstrates these points well over the 1978-93 period. Officially, long-term debt carried by the company increased a great deal, from US$796 million in 1979 to $2.322 billion in 1993. But even this doesn't tell the whole story. The company also increased its use of preference shares (from US$155 to 353 million) which are really guaranteed dividend shares that work like company bonds; the company was able to use accelerated depreciation provisions under the corporate tax system, to write off its plant and equipment investments very quickly, so carried large entries on its books for "deferred taxation" (another US$888 million in 1993) — really representing capital left in Alcan hands that would otherwise have gone to pay corporate tax; this, in effect, was a huge loan from the government.[4]

Moreover, Alcan was able to limit the effects of this borrowing on company prospects in at least two ways. First, interest payments it had to make on its loans were deducted from revenues as an operating expense — that meant the corporate tax that would otherwise be paid on that surplus of revenue over operating costs was reduced further, and these tax savings contributed to paying the interest costs. Second, Alcan's accountants could determine that the company's net assets were undervalued by existing equity levels, and declare a revaluation upward of the value of those net assets, and reflect this by giving more shares to shareholders to reflect this increased value — as in the three-for-every-two "share split" Alcan undertook in 1988.

This then made the company's long-term debt look less serious than previously, as the "debt-equity ratio" declined (in the Alcan case from 37 per cent in 1985 to 26 per cent by 1989).[5]

In addition, Alcan had a capacity to increase prices for its products under certain circumstances — and the most recent Alcan annual report (1993) indicates that this has been the case in the last few years. Again the result is that the debt of Alcan, taken as a percentage of sales revenue, looks to have decreased and to have become more easily managed within Alcan's overall business performance.

Similar points can be made with respect to other major Canadian corporations analyzed as part of this study.

A total of eight of the largest Canadian-controlled manufacturing and resource corporations was selected for analysis, representing over $40 billion in sales revenue and over $17 billion in equity capital in the 1993 financial year (Alcan, Northern Telecom and Inco had equity capital levels of $2.5 — 4 billion in 1993; Moore Corporation, Dofasco and George Weston were in the $1 — 2 billion range; and Stelco and Dominion Textiles were between $450 million and $1 billion).

These eight corporate giants increased their total long-term debt from $4.6 billion in 1980 to $9.55 billion in 1993, a jump of 108 per cent; their debt/equity ratio increased from 46.3 per cent in 1980 to a

GRAPH 1: LONG-TERM DEBT, 1980-93
Eight Major Canadian-Controlled Firms

Source: Company Annual Reports

GRAPH 2: DEBT ANALYSIS, 1980-93
Eight Major Canadian-Controlled Firms

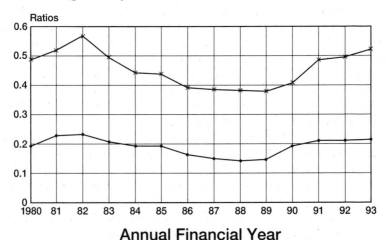

Source: Company Annual Reports

considerably higher 55.0 per cent in 1993. And this *understated* the real increase in debt, in ways noted above. In the case of Alcan, for instance, deferred tax increased from $614 million in 1980 to $1.174 billion in 1993, a further $563 million increase; Dofasco's deferred taxes jumped by $96 million.

Taking six companies for which the information was available, moreover, these firms were able to deduct *$719.7 million* from their income to cover the interest costs on this long-term debt — and this does not include the figure for the largest borrower, Northern Telecom.

Another point that is striking is that there is little relationship between accelerated debt levels and company profitability. Moore Corporation, which maintained by far the lowest debt levels, and actually decreased these over the 1980-93 period, went from solid, quite profitable performance from 1980 through 1989 into a period of difficulty leading to losses of $103 million by 1993. On the other hand, George Weston, which had increased its debt load much more than average (by 155 per cent between 1980 and 1993) maintained a reasonable though varied profitability throughout the entire period. Stelco, which kept its debts down, lost money from 1990 through 1993, while its steel competitor Dofasco increased its debtload by 289 per cent (to 72 per cent of its equity) and had a *positive* net income of $138.6 million in 1993 after three years of losses.

Conversely, Inco reduced its debt load and was profitable (making $37 million in 1993) while Alcan increased its debts and was losing money by 1991-93.[6] The clear conclusion to come to is that debts did not necessarily mean disaster for large Canadian corporations — it all depended on other circumstances that determined whether the debts could be managed, and help a corporation cope better with marketplace challenges.

But the main conclusion to stress is the flexibility with which corporate Canada could approach their debt question, compared to the public sector. Consider a simple contrast.

Suppose the federal government borrows $4 million to expand the Great Lakes Institute at the University of Windsor, so it can do faster and more accurate tests for toxic chemicals in the St. Clair\Detroit River system, and so equipment can be purchased to upgrade research aimed at cleaning up the river system. That is a full expenditure item carried at once on the books of the government.

There is no way to have taxpayers subsidize this further through accelerated depreciation. The government has no place it can deduct interest costs; it simply must pay them. There is no equity market the government can turn to for funding that will not look like increased debt. And there is no way the government can make the debt look smaller by a share split to increase the equity capital against which the debt is measured.

Nor can the public sector generally obtain increased money benefits from the output of the Great Lakes Institute expansion.

So both private and public sectors borrow — but the similarities stop there. The private sector uses many mechanisms for borrowings, making overall debt-equivalent levels hard to track; the private sector can use the tax system to have ordinary taxpayers pay a big share of borrowing costs; and the private sector can see to it there are money benefits for what is spent. As the next section discusses more fully, the public sector cannot match this strategic approach.

The Bias Against Public Sector Output

In 1985, there was a significant water pollution emergency in the St. Clair/Detroit River system running from Sarnia, past Windsor and south to Amherstburg and the entry to Lake Erie. Dow Chemical released a great deal of laundry cleaning agent into the St. Clair River, leaving high levels of chemical residue in the river system that included dioxins and furans of great concern to environmental experts.[7]

The general public may never have known about this danger, had not a brave informant from the Great Lakes Institute come forward to tell me about it because I was his MP. I raised urgent private concerns in both Toronto and Ottawa, and eventually had to take the information into public questions in the House of Commons to get official confirmation, and serious government action on this large spill — the clean-up of which eventually cost Dow Chemical over $1 million.

Any realistic assessment of the benefits of the Great Lakes Institute would have to stress such environmental watchdog and research activities contributed by staff there.

Yet how does our economy and its economic measuring agencies judge the value of the output of the Institute? The only measure reported is the cost of inputs to the Institute. Thus Statistics Canada will measure output of this public sector institution by costing inputs to it.

The contrast with the private sector is dramatic. Above we discussed federal government borrowing of $4 million to expand and improve the Institute. Now suppose Magna International, also in the Windsor area, were to seek $4 million to expand its auto parts plant. In obtaining the money, part (or all) of it could come either from a straight issuing of equity shares — in which case no increase of debt would be involved — or from an issuing of preference shares — which would be much the same as long-term financing, requiring a set return each year, but would not be called debt on the company books.

Moreover, if the company borrowed the money, it could soon write most of it off using accelerated depreciation provisions in the corporate tax system — which would mean in reality that taxpayers would cover a large portion of the cost via foregone tax revenue from Magna. Within a few years, only a small portion of the borrowing would be carried on the books as long-term debt. And a few years later, Magna's accountants might be able to say the value of company assets had increased, so there should be a share split, and the size of the loan would look even less significant as a proportion of (now larger) shareholders' equity in the company. Meanwhile, interest on the loan could be deducted as an operating expense from corporate taxes owing, thereby having ordinary taxpayers cover yet more of the private corporate costs of borrowing.

In any event, there would be a stream of income associated with the Magna loan, and Magna would have some capacity to raise prices and\or lower costs as a result of the loan and expansion.

Compare that with the public sector borrowing for the Institute. There would be benefits from the improved water testing and eventually the improved water quality. These might even be very large benefits, measured in terms of better health, fewer days in hospital, a more productive workforce and fewer children born with disabilities; but these are benefits you cannot put a price tag on, for which to go out and present individual bills. They are what economists call *public goods* and are not measured in our national economic statistics. There is an important intellectual stream in economics that has worked with this notion of "public goods" in a rigorous way. Social cost-benefit analysis has been used in assessing large resource development projects in Canada,[8] and the technique has also been employed in project appraisal in developing countries.[9] But there has been no real transfer to fiscal policy of the key insight — that many benefits of public projects, though they cannot be sold on a market, can still be estimated (if only roughly) as a public or social benefit.

Public goods clearly exist. Almost anyone will admit that in theory. But they are systematically undervalued in the market-oriented decision-making process in our society.

Thus we reduce policing in our cities — because of budget pressures — at the same time that Canadian concerns about crime are growing. We cut back fire protection at our airports — to save money

— at the same time as deregulation is supposed to be increasing the number of aircraft using those facilities. We cut anti-pollution efforts under the Green Plan, even as Great Lakes environmental problems are identified as worse than previously believed.

All of these are examples where, because our society cannot measure the real benefits of public goods (urban security, fire protection and environmental improvement, etc.) we therefore cannot see that we are almost certainly making social profits on public money invested in these three areas. And our decision-makers find it impossible to see that budget cuts have social costs much greater than the measured budgetary savings.

This bias against public sector activities, because they cannot be measured and sold on an individualistic basis in the marketplace, leads to systematic cutting back of important social priorities provided by the public sector, while far less essential private sector activities go forward (providing novelty rickshaw drivers in Canadian cities, for example, or operating yet another specialty cable TV service).

This inability of a market-based society to cope with social costs and benefits, and to measure public goods with any care, can lead, at its extreme, to complete social collapse. So much of the ultimate value of any society to the people who live in it depends on a strong degree of community responsibility and social cohesion; that's what allows you to go about your life with the general expectation that armed bands are not going to sweep down out of the hills and carry off what you have built — that's what underlies expectations that you can walk down most streets, and buy groceries in a store that will not poison you.

Yet that social cohesion is ultimately a public good — which no longer exists in much of Bosnia or Rwanda or Haiti. And it may be a public good which no longer exists in some U.S. inner-city areas.

Canadians should not be naive. If we continue to undervalue, in the systematic way our governments are doing so, the public goods that the public sector produces — from urban transport to security to equal access to health to good schooling to a cleaner environment — then social cohesion in this country could be lost, too. We have already had warnings in Canada — from rioting in Toronto, to sports outbursts in Vancouver, to misogynist killers in Montréal. These warnings deserve to be heard.

There are other reasons to be concerned about the bias against the public sector, too. One factor is distributional. The market responds to the existing distribution of wealth and income. One dollar represents one vote; and that means in effect that market dynamics are shaped by the top 25 per cent of income earners who control the majority of Canadian family income. Public goods, on the other hand, *should* respond to one person/one vote, and be much more egalitarian in their distributional impact.

Allowing for the complex realities of more articulate citizens having more impact on the allocation of public goods, this may not be as clear-cut in practice as theory might predict, but certainly the potential pressure is there for public goods to be allotted in a much more even-handed way.

That, of course, points to another fundamental problem in the provision of public goods. The majority of Canadian income is in the hands of a distinct minority of Canadian families. Yet if all public sector goods are to be financed by taxes, then the Canadian political economy requires a distinct minority to pay most of the taxes to finance public goods — which will benefit *all* Canadians more equally. It is heroic to expect such a pattern to persist over the long run.

There are three powerful biases, then, working against the provision of public goods via the public sector. First, borrowing by the public sector is quite clear-cut, cannot be reduced by subtle subsidies from another part of the economy (unlike private sector debt which can benefit from tax benefits from the public sector) and takes the form of bonds or treasury bills with fixed interest and payback obligations unlike the more flexible equity capital the private sector can access. This tends to make such borrowing easily noted and an open target for attack, compared to private sector moves to access the capital market.

Second, the output of the public sector is not accurately measured (by using the analytical tools of social cost-benefit analysis, for example.) Instead the value of public goods is systematically undervalued in economic and fiscal reporting. This makes the level of borrowing by the public sector seem larger than it should be, relative to the value of the net benefits from that borrowing. And again there is no way the public sector can easily correct this impression, compared to the ease with which net assets are revalued and share-splits increase equity in the case of the private sector.

Finally, third, while distributional equity considerations favour public sector activities, the reality of a minority of better-off taxpayers having to pay for benefits shared by all Canadians works against tax-financing as the exclusive means of financing a strong and active public sector.

Some consequences of this bias against the public sector have already been noted, in discussing the threats to social cohesion associated with large cutbacks. But another set of threatening economic effects also deserve emphasis, and are discussed in the next section.

The Public Sector and Sustainable Development

The deficit is usually discussed, in economic policy terms, in a macroeconomic framework where overall demand in the Canadian economy can be influenced by deficit levels in federal and provincial budgets.

There is general agreement among economists that a significant increase in deficit levels can increase overall demand to some extent and have some positive impact on employment levels in Canada (given unemployed labour and other resources in the country) — while a general reduction in deficit levels, in the same context, would have some negative effect on jobs in Canada. This counter-cyclical role of fiscal policy must not be ignored, especially with over 10 per cent of the workforce unemployed. The reality is, however, that Canada is now such an open economy, so integrated by the free trade deal, North American Free Trade Agreement (NAFTA) and General Agreement on Tariffs and Trade (GATT) into a continental and global economy, that these Keynesian effects on overall demand and thus on Canadian jobs are likely to diffuse themselves very quickly throughout all of North America. So it may well be that the short-run macroeconomic impact of deficit levels is less important in 1994-95 than the effects of deficit policy on the public sector as a longer-run factor in shaping the broad direction of Canadian development.

The large levels of short-term capital shifting throughout the international capital market, often in response to haphazard political developments, or misleading economic signals, also mean that interest rates can be buffetted dramatically, too — even if governments are willing to see fairly wide swings in currency values (and that is often *not* the case). Thus monetary developments may often outweigh fiscal policy effects that countercyclical budget deficits may be meant to counter.

None of this makes the basic Keynesian framework invalid — just much less effective as a source of policy instruments for achieving full employment. Thus the constraints on Keynesian fiscal management may not be the major way in which the new assualts on the public sector and its role are having its main long-term economic impact on people.

So far the bias against the public sector seems to be showing up in five main areas — policy spheres where cutbacks either are hitting adversely (education, unemployment insurance and health care), or where essential initiatives are not being taken (childcare and community economic development). These are all areas of profound importance for the long term future of sustainable Canadian development.

The problems with Canadian government performance in the education policy area have been widely stressed in recent years. The Michael Porter study on Canadian competitiveness for the Business Council on National Issues, which stressed the private sector as a focus for Canadian economic growth initiatives, concluded that Canada's "education and training systems have failed to respond adequately to the challenges posed by the contemporary global economy".[10] The same point has been underlined by the business-labour consensus report on economic restructuring of the Canadian Labour Market and Productivity Centre,[11] and by much other political and economic policy commentary.

Yet, as Judy Wasylycia-Leis shows in her social policy chapter, education is an area where federal government transfer payment freezes and associated provincial budget cuts, have significantly reduced public sector efforts. This is in dramatic contradiction to the arguments of analysts like Robert Reich, who have stressed the importance of human capital improvements as sources of international competitiveness in the struggle to attract increasingly footloose private capital investments (and therefore jobs) to locate in our national jurisdiction. Such emphasis on growing skills is also essential if community prosperity is to be possible in a context of increasing natural resource constraints and higher long-term energy pricing, designed to stabilize and reduce future ecological damage.

Wasylycia-Leis makes the same point about health care expenditure, another important source of long-run competitive advantage for Canadian-based enterprises. Representatives of large U.S. auto firms have stressed to me the importance of the efficient Canadian medicare system in their decisions to locate production in Canada rather than the U.S., with its far more expensive and wasteful private health plans. But Canadian governments nevertheless continue to cut back service under our system, despite the obvious negative impact in the longer-run on such investment location decisions.

The same basic point holds true where child care initiatives and unemployment insurance are concerned. Expansion of good, stimulating and affordable childcare facilities is essential to early childhood development of co-operative skills and learning capacities; the economic impact in the longer-run would be immense, as the high productivity and ecological consciousness in the Scandinavian economies demonstrates. And the same is true of generous and efficient unemployment benefits; again, Porter's BCNI study makes the point that Sweden directs 70 per cent of its labour market expenditures to training and skills upgrading, and just 30 per cent to income support —

while fully 75 per cent of Canada's allocations go to income support and only 25 per cent to training and job creation.[12] Yet Canada's plans to reform the unemployment system are starting from a fundamental goal of cutting $6 billion in overall expenditures, rather than aiming to make the system more effective at labour restructuring by more generous support for training purposes.

The other policy area which sustainable development concern makes a priority is community development initiatives. Coro Strandberg, in her chapter, discusses the wide range of local efforts already underway across Canada, showing that community-based development has been accumulating experience and credibility in Canada — and that the result can be bottom-up ways to build new jobs for the longer-run. To expand more significantly, and to become an important factor in Canadian development, however, this CED movement requires support from provincial and federal levels of government — both to improve technical support networks that can assist local efforts, and to broaden access to capital markets for new community-based initiatives.

In short, there are important areas for expansion and initiative for the public sector, if a broadly-based skills and employment intensive development process is to move forward in Canada. And these areas cannot come at the expense of important existing contributions made by the public sector to the Canadian economy — such as environmental protection and research, science and technology support, support to Aboriginal economic development and land claims settlements, employment equity objectives, and research and income security funding for family farming.

New Policy Initiatives

So far this chapter has presented a bleak assessment of the "march of events" in Canada (to return to the opening quote from Galbraith).

The evidence shows that the private sector has relied heavily on increased use of outside capital, much of it borrowed, but in complex ways and using mechanisms in the tax system (and elsewhere) that have often disguised this reliance on debt. The much more clear-cut, open way in which public-sector borrowing has taken place, without writing it off against tax liabilities, is one bias against the public sector.

The other bias against public sector activities is that the net social benefits of the provision of "public goods" have not been measured in any ongoing systematic way in our national economic statistics, because it has not been possible to measure value to individual

Canadians through the prices they are prepared to pay in a functioning market situation. This has meant a consistent undervaluation of the net social value of public sector activities (since the value of these is simply measured by the cost of the inputs that go into producing these goods or services) and it has meant a gross and continuing over-valuation of the cost-savings of public sector cutbacks (since the social benefits lost from the activities eliminated are not valued, to set against the savings made). This process, it was suggested, can have dangerous consequences at an extreme, leading to the breakdown of social cohesion in Canada. This market failure to measure the costs and benefits of community stewardship is especially worrying in the context of environmental pressures in an increasingly fragile and overloaded world ecological system.

The third section traced the impact of these biases against public sector activities in examining Canadian sustainable development priorities — suggesting that the result is underinvestment in important areas for future economic sustainability such as education/training, labour adjustment and health care — and the failure of Canadian governments to take national initiatives in the two important areas for our future economy of child care and community economic development.

So how does this "march of events" affect the conventional wisdom that budget deficits are disastrous?

On the one hand, it helps explain why no sensible national government seems truly willing in practice to take the extremely harsh steps needed to eliminate the federal budget deficit — despite the rhetoric from Michael Wilson or from Paul Martin. This is the same imposition of reality over wishes that made Herbert Hoover run budget deficits in the start of the Great Depression in the U.S., despite his stated views that deficit elimination was crucial. But it also does point to the need for new policy instruments to help redress the biases in a market economy against key public goods provision from the public sector.

This is not a case for spending more public money to put people back to work through the impact of the Keynesian multiplier (given the high rate of leakages from the Canadian economy in the world of 1995).

But there is a strong case to, in effect, restructure capital markets in Canada — by creating a new National Investment Fund, to undertake crucial public goods investments with important benefits for sustainable development over the longer run — and by permitting municipalities and local regions to establish Community Economic Development funds for financing of local economic initiatives.

These new Funds would offer bonds on Canadian capital markets which would be tax-free — in the way that Municipal bonds in the U.S. are tax free — and would thereby provide powerful incentives for savings to flow into them, at lower interest costs than are offered in the normal capital market.

The resulting National Investment Fund would then be able to provide capital for schools, health facilities, child care centres, training institutes, environment research institutes — and all manner of other important social infrastructure investments. And the financing would come from Canadian — not foreign — sources. Both the federal and provincial governments would be able to access the fund, and would co-operate in its management. As for Community Economic Development Funds, these would be approved via provincial-federal agreement, but would be run by local committees responsible to the local community and to investors choosing to invest in that particular fund.

Over time, such a change in Canadian capital markets could be of immense importance. It would spur sustainable development through the emphasis on small-scale, locally-based enterprises (many with a service and information bias), and by promoting improved training and quality-of-life for parents, children and displaced workers benefitting from improvements in their skills, learning and employment options.

Above all, it would to a considerable extent overcome the biases against public sector activities in Canada, and thereby make our society a better place to live. This direction of change could be a crucial step to realizing many of the environmental, social, equity and community development goals presented in this book. It would also respond to the community-based, bottom-up vision that so many Canadians seem to be fighting for as they fashion a new kind of progressive politics for the future.

There will be, in some places there already is, a movement for profound change as dramatic as when women fought for votes 75 years ago. Communities of people are learning they have the power to say no; they are learning they have the power to bargain hard with giant corporations and powerful government elites — and often to win.

Above all, step by step, Canadian communities are beginning to see that they can shape their own future. That's what the progressive politics of this next decade will be about, more power for people in their communities.

That's what progressive politics must be about, as our world becomes more and more vulnerable to the pressures of past choices that are simply not sustainable in the future — as disappearing fish stocks on our coasts, shrinking forests and failing nuclear plants make only too clear. The push by people for power to make changes for their own communities that I saw growing in Windsor and elsewhere represents what Canada needs.

We need to reshape a new ethic of mutual caring in the 21st century. Sir Wilfrid Laurier talked about this 20th century belonging to Canada. For the sake of us all, the next century must belong to the world. And the grassroots drive for community social responsibility that has been growing throughout Canada can help make this happen.

This article has pointed to new financial initiatives that could help realize this vision.

After periods as Associate Professor of Economics, and then Associate Director of the International Development Research Centre, Steven Langdon was elected to serve as Member of Parliament for the federal riding of Essex Windsor in 1984 and 1988, becoming New Democrat Trade critic and Finance critic. He now runs an economic analysis and training firm, and is Adjunct Professor of Public Administration at Carleton University in Ottawa.

ENDNOTES

1. See *The Budget 1992,* Government of Canada (Ottawa, 1992), p. 127.
2. See *North-South: A Program for Survival, The Report of the Independent Commission on International Development Issues under the Chairmanship of Willy Brandt,* (The MIT Press: Cambridge, 1980) pp. 208, 238.
3. *The Budget 1992,* p. 63.
4. See Alcan Corporation, *Annual Reports,* 1993 and 1989.
5. See Alcan, *Annual Report,* 1989.
6. This information is drawn from annual reports of the various corporations noted, as collected and analyzed by Jonathan Langdon.
7. See *Government of Canada/Province of Ontario, St. Clair River Pollution Investigation (Sarnia Area),* (Ottawa, 1986.)
8. See W.R.D. Sewell, John Davis, A.D. Scott and R.W. Ross, *Guide to Benefit-Cost Analysis,* (Resources for Tomorrow Conference: Information Canada, Ottawa, 1965) chap. 6.
9. See I.M.D. Little and J.A. Mirrlees, *Project Appraisal and Planning for Developing Countries,* (Heinemann Educational Books: London, 1974,) chap. 16.
10. Michael Porter, *Canada at the Crossroads - The Reality of a New Competitive Environment,* (Business Council on National Issues: Ottawa, 1991,) p. 89.
11. See *Canada: Meeting the Challenge of Change,* (Canadian Labour Market and Productivity Centre Economic Restructuring Committee: Ottawa, 1993.)
12. Porter, op. cit., pp. 57-58.

New Zealand's New Right Revolution

by Murray Dobbin

Murray Dobbin has been a social activist in Saskatchewan for 25 years and is also a freelance journalist. Over the last three years, he has written a book on Preston Manning and the Reform Party, and another one on Conservative leader Kim Campbell. Dobbin visited New Zealand in February and March of 1994, interviewing New Zealanders in preparation for a radio documentary on their country. The following is an edited version of talk given August 29, 1994, to a conference on the value of public services co-sponsored and hosted by the Public Service Alliance of Canada.

I became interested in doing a documentary on New Zealand precisely because of the kind of information we have been getting about New Zealand, the alleged debt crisis and how New Zealand has been promoted as the way Canada should go. I find it particularly outrageous that Sir Roger Douglas, who is seen by many New Zealanders as a man who has implemented the destruction of his own country, now comes to Canada and tells us how to do the same thing here.

I want to, number one, debunk the myth that the changes in New Zealand were due to a debt crisis. Secondly, I want to examine what New Zealanders refer to as the political coup which heralded the changes, and look at the roots of that change in the American neo-conservative universities. Next, I want to briefly look at some of the ideological premises that underpin the revolution that took place in New Zealand over the last nine years, and specifically at the impact on public and social services, in particular, health, education and welfare. I also want to comment briefly about the impact on community and the political culture in New Zealand. And lastly, I want to make the connection between the New Zealand experience, the Reform Party and what has happened in Alberta under Ralph Klein.

First, the debt crisis. Promoters of the changes in New Zealand say they had a debt crisis in 1984. The public debt in 1984 was $22 billion. Even after selling off $16 billion in public assets, New Zealand's public debt today is $46 billion. In other words, the real debt level is more like $54 billion. So if they had a crisis in 1984, you have to create a new language to describe what they have today.

What they had in New Zealand in 1984 was not a debt crisis but a currency crisis created, in part, by Sir Roger Douglas himself. Douglas released, accidentally he said, a paper saying that the Labour Government, if elected, would devalue the New Zealand dollar. There was a run on the currency which created a short-term crisis after the election when international lenders temporarily refused to cover some of the country's outstanding loans.

That temporary crisis gave a group of bureaucrats, Labour politicians and key figures in the new business elite in New Zealand a perfect opportunity to implement a sweeping neo-conservative agenda. It included the elimination of all subsidies, which devastated first the farm sector but then other sectors as well, and the almost total deregulation of the financial sector. New Zealand now has the most deregulated financial sector of any of the Organization for Economic Co-operation and Development (OECD) countries. The changes implemented also involved the devaluation of the New Zealand dollar, a cut in taxes for corporations and the wealthy of 50 per cent, the commercialization of government enterprises and departments, and the elimination of import substitution protection for New Zealand manufacturers.

People have called the implementation of this agenda a political coup, but this description is not mere paranoia. In fact, when I interviewed David Langey, who was the prime minister at the time, he didn't object to that word and actually referred to the changes as a "revolution."

There were three groups in New Zealand who implemented this revolution: one was a small group of six or seven bureaucrats in the Finance Department (called the Treasury) in the Central Bank; Labour Finance Minister Roger Douglas and four or five senior Labour Ministers, plus the new business elite. They came together in what was called the "Wednesday Club," which met about every three weeks to discuss neo-conservative ideology and how it should be implemented in the New Zealand context. The leaders of this group were the Treasury bureaucrats, all of whom were trained at monetarist schools in the U.S. and who had known each other for many years. It was the peculiar circumstances of the currency crisis, that allowed this group to implement its agenda very quickly.

It is really interesting to hear how this ideology was sold in New Zealand, because the technique would be very familiar to Canadians. The TINA argument — There Is No Alternative — that way of thinking is as common in Canada as it is in New Zealand. As well, New Zealand neo-conservatives completely captured progressive language in the selling of their reforms. So the radical changes were not promoted as a neo-conservative agenda because, as we know, they couldn't be sold on that basis. Instead the changes were sold on the grounds of efficiency, as promoting choice, as enhancing the country's ability to compete internationally, all of the same language as we hear today in Canada. And, of course, the use of the word "reform" was repeated over and over again.

One of the major weapons, there as here, was what I call, in relationship to the Canadian experience, "debt terrorism" — a constant reference to the debt as an argument for cutting back everything, saying that we can't possibly afford these things anymore.

One of the reasons the debt is so huge in New Zealand is that these policies ended up eliminating half of New Zealand's manufacturing jobs over a two-to-three year period and creating enormous unemployment. As a result, the country now has a revenue crisis just like we have had in Canada for the last 15 years.

Jim Anderton, a former Labour Party MP and now the leader of a coalition of parties opposing the new-right revolution, told me that he spoke to a Japanese financier about the massive deregulation of 1985. The financier responded by saying that if Japan had implemented the kind of deregulations that New Zealand did, 90 per cent of Japanese businesses would have gone bankrupt. Suddenly, an over-regulated economy was completely deregulated. All kinds of manufacturers, small and middle manufacturers who were, in terms that you would normally judge these things, efficient operators, went out of business because with financial deregulation, literally billions of dollars of foreign currency poured into the country to buy up assets. Interest rates were raised to 30 per cent to try to cool the economy off further exacerbating the debt problem.

The first phase of the "reforms" was sold by references to the debt. But more recently the word "choice" is one that has been used to sell reform in New Zealand, more than it has to this point in Canada. That idea had a certain resonance in New Zealand because the country's strong tradition of egalitarianism resulted in a certain uniformity and lack of consumer sophistication. Egalitarianism in New Zealand was established really through the policies of the first Labour government back in 1937. Medicare, progressive labour legislation, publicly-funded education and import protection for industries, all were established back the late 30s, so for 50 years consumer choice was extremely restricted. For example, one person I interviewed said that nearly everyone had the same couch; you couldn't even get a different colour. All the houses looked the same. So egalitarianism had that kind of price. And there was a real sense in which the neo-conservative revolution allowed the middle class to begin to have the same kinds of choices as North American consumers do.

Consumer choice was used to sell all kinds of other things as well — a partial privatization of education, a partial privatization of medicare, all these things were put in terms of "choice" which of course sounds like a positive concept.

The most important difference, I suppose, between the Canadian and New Zealand experience is that, there, ideology is used much more explicitly. Some of you will be familiar with "public choice theory" and "agency theory," which essentially portray human beings as "utility maximizers"; in other words, we are all selfish and in all the things we do, we express a very narrow self-interest. Public choice theory has worked its way through the whole public policy process in New Zealand so that all public policy now rests on this assumption.

One of the results of public choice ideology is something we have also experienced in Canada: the attack on so-called "interest groups," groups dismissed as "special" and "vested interest" groups. The impact in New Zealand is that if you have expertise in an area, such as health or education, or measures to fight poverty, you are almost automatically excluded from the public policy process, because it is assumed that you are a "vested interest" defending the status quo. Rather than bring in health experts in New Zealand into the health policy process, they brought in Americans who don't have a vested interest, but also don't know a thing about New Zealand or how its health care system has worked over the decades.

And so you have this incredible imposition of a foreign model on New Zealand which takes no account of the political culture, no account of how medicare has been run or of any of its successes. In the case of medicare, the National Party government brought these foreign "experts" in for something like *48 hours* and then based health policy on 48 hours of consulting with American health economists. This is an indication of how fast some of this revolutionary policy was put together.

"Agency theory" is very similar to "choice" theory in that it assumes that the norm in human and inter-agency relationships is an unethical, dishonest one. The key reform in health care, for example, has focused on dividing the purchaser and provider of health services. As a result, the purchaser of services focuses an enormous amount of attention on ensuring that the providers of services aren't cheating them. Government policy is therefore based on what I think is an extremely cynical view of human nature, a view which simply cannot be sustained either in our own experience or in any empirical study. We all exhibit all kinds of actions that are not narrowly self-interested — from family commitments to volunteer community work. But that is not accepted by the ideologues behind the changes in New Zealand.

I just wanted to touch on health care and education, in particular. In relation to health care, there is now a preoccupation with the notion of separation of purchaser and provider. There are now four appointed regional health authorities which replaced 14 elected health boards. They "purchase" services from public, private or volunteer providers by letting contracts out accepting the lowest bid. There has been a rapid and fairly ruthless commercialization of health care, and of hospitals in particular. User fees were implemented for GP consultations, for prescription drugs, for medical tests, on hospital stays, and so many rules introduced that it was very hard to find anyone who actually understood all of what this meant. The rules regarding payment schedules for health services have become so complicated it is difficult even for those in the field to sort out the system. When I was there, the government had to put in an extra half billion dollars into the regional health authorities because they were already broke half-way through the year.

There is a competitive model for services. So you could have the absurd situation of there being two CAT scanners, next door to each other, both trying to out-bid the other for services asked for by the regional health authority. And the user fees, especially on prescription drugs, have caused enormous hardship for low-income people. There are hundreds of cases of people leaving prescription drugs on the counter at the drug store, because they were faced with the decision of either buying medication for one sick child or feeding three children. The regional health authorities now face two fundamentally conflicting goals: one is the efficient purchase on the market of services, and, at the same time, the responsibility for making care accessible to everyone. These are quite contradictory principles, and the regional health authorities have made it clear that they are finding it very difficult to define where the line should be drawn between these two objectives.

In education "reform," New Zealand has moved half-way to a voucher system. The government, which has a one-seat majority at this point, has not been able to go forward with this. But what now exists in education is a user-pay system plus complete parent choice.

Parents now have the choice of sending their kids to any school they choose, and they also have to pay a fee to the school for each child. The result is that geographic determination of school populations is replaced by social and economic class determination. In a mixed class neighbourhood, for example, the neighbourhood school suddenly finds itself impoverished, because word gets around that there is a good school in some other neighbourhood, a more exclusively middle-class neighbourhood. Middle class people in the mixed neighbourhood send their children to the school out of the neighbourhood. What initially might have been only a rumour becomes a self-fulfilling prophecy: if it wasn't actually a "good" school before, it becomes a good school, because now you have more and more middle class people willing to pay higher fees to the school. As a result, you get tremendous disparities in the quality of education.

While I was in New Zealand the Anglican church released a study showing that the average funding per student (including state funding) in poor neighbourhoods was $40 and in middle class schools the average was $200. With this increasing disparity, some schools now have to raise extra money and have fund-raising events just to fix holes in the roof.

The effect of this policy has really been the creation, with public funds, of a quasi-private school system. The wealthier schools, in the middle class and upper middle class areas, because so many people want to go to them, have the ability to cut off registration of students. So they can cut them off on any basis they want. There is no rule that says you have to take any particular student. You have discretionary authority to cut off registration, which means schools in high demand can pick and choose students at will. Such discretion works to reinforce the class determination of school populations.

To add to the dramatic deterioration of educational standards for low income and working poor parents, the government has deregulated labour in the education field. Schools can now hire teachers who do not have professional qualifications. Schools facing funding crises are tempted to hire less qualified people to save money.

In the area of welfare, there was in effect a 25 per cent cut virtually overnight, which social researchers have suggested increased the poverty rate by 40 per cent virtually within a period of a month. There is an extremely complex targeting of the welfare system now, so complicated that even those who work with people on welfare are constantly trying to figure out the system. You get a basic rate and you virtually have to prove a need for every other payment, whether it is for heat or electricity or any number of possible extra needs. Most needs beyond a very minimal payment are considered "special" and you have to demonstrate that you deserve them.

Those I interviewed working with the poor point out that in the first few years people expected the problem to be temporary, because the Labour government kept saying "prosperity is just around the corner." But New Zealand is creating a permanent under-class.

Now poor people have begun to realize that their situation is not temporary. This has resulted in tremendous demoralization and health problems resulting from depression and family violence. One woman I spoke to who was working at a food bank told me a story about a woman who had gone without electricity for a full year. The utility had cut her off because she had a $700 electricity bill. She had tried to cope without electricity because it was impossible for her to imagine how she would ever pay this amount. So a previously middle class woman became completely immobilized by her poverty; it was only when someone else found out that she had been living without electricity that she got the help she needed.

I heard many personal stories that brought home the real effects of New Zealand's revolution. I learned about all kinds of families who simply quit eating in the last two days before they get their next welfare cheque. With one family I met, the school had finally sent the children home. The mother was ordered not to send the children to school because they had been steadily losing weight, couldn't concentrate and brought no lunches. It turns out that the mother had been feeding them oatmeal porridge both in the morning and for the evening meal for a month because that was all she could afford.

In terms of the statistical picture, the New Right Revolution in New Zealand has given that country some dubious honours on the human misery scale.

- New Zealand now has the highest youth suicide rate in the world.

- It has one of the highest violent crime rates of all developed countries. A Dutch study suggested that New Zealand averaged first or second in most categories including first in violent crime and burglaries. New Zealanders were second in terms of the percentage of citizens afraid to leave their homes at night.

- Twenty-six per cent of New Zealand children are now in some way dependent on a welfare benefit. There has been a dramatic increase in child prostitution, in part because you can't get a benefit (social assistance) unless you are 19 years old. You can't get a full benefit until you are 24 years old, forcing young adults to rely on their families if they can't get work.

Women are, by far, the most affected by all these changes. Phillida Bunkle, a feminist academic and activist I spoke to, said that the changes have completely turned back the clock. The way she put it was "you either have people dying in the streets or women look after them." The government has stated that it wants to see families shoulder more of the burden for social services, which basically means it will be women having to cope with the impacts of the destruction of social services.

With the cuts to social services and higher unemployment, there has been a tremendous increase in poverty among women. If you combine race and gender the result is even more dramatic: 26 per cent of Maori women live on a benefit; six per cent of white men do. So there is a tremendous racial and gender bias in terms of how poverty is distributed in New Zealand.

I just want to go through quickly the four traditional ways that we look at economies to see if these policies have succeeded. We'll not only talk about the debt — as I've pointed out, it was a catastrophe in terms of the increase in debt. In terms of unemployment, there was four per cent unemployment in 1984. By early 1986, it was over 12 per cent. The current government now claims that it is 9.5 per cent, but independent research suggests that the rate is closer to 16 per cent. That doesn't count the 120,000 workers who left New Zealand in the first four years after the reforms were implemented.

New Zealand had the worst jobs record in the OECD throughout most of the mid-to-late 1980s, and the new jobs that are created are largely low-wage and part-time. Economic growth in New Zealand between 1987 and 1992 was negative. It was minus one per cent at the same time that the OECD average was nearly twenty per cent growth. The only success that New Zealand has enjoyed, in terms of their criteria, is inflation — currently running at about one per cent. But you would expect to have low inflation if you beat the economy into the ground, which is exactly what two successive governments did.

The implementation of a full-fledged New Right agenda is explicitly an attack on community. The schools example is perhaps the most graphic in its effects. New Zealand education policy severely undermines the whole notion of neighbourhood, since those who can afford to are now sending their children outside of the neighbourhood to good schools.

In addition to social and economic policies, government encouragement of stock market investment through tax policy and privatization was a deliberate attempt to "sell" the benefits of capitalism through individual gain, just as it was in Britain where Margaret Thatcher set as her goal to have more shareholders in Britain than union members. Especially up to the 1987 stock market crash (which affected New Zealand more than any other developed nation), there was a tremendous amount of speculation and profit taking. Share-market clubs attracted all kinds of people unaccustomed to such activity — teachers, union members, other professionals, got caught in what many described to me as a "frenzy" of speculation.

The explicit and implicit attack on the notion of community has created a class consciousness — and visible class divisions — in New Zealand that didn't exist before, a meanness of spirit which many people talked to me about. Privatization of New Zealand's government services and crown corporations — amounting to $16 billion in asset sales — was implicitly a rejection of the notion of community owning anything or producing anything in common.

The preoccupation with the concept of choice plays very strongly to a strong individualism in New Zealand. But people are finding that while you may have increased choice of consumer goods (if you have money), however increasingly you don't have a choice over what kind of community or what kind of society you want to live in. Both major parties, the National Party and the Labour Party have the same policies. In effect, what you have in New Zealand is a commercialized political culture. You are now a consumer of goods but have little or no choice over social or political objectives. People quoted to me Margaret Thatcher's statement that there is no such thing as society, just individuals with property and their families, describing it as a notion that is alive and well amongst a certain class of people in New Zealand.

Along with all of these economic and social changes has come an explicit, and quite ferocious, attack on democracy and democratic institutions. The labour market has been totally deregulated. You cannot find the word "union" in labour legislation in New Zealand at all. Employers now are free to bargain with individual employees. Employees can appoint an agent, but the employer is no longer obliged to deal with that agent. As a result, in the space of three years, the percentage of unionized workers has dropped from over 45 per cent to less than 28 per cent and it is still falling.

Similarly, as I mentioned earlier, the ideological attack has been based on the TINA argument — There Is No Alternative — and the deliberate use of misleading language. So there is that cultural attack on the notion of democracy. It has struck me that if it is true what neo-conservatives are saying and there is no alternative to their policies, then there is little point in having elections. Certainly that sense is very strong among many New Zealanders as well. And as far as democratic institutions involved in non-electoral politics, they are subjected to the attack being made on "special interest" groups.

The anti-democratic methods used to implement the New Right agenda were revealed in a speech made by Sir Roger Douglas, the former New Zealand finance minister, when he was the keynote speaker at the Reform Party Convention in Canada in 1991. Douglas was the only speaker introduced personally by Preston Manning who said "Listen very carefully to this man. He not only talks about structural adjustment and reform. He's done it."

Douglas advised the Reform Party Convention that if they ever became the government that they should implement their agenda as quickly as possible to avoid interest group organizing against them.

He also advised them not to reveal their agenda, and argued for retroactive consensus — another oxymoron, like progressive conservative. He said, "Consensus for quality decisions is built after they are taken." And that is exactly what both governments in New Zealand did in the 1980s. Both the Labour and the National governments engaged in retroactive consensus, a process by which governments do not reveal their real agenda, implement policies they know are unpopular in a blitzkrieg that demoralizes opposition, and then takes the lack of resistance as a sign of support.

There is another aspect of the fight against democracy. There has been a tremendous determination by the New Right in New Zealand to deliberately and systematically get control of the key institutions. They seized control of the Labour party government first and then moved quickly to place key people in the National Party opposition. They now have virtual control in terms of those government departments and agencies that still exist. Officials with the Finance Department, where the revolution began, comment publicly on almost every area of public policy, in particular education and health.

Those who buck the correct political line suddenly find themselves on closed career paths, cut off from government contracts and even shut out of social circles. I heard stories about people who used to be invited to Christmas parties, who for the last 20 years have been invited to the staff Christmas party, and all of a sudden they didn't get invited any more because they were not towing the ideological line. So there is a real sense in which there is an attack on any alternative view at all. We have experienced that in Canada as well, but I think it is much more explicit and much more ferocious in New Zealand than it has been here. And, of course, in terms of an attack on democracy, the creation of enormous poverty disenfranchises hundreds of thousands of people as well — people for whom any effective participation in political life becomes a luxury they cannot afford.

Media concentration has been the same in New Zealand that it has been here. There is almost universal support within the media for this whole notion of choice. There was an editorial in a major daily while I was there that seemed to sum up the new right agenda argument by stating flatly: "Fairness is not the issue. Choice is the issue." So that ideology seems to have really permeated the media elite in New Zealand.

There is an obvious parallel in Canada to what has happened in New Zealand — a sort of New Zealand in waiting. The Reform Party policy book prescribes almost exactly what has happened in New Zealand.

And that if we want to imagine what it would be like to have a Reform government in Canada, we just have to look at New Zealand.

Indeed, we don't have to imagine very hard — we can just look at Alberta, because Sir Roger Douglas is advising the Alberta government, and what is happening in Alberta is much the same as what has happened in New Zealand. The fact that Sir Roger Douglas (he was knighted by Margaret Thatcher for doing things even she dared not attempt in Britain) advises the Alberta government, gives speeches to the Reform party and regularly addresses conservative Canadian audiences suggests the internationalization of this free market ideology.

There is an international network of neo-conservatives. It's not a conspiracy, but they communicate a great deal and share experiences. The first experience with this kind of top-down right wing revolution was actually right here in Canada. I don't know whether the New Zealand government learned from it or not, but the Bill Bennett Government of 1983 approached so-called "restructuring" in precisely the same way as Roger Douglas: a hidden agenda, implementation of it virtually overnight. Bennett had hoped that groups wouldn't be able to mobilize against such an onslaught, and of course he badly misjudged that. But certainly neo-conservatives, including Milton Freidman, wrote about the B.C. experience. The six or seven key senior officials in the Treasury, which is the Finance Department, and the New Zealand central bank I had earlier talked about, all had received their education at the Chicago School and other monetary schools in the United States.

A woman who was a contemporary of them, who had also received her training in the States, suggests that these men were completely bowled over by the kind of consumer goods available in the United States, and by the ideology, and came back wanting to "modernize" New Zealand. Embarrassed by the small-town quality of their egalitarian society, they were going to transform New Zealand into a modern, entrepreneurial nation. It should be acknowledged that many of the regulations in New Zealand had created a relatively stagnant economy. And so the new financial elite was chomping at the bit for change. As a result there was tremendous appeal in New Right ideology and, of course, having gone to those American schools they have associates in the United States with whom they communicate.

I think that there has been a decision by neo-conservatives to promote New Zealand as the way to go. It is a strategy that is having some success. Both Bob Rae and Roy Romanow have obliged their caucus and cabinet to view a very distorted interpretation of the New Zealand experience in the form of documentary aired by the program "W5." And I gather, from people I have talked to, that New Zealand is popping up in policy discussions within the federal Liberal Government now as well.

In the first Labour Government, from 1984 to 1987, there was very little resistance to the New Right initiatives, in part because it was a Labour government implementing them. In their first term of government, Labour had very progressive social legislation, including the most progressive Aboriginal legislation in the history of New Zealand. There were many policy areas in which the government was doing the kinds of things that social democrats are expected to do. And there was a lack of familiarity with the political language of neo-conservatism in the political culture to deal with a lot of the changes. New Zealand is characterized by a very practical approach to political and social questions and despite its long history of social democratic policies, the political culture is not accustomed to the concepts of "Left" and "Right." Financial deregulation, commercialization (which led inevitably to privatization), regressive taxes all caught many people, including many on the left, off-guard.

As one commentator put it, New Zealanders were not adept at operating politically outside the context of the long-standing political consensus. That consensus was established over 50 years ago. In 1937, virtually all New Zealand's social welfare institutions were established by the first Labour Government. From 1937 on, there was little need for social movements to push for job creation, protection for labour, medicare, access to education or similar progressive initiatives. Many of these things were implemented so long ago and were taken so much for granted, that people were at a loss to know how to defend them from those who unilaterally broke with that historical consensus.

The Left, for five or six years had been concentrating on things like feminist issues, issues of race, human rights, international issues, apartheid in South Africa. I think the Left was caught off-balance because it did not have a fully developed and comprehensive economic policy, which was the advantage of the Right. One of their strengths was they had this whole package. They were able and prepared to say: "This is what we need to do in each of these many areas, and this is why we need to do it."

In addition, the previous National Party government of Robert Muldoon had been extremely intrusive in its policies and government intervention had become associated with an extremely unpopular prime minister. People were expecting change and were willing to suspend their judgment — along the lines of, "We'll put up with some short term pain, and see if the situation will get better."

In its second term, the Labour government engaged in massive privatization, which they hadn't in the first term. They lost popular support in 1990 and also lost the support of business, because they refused to implement the social policy aspects of the New Right agenda which included the deregulation of labour. After Labour lost the 1990 election, real opposition began to the neo-conservative agenda began to build, in part because of the severe poverty created by the National Party's vicious cuts to welfare and the partial privatization of medicare and education.

Whereas, in Canada a lot of the opposition to the New Right policies of Brian Mulroney was expressed through social movements, in New Zealand it has been expressed largely through the creation of new political parties. There is now a party called the Alliance, consisting of a New Labour Party, founded by Jim Anderton, a former Labour MP and colleague of Sir Roger Douglas, and the only Labour politician to consistently oppose the changes; a Maori Party; a Green Party; a Social Credit Party now called the Democratic Party which focuses on monetary policy; and a Liberal Party. They got 18 per cent of the vote in the 1993 in their first ever challenge to the old line parties, running on an set of policies which were explicitly aimed at reversing New Right initiatives.

But the key victory in the 1993 election was the referendum vote in favour of proportional representation. The next election, which constitutionally has to be held in 1996, must be held on the basis of proportional representation. The Alliance now has between 30 and 34 per cent of the popular vote in the polls and Jim Anderton has an approval rating of over 70 per cent as the most popular person for

Prime Minister. Unless things change dramatically in the next couple of years, there is almost certain to be a minority government in the next parliament, and most commentators that I spoke to in New Zealand thought there was a strong likelihood of a minority Alliance government.

But nothing is guaranteed. The fact that the National Party is still leading in the polls ahead of the Alliance (by four per cent) and the Labour Party (which is now down an historic low of 20 per cent), demonstrates that there is a significant sector of the New Zealand population which supports the revolution in that country. In the past year the economy has grown at 5 per cent — a long overdue recovery from seven years of negative and zero growth. Whatever the outcome of the next election, politics in New Zealand leading up to that vote will fascinating. As union leader and historian Tony Simpson said to me, New Zealand will either cease to be a democracy at all or it will become so radically democratic that it will make past social democratic governments look mild in comparison.

The Public Sector and the Labour Movement:
Shifting the Perspective

by Daryl T. Bean
President
Public Service Alliance of Canada

The past few years have seen remarkable changes in the Canadian labour movement. The influx of public sector workers continues to be a source not only of numbers but of new ideas and approaches in the house of labour. With some private-sector allies, notably the Canadian Auto Workers, we have brought with us a new emphasis on coalition-building, an escalating disillusionment with business-as-usual electoral politics, a growing recognition of the need to democratize our own structures, and an (unsurprizing) insistence on the need for a strong and effective public service. This new perspective did not arrive out of thin air. It is not the result of wild theorizing by leaders out of touch with reality, but evolved naturally out of our concrete experience as public sector workers.

Government as Employer

Having a government as an employer almost inevitably means, first of all, that our role as a bargaining agent is never simply confined to the realm of collective bargaining proper — particularly these days! When an employer has the power to legislate its will, and indeed does just that, more and more, as a matter of course then a strong response from the membership, and from the labour movement as a whole, is called for if the union is to advance in any significant way. For our leaders, this has meant a shift in some cases from a business-union approach to a membership-focussed one. For our members, long wary of politics because their public service culture, fortified by regulations, has discouraged political involvement, it has become increasingly clear that having a political employer means that we need to be political too.

To a large extent, also, our perspective arises from the nature of the work we do. Our members both produce services to the public, and, as part of that public, consume them as well. Thus the concepts of public need and of quality have an immediate meaning for us. We can see first-hand what cutbacks, downsizing, contracting-out and privatization do both to members and to the services we provide. "The bottom line" of the private sector profit-and-loss-model doesn't square with most of our work: it is difficult to see, for example, how ambulance services to the North or Coast Guard patrols rescuing people from the seas can be made "profitable" in any meaningful sense of the word.

In addition, the type of work we do makes us somewhat resistant to the popular view, pushed by business and unfortunately shared by some of our sisters and brothers in the private sector, that the state is in essence an obstacle to progress and productivity. Our members oppose in their bones, in other words, the corporate ideology which the Conservatives, and now the Liberals are determined to implement.

Mean Times

The current political climate has shifted several degrees to the right in the past few years, however. We are living in what was aptly termed in a recent Canadian Labour Congress (CLC) policy paper, "the mean society." Buzz-phrases like "global competitiveness" are bandied about to justify rollbacks and closures in the private sector, the North American Free Trade Agreement (NAFTA) has widened the free trade hemorrhage. Unemployment is high; the response is to slash Unemployment Insurance benefits. In such times we workers can be easily divided among ourselves.

The image of "fat-cat" public employees, diminished somewhat during our strike by media exposure of "real people" on the picket lines, has returned full-force. Rather than seeing our gain of employment security as a victory for workers, those whose lives have been made precarious by the corporate agenda have been encouraged to regard this as somehow unfair to them. Our opposition to the abrogation of collective bargaining, or to unilateral government overrides of collective agreements, is portrayed not as resistance to an escalating assault on basic union rights, but as the whining of a privileged group. In attacking the Ontario public service unions during the "social contract" controversy, for example, labour historian Desmond Morton insultingly noted that the New Democratic Party government of Bob Rae had a wider agenda than their "care and feeding." Groups of workers, in other words, are set up to compare their degrees of pain, not to confront the common source of that pain.

So we have a more complex task on our hands than merely confronting the employer. Attitudes shaped by government and the corporate sector, and retailed through the media, have helped to isolate us to some degree from other working people. And for our part, we have been slow, too slow, in reaching out at the community level to build links which all of us need. We are divided — and we are ruled.

The Politics of Public Sector Unionism

Many private-sector unions consider political activity second-nature. Support for the New Democratic Party is traditional, and money and volunteers can be counted on both at election time and between elections. The fate of the NDP, in fact, has until recently been so publicly intertwined with the fate of the labour movement that hostile commentators have accused the party of being the captive of "big labour."

With the inception of the Ontario government's so-called "social contract," however, many public sector workers have asked just who is the captive and who the captor. The have seen several influential CLC affiliates making their view very clear that, regardless of the Rae government's attack on the public sector, the NDP remains labour's only ally, however imperfect, in the political process, and must continue to have labour's support. There has seemed, to these affiliates to be no other viable option, no new political strategy available. While the Public Service Alliance of Canada (PSAC) fully recognizes the progressive labour, employment equity, pay equity and other positive legislation enacted by the Ontario NDP government, there are fundamental workers' rights, such as collective bargaining, which no government, regardless of its political stripe, has the right to deny.

A number of public sector unions, including PSAC, cannot by law support a political party, and this prohibition has had the effect, in the past, of placing a good deal of political activity outside the sphere of what the rank and file considers legitimate union activity. Moreover, it has set us apart, in some ways, from the mainstream of the Canadian labour movement, which has long considered political activity a necessary aspect of fighting for their members.

The Alliance has, however, found ways of participating in the electoral process. Two conventions mandated the PSAC to work for the defeat of the Progressive Conservative government, and in the last election, our union supported candidates in a number of ridings who had met basic pro-labour criteria. While it could be predicted that some of our members would be concerned that this was not "legitimate" union activity, a concern of a different character was raised by some activists: in light of the Liberal record of the past (the Anti-Inflation Board, 6 and 5) and the NDP record in Ontario, is it not a risky proposition to endorse candidates from any political party?

In fact, a critique of electoral politics is beginning to gather momentum, indicated by the historic "Peoples' Agenda" demonstration on Parliament Hill on May 15, 1993, and in part by the rapid betrayal of the Liberal Party of their pro-labour promises, from free collective bargaining in the federal public sector, to re-negotiating the free trade deals, to abolishing the Goods and Services Tax. Our members are frustrated and critical of a process which has prevented us from moving forward for considerable time, and from holding those in power accountable in any way once an election takes place. Although it would be wrong to suggest that the membership has lined up behind a specific alternative strategy, it is clear that many of our activists, at least, want a new way of doing politics. Political parties, of whatever stripe, have shown themselves incapable of or unwilling to deliver the goods once in office.

In this context, it has become imperative to us to begin to develop this new politics in our own union. We have discovered from experience that we cannot make headway with the strategies of the past. We cannot put all our energies and our faith in an electoral process which has played us for fools again and again. Learning the lesson of solidarity all over, we are expanding our efforts to reach out to the rest of the labour movement, to our social partners, to the communities in which we live.

Starting at Home

All of this, we have come to realize, must start in our own union; like charity, solidarity begins at home.

Only the members can make the union strong. Our membership is a widely varied one. Virtually every trade and occupation that can be found in the private sector can be found in our own ranks as well. Women make up nearly one half of our total membership. Activists among them have been responsible for an ongoing educational process which has led to the formation of regional women's committees, the holding of regional and national women's conferences, courses designated to raise the awareness of our membership about women's issues, that the placing of issues such as pay equity and sexual harassment high on the Alliance agenda. Other equality-seeking groups have organized regional networks: gay men, lesbians and bisexuals; members with disabilities, Aboriginal members, and visible minority members. This energy from the rank and file has been nothing but beneficial for our union, and continues to help educate all of us. Where fears were raised initially by some that the particular issues raised by each of these constituency groups would divide us, we have found instead that the increasing understanding brings with it a deeper solidarity among the membership as a whole.

This on-going internal experience has made it easier for us to develop a perspective which extends beyond our own "borders." From the perspectives and lived experiences of women and other equality-seeking groups, we have come to recognize that the forces which oppress them are linked to the forces which we as working people face together, in the workplace, in the streets, in our own homes. To use the current phrase, we have begun to "make the links."

But there is another aspect to this increased awareness, too, and one which is bound to cause stresses and strains in any organization. When members are made the focus of our union, we must expect that demands for more democratic structures are bound to follow. It has been our experience, certainly, that activist members want a more accountable leadership, a better flow of communication between members and leaders, and more say in the day-to-day running of the union as well as in determining the direction we take in the future. At our most recent Convention, changes have been approved which, when fully implemented, will place most of the top Alliance leadership in the regions which they will represent, and will set up representative councils in each region if the members there so desire.

This kind of structural change flows directly from encouraging the increasing involvement of members. The need for change to continue is, in my view, urgent. Having reached an impasse at present with the federal government, the disaffection of some of our members is growing, and their frustration and anger is too often directed against their own union. Members must be persuaded that they have a real stake in their union, that their involvement is not only wanted but needed, and that their issues are taken seriously.

Thus, the relatively rapid changes which we have experienced internally as a public sector union can be expected to continue, and our perspective as a union will continue to broaden and be more inclusive. As we face radical changes in the work process, workplace reorganization, management brainwashing techniques such as Total Quality Management (TQM) and so on, our members need a higher level of union education and a greater degree of commitment than ever before. This can only come about if our structures serve the members, and not vice-versa.

Building a Base for Social Change

Our experience, as I have tried to outline here, has inevitably led us in the direction of social activism. Indeed, such activism may be the key to our survival as a union. It is certainly my view that we need a large and powerful broad-based coalition of working people to resist the corporate agenda. But this is far from being a universally held view within the labour movement.

Much has been made, of late, of a supposed split between public and private sector unionists, notably over the question of continued support for the NDP. Wile it is true that the public and private sector experiences are in some respect very different, it is misleading in the extreme to suggest, as some have done, that our interests are divergent as well. To begin with, the large CAW private-sector union has aligned itself with the major public sector unions; and the public sector Service Employees International Union (SEIU) has joined forces with large private sector unions such as the Communications, Energy, and Paperworkers (CEP) and the United Steel Workers of America (USWA) on the other side of a debate which is essentially strategic and ideological.

While no one is suggesting abandoning electoral politics altogether — in fact, public and private sector affiliates recently agreed to continued support for the NDP, based, however, on a serious, membership-based re-evaluation over time — the question is one of degree. Some affiliates can see no alternative to business as usual, and support the labour status quo. The problem for a union like ours, however, is that the status-quo just isn't working. The status-quo is legislated wage freezes, a unilateral and indefinite cessation of all pretense at genuine negotiation by an employer which can and has legislated its own way time and again. It is a continuing refusal to budge even on items of health and safety (employees on Parliament Hill continue to breathe asbestos, but the health and safety provisions of the Canada Labour Code have not been extended to cover them) to simple respect (Prime Minister Jean Chrétein curtly refused to lower flags for the April 28 Day of Mourning). The status-quo for much of the Canadian public sector, in fact is the continuing abuse of power by various governments which deny basic union rights to a significant section of the Canadian labour movement. Simply supporting this or that political party does not, to put it bluntly, seem like much of a strategy to us.

A number of public sector unions, by virtue of our history, are forced to look for an alternative strategy. Our union is strongly supportive of the direction indicated in the May 15 demonstration on Parliament Hill because, for us at least, there is simply no alternative. A social movement, based on coalition principles, must be built. The Alliance is already working in coalition with a number of social partners, including the National Action Committee on the Status of Women, the National Anti-Poverty Organization and the Action Canada Network. The task that lies ahead, however, is to involve the membership, regional activists in particular, in building such coalitions in their own communities. A movement, after all, is not leaders working together, but members working together.

In this respect, the work already done internally is paying dividends. Necessary person-to-person contacts are already in place, because activist members in the various constituency groups tend to be active also in a number of associations and organizations which promote their immediate issues and concerns. By reaching out to our own membership, therefore, we are already actively involved in the process of coalition-building.

We consider it a priority, as well, to deepen our involvement in District Labour Councils and Federations of Labour, and by so doing, to establish links of solidarity with the rank-and-file of other unions. Finally, we believe it is essential to organize the unorganized, and, like other unions, are continuing our efforts in this regard.

A New Politics

In none of the foregoing do I wish to suggest that PSAC has already succeeded in transforming itself into the union we would like to be, nor that we have develop our links with the wider community to anywhere near the degree that is necessary. What we have done is set the course. We have much further to go, both in motivating and mobilizing our membership, and in establishing the full partnership with other unions, progressive organizations and communities which we would like.

Given the crisis confronting workers in both the private and public sectors, it is essential that we resolve our tactical differences and develop a common strategy to confront the corporate agenda which is wrecking the lives of Canadian working people. The CLC resolution setting in motion a reassessment of our relationship to the NDP has restored some harmony. Now is the time to move ahead, building a social movement on the ground, and making the necessary and some-times painful changes in our structures, our approaches, our assumptions and our philosophies which will facilitate this.

It is worth pointing out that we can all learn a lesson in this respect from that most unlikely sources, the Reform Party of Canada. Their organizers began by building a grassroots movement of their own. They made the coalitions, they gave people a sense that they counted in the movement (even if it is, in this case an illusion), they presented clear alternatives, they staged rallies, they worked the media, and they came within an inch of forming the official opposition in Parliament as a result.

If the Reform Party is capable, in such a short space of time, of creating a movement and from that secure base sending more than fifty members to Parliament, then surely with our organizing experience, our resources, our vision, our increasing connections to the rest of the community, the labour movement can play a vital role in remaking society.

In fact, we really have very little choice. Those in power continue to make a world in their image: cutbacks, privatization, erosion of the social safety net, a return to the dog-eat-dog savagery of the unrestricted market. Now that market has become increasingly globalized, and the centres of power are more difficult to confront. A complete alternative vision, therefore, must look to international, as well as national, solidarity, the building of which is a task which is truly only in the most tentative stages. But if we do not head in this direction, and keep our eyes on our own vision of the future, and use all the resources at our command (our sheer numbers being our greatest potential weapon), we truly face what one writer has called "the end of history": in other words, no future at all.

The alternative to our aspirations and values lies all around us: waste, devastation and want, a polluted landscape littered with food-banks and inhabited by a marginalized and dispossessed majority. How can we do otherwise but resist? Yet our own humane, democratic and creative vision of the future can only be implemented if we are prepared to grasp the enormity of our common task, resolve our differences and work together. Only then will the grim "end of history" turn out to be the beginning of real history, a history made with our own hands, and one which is worthy of our dreams.

Some Last Thoughts

. . . .

F ree enterprise means unrestricted competition; the race to the swift and the battle to the strong. You hear members of the House of Commons, in this debate, talking about going back to free enterprise. We have never left it. We have had in Canada both the major line parties in power administering a system of private enterprise since Confederation. What has been the result?

This system produced in this country a state of affairs in which we had a million people on relief previous to 1939, people who were ill-fed, ill-clad, and ill-housed and, when war broke out, according to government figures, 46% of the men called for service were rejected because that depression had left physical and psychological scars which will never be erased . . . .

I want to emphasize here that we do not want to destroy things as they are, we want to change things as they are, and to make sure we shall never go back to things as they were (in 1939).

Clarie Gillis, *MP for Cape Breton South, 1953*
(the miners' leader, who in 1934 led United Mine Workers District 26
into the first-ever union affiliation with the CCF in Canada)

I have always welcomed having inside the party a group of people who keep pushing the party into being more aggressive and more radical. It is very easy for politicians not to rock the boat. . . . So we need people in the party who will say, "Just a moment, these were our long-term objectives. We haven't reached them yet, and we're not moving fast enough. Can't we speed the process up?"

Tommy Douglas, *First National NDP Leader, 1971*